A beacon of neutral democratic ideals, Costa Rica stands out in a turbulent region; as far back as the 1930s one commentator called it the 'Switzerland of Central America'. Whatever its political credentials and claims to neutrality, this country is undeniably a nature-lovers' paradise: you'll find moss-draped cloudforest on the slopes of Monteverde, where the red and green sacred quetzal bird hides in the treetops and hummingbirds busy round drinking nectar, there's rainforest wilderness on the Osa Peninsula and remote turtle-nesting beaches on the north Atlantic and Pacific coasts. The country's volcanic peaks range from the gentle steaming lagoons of Irazú and Poás to the explosive Arenal, just outside La Fortuna.

Travellers looking to combine nature and comfort should head to the endless sand and surf beaches of the Nicoya Peninsula, Quepos and Parque Nacional Manuel Antonio, or to the off-beat strands of the Caribbean. For adrenalin junkies there's whitewater rafting, trekking and coast-to-coast mountain biking, and the chance to climb the barren *páramo* savannahs to the peak of Cerro Chirripó.

Historically Costa Rica has avoided the extremes of external influences. The Spanish found no mineral wealth here or compliant indigenous labour to work the land. Hard conditions and poverty forced both conquerors and conquered to work and live side by side. It was only with the arrival of wealth from the magic coffee bean in the central highlands that a landed gentry arose to conflict with the interests of a liberal merchant class.

As a result, Costa Rica's architectural highlights are somewhat limited compared to much of the region, concentrated in the churches that dot the central highlands. But, just like the country's natural nuances that host incredible diversity, the architectural differences are subtle. And just like the natural wonders, you'll have to look harder to truly appreciate them.

Richard Arghiris

Best of
Costa Rica

❶ Volcán Arenal

After decades of almost constant violent eruption, Volcán Arenal, one of Costa Rica's most iconic attractions, fell into a slumber in 2011. Recent murmurings indicate it may be about to blow its top again, but until then, you can hike through diverse ecosystems in the day, then bask in nearby hot springs. Page 67.

❷ Monteverde

Monteverde provides a brief insight into the magnificent diversity of the highlands, including over 400 species of bird, the highlight being the resplendent – but elusive – quetzal. For a bird's eye view, soar through the spectacular misty cloudforest canopy on a high-speed zip-line. Page 78.

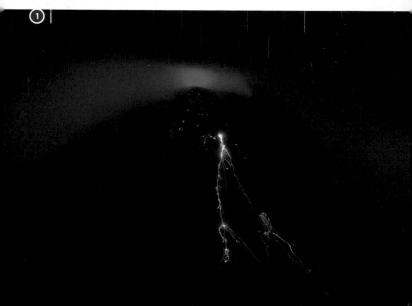

Footprint Handbook

Costa Rica

RICHARD ARGHIRIS

This is
Costa Rica

❸ Beachlife

Beach lovers and surfers can pick pretty much any spot from the northern Nicoya Peninsula down the Central Pacific coastline and find a personally tailored version of paradise with lively resorts and quiet hideaways catering for all budgets, tastes and energy levels, all with some of the best sunsets on the planet. Pages 94, 106, 120 and 151.

❹ Parque Nacional Chirripó

Travelling overland down the mountainous spine of the country, a barren *páramo* wilderness at the heart of the continental divide, you'll be able to enjoy sweeping views of Chirripó Grande, the country's highest peak and a serious challenge for trekkers. Page 124.

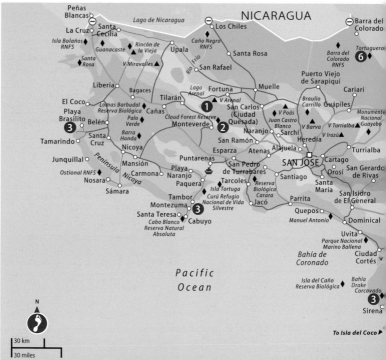

❺ Puerto Jiménez and Península de Osa

Located on a remote Pacific peninsula, the pristine Parque Nacional Corcovado is a moment of magic for both adventurers and wildlife lovers, where you can encounter sublime rainforest fauna. Gateway to Corcovado is Puerto Jiménez, a relaxed former mining town with a frontier feel. Page 133.

❻ Parque Nacional Tortuguero

The canals of Tortuguero are likely to provide quiet moments of awestruck contemplation as you encounter the wildlife and vegetation of this aquatic inland waterworld, while on the coast prehistoric turtles lumber out of the surf to nest on the beaches as they have done for millions of years. Page 145.

Caribbean Sea

Siquirres
Matina
Puerto Limón
Barbilla
Cahuita
Puerto Viejo de Talamanca
Bribri ❸
Hitoy-Cerere Reserva Biológica
Chirripó Grande
La Amistad ❹
Buenos Aires
PANAMA
Palmar Norte
Paso Real
Coto Brus
Palmar Sur
Iahillo
San Vito
Piedras Blancas Golfito RNFS
Ciudad Neily
Península de Osa ❺
Golfito
Paso Canoas
Puerto Jiménez
Carate
Pta Banco
Punta Burica

Surfer, Playa Negra

Route planner

Choosing where to go in Costa Rica is tantamount to being a child in a huge sweet shop – the choice is daunting and you want to do it all … immediately. Given all the options, it's worth doing a bit of planning. Obviously, the more time you have the better, but one of the great things about Costa Rica is its diversity-to-size ratio. Even with just a few days, you would have time to visit a couple of highland spots and a beach before heading home. Ideally, you would spend two or three weeks in Costa Rica; four to five weeks would be much more relaxing.

Ten days

Central Valley, cloudforest and beaches

Seeing a cross-section of Costa Rica in 10 days could be tough. Space it out and it could be ideal. After a day in San José or a nearby town of the Central Valley, it's a short trip north to Fortuna taking in the craft capital of Sarchí, and the topiary creations of Zarcero en route. A couple of days in Fortuna allows plenty of time to see the Arenal volcano and the nearby waterfall, and still have time for a day trip north to the wetlands of Caño Negro Wildlife Reserve close to the Nicaraguan border, before heading round Lake Arenal to Santa Elena for a couple of days exploring the delights of the cloudforest in the Monteverde area.

Heading further north you could have a few days' adventure at one of the lodges close to Rincón de la Vieja hiking through the national park, or simply taking it easy.

With just a few days left, head out to the Nicoya Peninsula and find a beach that takes your fancy. Tamarindo is a lively spot, while Playa del Coco is a good budget option. Sámara and Nosara are slightly pricier but offer peace and quiet. Enjoy some genuine rest and relaxation, with the occasional local excursion, before heading back to San José (40 minutes by plane or half a day overland).

Two weeks

A few extra days couple would allow you to tag on a trip to Parque Nacional Tortuguero on the Caribbean to the suggested itinerary, above. Alternatively, after visiting Arenal and Monteverde, you could head out to Tortuguero National Park before going south to relax on the quieter beaches and at one of the secluded homely lodges.

Two weeks is long enough to consider doing a fly-drive option. Take the first week to acclimatize yourself to Costa Rica, seeing a couple of places that you can't reach in a private vehicle, and then head out on your own to explore and enjoy the freedom of going left, right, straight on or backwards whenever you please.

Three weeks
Mountain peaks, lush rainforest and Pacific beaches

You are now moving into the realms of really being able to explore. After a brief foray through the Central Valley exploring the delights of the region, head out to Arenal and Monteverde and make your way slowly south down the Pan-American Highway through San Isidro de El General. Hikers can stop off for a few days to knock off Chirripó, while others can explore the quieter options of this forgotten region. Continue south through the scenic Coto Brus Valley to San Vito and finally to Golfito, where you can step out to explore the coast or tramp through the rainforest of Parque Nacional Corcovado.

Awestruck and amazed, head up the coastal road slowly taking in Dominical, Jacó or Manuel Antonio – depending on whether you like deserted, busy or popular – to enjoy the beach before heading back to San José.

When to go

Climate

In general, the best time to visit is December to February. This is during the dry season (December to April), but before the temperatures really rise (March and April). Two main factors contribute to the local climatic conditions: altitude and location. The climate varies from the heat and humidity of the Caribbean and Atlantic lowlands, usually around the mid-20°Cs, falling to the warm temperate Meseta Central with chilly temperatures at greater heights – in the Cordillera Talamanca, the average temperature is below 16°C. On the Pacific side there is a well-defined wet season (May-November). The wetter Atlantic side has no specific dry season but there is less rainfall between March and September.

Weather San José

January	February	March	April	May	June
23°C 14°C 10mm	24°C 14°C 0mm	26°C 15°C 20mm	26°C 16°C 40mm	26°C 16°C 220mm	26°C 16°C 240mm

July	August	September	October	November	December
25°C 16°C 210mm	25°C 16°C 240mm	26°C 16°C 300mm	25°C 15°C 290mm	25°C 15°C 140mm	23°C 14°C 40mm

Bank holidays are cause for celebration everywhere and Costa Rica is no different. On national holidays, banks, government offices and stores close down so make sure you have enough money. National holidays are listed here, regional and local festivals are listed in the relevant chapter. Large festivals tend to go big on processions, costumes and traditional marching bands, but find a small town and you'll get horse racing, bull-friendly bull fighting (where the lucky beast leaves the ring exhausted but alive) and a chance to rub shoulders with the townsfolk at a more intimate gathering.

The main holiday period is Christmas and New Year, and Easter week, when much of San José decants from the highlands to the beaches. Book accommodation well in advance at this time of year.

Festival calendar

January

1 January New Year's Day.
Late January/early February **Fiesta de los Diablitos**, in the small towns of Boruca and Rey Curre, southern Costa Rica, symbolic of the fight between cultures, religion and colonization.

March

March (second Sunday) **National Oxcart Day**, with colourful processions and music in Escazú.
March/April **Maundy Thursday** and **Good Friday**, Easter Week.

April

11 April **Juan Santamaría Day**, celebrating the victorious Battle of Rivas against William Walker in 1856.

May

1 May **Labour Day**, which apparently heralds the President's State of the Nation address, cricket matches and a day off.

July

25 July **Annexation of Guanacaste**, celebrating Guanacaste's decision to stay with Costa Rica rather than Nicaragua in 1824.

August

2 August **Virgin Mary Queen of Angels**, Patron of Costa Rica celebrated with religious pilgrimages to the Basilica in Cartago.
15 August **Day of the Virgin Mary's Assumption to Heaven** and **Mother's Day**.

September

15 September **Independence Day**, with parades and marching bands through the streets of San José.

October

12 October **Día de la Raza (Columbus Day)** celebrated with particular gusto in the Caribbean city of Puerto Limón, the week before and after Columbus Day.

There's music, dance, street processions and general festivities. Hotels book up, but it's definitely worth making the effort to go.

November
2 November All Souls' Day, the Day of the Dead, showing respect to those who have passed on.

December
25 December Christmas, celebrations build before and continue in the week after, particularly in San José but also on a smaller scale throughout much of the country.
31 December, 1 and 2 January La Danza de los Diablitos, a festival with traditional masks, costumes, music and dancing in the Indian village of Boruca.

What to do

Many options in Costa Rica have been packaged to create two-, three- or four-day trips. By mixing and matching, you create a tailor-made trip to match the pace you want. A suggested itinerary might include: two or three days' whitewater rafting on the Pacuare or Reventazón rivers near Turrialba, followed by a flight down to Palmar Sur or Puerto Jiménez for some trekking through Parque Nacional Corcovado before heading to Drake for some relaxing diving.

Ballooning and bungee jumping

If you're looking for a last big-spending celebration, hot-air-balloon rides take you over the trees near Arenal Volcano and also the Turrialba region. Contact **Serendipity Adventures**, T2556-2222, www.serendipity adventures.com. The final suggestion is to jump off a bridge. Bungee jumping, that is, off the Colorado bridge, close to Grecia in the Meseta Central (see page 49).

Canopy tours

The rainforest canopy is where most of Costa Rica's wildlife action takes place and there are now a multitude of ways of getting you up there. The calmest is probably exploring on a suspension bridge, strung out along the trees where you are free to walk at leisure, or on an aerial tram, which is essentially an adapted ski lift. The best high-adrenalin option is the zip-wire, which lets you whizz down high-tension steel cables strung between forest giants. You won't see much as you soar through the air, but it is good fun and you do get close to the forest canopy. Most of the country's canopy tour companies are concentrated in Santa Elena and Fortuna.

Diving, snorkelling and swimming

There is swimming on both Atlantic and Pacific coasts. Offshore, sea kayaking is increasingly popular. Snorkelling and scuba-diving are offered by several hotels and most beach tour offices, but you have to pick your spot carefully. Anywhere near a river will suffer from poor visibility and the coral reef has died in many places because of agricultural pollutants washed downstream, particularly on the Caribbean coast. Generally, on the Caribbean side, you can see wrecks and coral reefs, particularly in the southeast towards the Panamanian border, while on the Pacific side you see large pelagics and sportfish. Live-aboard dive boats

Best surf breaks

Pavones

Hidden away on the south Pacific coast, Pavones is a legendary left point break that rides for up to 800 m on a good swell. It's the longest ride in Costa Rica, and being a fickle fiend, it's also the longest wait; when there's no swell its popularity can lead to a crowded line up. However, as luck would have it, there are a number of other left handers around the point and also a beach break which can be bigger than the point itself. And Pavones is just the right sort of laid-back town you'll want to wait in on quiet days.

Salsa Brava

Over on the Caribbean side, offshore of Puerto Viejo de Talamanca, Salsa Brava reef break is known for its size and power. It's the biggest wave in Costa Rica, and definitely not for novices (the powerful wave breaks over coral – you may need to pack a spare board for this one). It needs a swell to work; the best time of year is from December to April. This is one of the most up-and-coming beach spots in Costa Rica.

Witches' Rock

At the northernmost point of the Nicoya Peninsula, Peña Bruja, mistakenly translated in the 1980s as 'Witches' Rock', is a famous break, with fast, hollow rights, and good lefts when it's smaller. A beautiful, remote and picturesque spot, the wave is off Playa Naranjo, in Santa Rosa National Park. Access is by 4WD during dry season (boat during the wet) and camping is available at the park ranger's station.

Playa Hermosa

Just south of Jacó (itself a great surf spot, well suited for the novice), Playa Hermosa provides a powerful and consistent beach break, with a hollow peak that could be compared to Puerto Escondido in Mexico. Sticking out into the Pacific, the spot is assured reliable swell. At times it's perfect. Playa Hermosa is your laid-back surf base, while Jacó provides a lively party atmosphere.

Playa Grande

Playa Grande, a short trip across the estuary from Tamarindo, provides one of the most consistent breaks in the country, with lefts and rights of good size (it's the most westerly point of Costa Rica and can get swells from the north, south and west). There's almost always something happening at Playa Grande except at the bottom of the tide. A few hotels in Playa Grande and lots in Tamarindo make it a good base from which to explore and take side trips.

Malpaís

Slowly and reluctantly emerging into the spotlight, Malpaís, on the southwest tip of the Nicoya Peninsula, provides one of the best all-round surfing experiences in the country. There are several breaks up and down a short stretch of beach, with good transport for moving between them. There are courses for beginners, and a good mix of lefts and rights for all levels of surfer. There's plenty going on in the area, and enough services to make it a good spot for a surf crowd, or a family looking for more than one activity by the beach.

Tortuguero National Park

If creeping along the coast in the middle of the night, with no torch, wasn't exciting enough, imagine seeing a massive leatherback turtle coming ashore to nest at Tortuguero National Park. Laboriously dragging itself up the beach to beyond the high watermark, it digs a deep hole to incubate the leathery eggs, and returns exhausted to the restful world of the ocean. See www.tortuguerovillage.com.

Marino Ballena National Park

Marino Ballena National Park in the southern central Pacific coast just doesn't make sense. Every December to April migrating northern hemisphere humpback whales visit, and from August to October their southern hemisphere cousins drop by. Add dolphins and turtles, and it's a veritable natural zoo. And yet barely anyone visits. True, you're not guaranteed a sighting, but when you do get one, it's a truly unforgettable experience. The area is less developed than much of Costa Rica, so the best accommodation is the rustic Hotel Canto de Ballenas, www.turismoruralcr.com.

Monteverde Cloud Forest Reserve

Whether you're with a guide, or exploring alone, Monteverde Cloud Forest Reserve, www.monteverdeinfo.com, offers the chance to discover a great wilderness. Wander the quieter trails passing trees cloaked in moss and epiphytes, drenched by passing clouds. Catch a glimpse of an exotic bird, spider or brightly coloured frog. Take a nocturnal tour to see tarantulas and other creatures of the night. Then get up early to experience the rainforest as dawn breaks. You can happily spend a day enthralled by the jungle, but for real adventure, head deep into the reserve and spend a few days at one of the field stations.

head for the islands of Caño and Isla del Coco. Divers are not permitted in national parks or reserves, nor within 500 m of the protected sea turtle zone north of Parque Nacional Tortuguero.

Fishing

For sport fishing, sailfish and marlin are targeted off the Pacific; snook and tarpon are caught in the Caribbean, the largest snook being found in September and October, mostly north of Limón (where there are fishing lodges), but also towards Panama. Exciting it may be, cheap it is not.

Anglers can save money in groups, since it is usually the same cost to rent a boat for one or four.

Nature tourism

There are many well-kept and well-guarded national parks and nature reserves that protect some samples of the extraordinarily varied Costa Rican ecosystems. In the north the variety is daunting and includes some of the last patches of dry tropical forest in the Parque Nacional Santa Rosa, the cloudforest of Monteverde and the Talamanca

Mount Chirripó

In their eagerness to provide good service and a warm welcome, Costa Ricans have taken much of the work out of exploration. However, you can't avoid the tough stuff if you want to climb Mount Chirripó in the central Talamancas. The trip starts from San Gerardo de Rivas, easily reached from San Isidro de El General. Allow at least one day up and one day down – more if you have the time. It's not a technical climb, more of a steady plod, but you have to keep moving. As you climb through the different ecosystems, from cloudforest to alpine *páramo*, you'll see plenty of birds – and hear even more. Listen out for the rriikkk-rriikk-rriikk of the toucans. It's a great trek, and leads to the highest point in Costa Rica.

Volcán Arenal

Volcán Arenal fell dormant in 2011, but new rumblings in 2014 indicate an eruption might be imminent. The volcano is a classic casualty of the nature documentary. Having peered down the crater of an explosive volcano at home on TV, could anything match that drama in real life? Probably not, but if Arenal is active, and if you can find a spot to sit, rest and watch, it is mighty impressive. By day, a steady gentle puff of smoke rises from the crater. At night, the dust trails reveal themselves to be molten lava, drawing a bright orange line crashing, smashing and splitting down the volcano. It might seem a long way off, but it can be deadly. Enjoy the geological spectacle.

Manuel Antonio National Park

Why does Costa Rica have so many national parks? Because there's so much to protect. For convenience and beauty, head for Manuel Antonio National Park, which has stunning beaches and rainforest side-by-side. Cahuita National Park on the Caribbean also has a forest-fringed beach, with clear waters and some of the best corals in Costa Rica. For challenging hiking, steaming mudpots and waterfalls head up to Rincón de la Vieja, a little to the east of Liberia. Choosing a favourite national park is like having to choose a favourite child. You can't – just love them all.

Mountains, and nine active volcanoes including Rincón de la Vieja, Poás, Irazú and of course Arenal. See also box, above.

Birdwatchers and butterfly lovers have long flocked to Costa Rica to see some of the 850 or so species of bird and untold varieties of butterfly. All of these can best be seen in the parks, together with monkeys, deer, coyotes, armadillos, anteaters, turtles, coatis, raccoons, snakes and, more rarely, wild pigs, wild cats and tapirs.

Although the national parks and other privately owned reserves are a main tourist attraction, many are in remote areas and not easy to get to on public transport; buses or coaches that do go tend to stay for a short time. There is a tendency for tour companies to dominate the National Park 'market' to the exclusion of other public transport. For tight budgets, try making up a party with others and sharing taxis or hiring a car.

Asociación de Voluntarios (ASVO), Paseo Colón, Toyota, 250 m north, T2222-3612, www.asvocr.org. Contact if you want to work as a volunteer in the parks, at US$20 per day for lodging and food plus US$30 registration. Bilingual tourist information and/or telephone numbers for individual national park offices is available by dialling T192.

Fundación de Parques Nacionales (FPN), 300 m north and 150 m east of Santa Teresita Church, Barrio Escalante, between Calles 23-25, San José, T2257-2239, www. fpn-cr.org. Monday-Friday 0800-1200, 1300-1700. Contact for information and permits to visit and/or camp or conduct research in the parks. Check in advance if your trip depends on gaining entrance.

Sistema Nacional de Areas de Conservación (SINAC), Avenida 15 Calle 1º, Barrio Tournón al costado Sur de la ULACIT, San José, T2522-6500, www.sinac.go.cr. Administers the National Park System (email in advance or call).

Rafting, kayaking and canoeing

The rivers of Costa Rica have proved to be highly popular for whitewater rafting, kayaking and canoeing, both for the thrill of the rapids and the wildlife interest of the quieter sections. The five most commonly run rivers are the Reventazón (and the Pascua section of it), Pacuare, Corobicí, Sarapiquí and El General. You can do a day trip but to reach the Grade IV and V rapids you usually have to take two to three days. The Reventazón is perhaps the most accessible but the Pacuare has been recommended as a more beautiful experience. The Corobicí is slower and popular with birdwatchers.

Ríos Tropicales (see page 43) has been recommended. For reasons of safety heavy rain may cause cancellations, so make sure your plans are flexible.

Spectator sports

Most fiestas end with **bullfighting** in the squares, with no horses used. Bullfights are held in San José during the Christmas period. There is no kill and spectators are permitted to enter the ring to chase, and be chased by, the bull.

Football (soccer) is the national sport (played every Sunday at 1100, September-May, at the Saprissa Stadium).

Surfing and windsurfing

Windsurfing is good along the Pacific coast, particularly in the bay close to La Cruz and world class on Lake Arenal, particularly the west end where hotels have equipment for hire.

Surfing is popular on the Pacific and southern Caribbean beaches, attracting professionals who follow storm surges along the coast. Beginners can take classes in some resorts like Tamarindo, Jacó and Dominical, and proficient surfers can get advice on waves from surf shops in these areas. See also box, page 15.

Shopping tips

There is certainly no shortage of souvenirs to buy in Costa Rica. Items range from small collectibles, fridge magnets, knick-knacks and T-shirts of the anthropomorphized gaudy-leaf frogs and "My Uncle went to Costa Rica and…" genre, to genuinely well-made wooden furniture and decorative pieces. Haggling is not entered into as a rule but you may find the occasional opportunity to flex your negotiating might.

The best buys are wooden items, ceramics and leather handicrafts. Many wooden handicrafts are made of rainforest hardwoods and deforestation is a critical problem. Coffee should have 'puro' on the packet or it may contain sugar or other additives.

Don't buy any archaeological artefacts or items made from endangered species including turtles, animal skins and coral.

What to buy

With row upon row of carefully decorated gifts sitting in neat rows it's easy to think Costa Rica is only full of mass-produced items. Look a little closer and you'll see the quirky touch and character of the hand-painted items.

The main place to buy gifts – for some the only place – is **Sarchí** in the Central Highlands. The town has become the artisan centre of the country, churning out creations of colourful, hand-decorated *carretas* (ox-carts). Don't worry about getting them home – they can be flat-packed and shipped if required, as can the sturdy wood and leather rocking chairs sitting on porches and balconies throughout the country.

You can buy gifts throughout the country. **Wooden carvings** are popular with decorative and functional pieces including bowls, trays and carvings, as well as recycled wood from coffee plants used to create figures and animals. Lightweight balsa is often carved into tropical wildlife creations.

Jewellery sets semi-precious jade in gold and silver, and jade, copper and bronze are used to create **pre-Columbian replicas**. Indigenous pieces are available in a few select places, including the deep red **ceramics** of the Chorotegas in Guaitil, the **masks** and **woven goods** of the Boruca, or the **carved gourds** or *jícara* of the Guaymi and Bribrí in the far south.

Textiles provide plenty of options beyond the simple T-shirt, with mats, table cloths and napkins. Although they're from Panama, vividly colourful *molas* (brightly coloured appliqués) are available in some parts of the south of the country.

Contemporary, traditional and religious **art** hangs off the walls of galleries dotted around **San José** and **Escazú**. A personal favourite is the vibrancy of Patricia Erickson. Ceramic creations include the colourful and slightly humourous pieces of Cecilia Figueres.

Music makes a good gift. For folklore you won't get a broader swatch than *Costa Rica Pura Vida*, sold in market squares and record shops. Less manic on the *marimba* is the ambient jazz feel of *Editus* who, with Panamanian Rubén Blades, won a Grammy for their album *Tiempos*.

Finally fill any spare space in your bag with freshly roasted **coffee**, **liquors** or **paper** and **envelopes** recycled from banana leaves.

Improve your travel photography

Taking pictures is a highlight for many travellers, yet too often the results turn out to be disappointing. Steve Davey, author of Footprint's *Travel Photography*, sets out his top rules for coming home with pictures you can be proud of.

Before you go

Don't waste precious travelling time and do your research before you leave. Find out what festivals or events might be happening or which day the weekly market takes place, and search online image sites such as Flickr to see whether places are best shot at the beginning or end of the day, and what vantage points you should consider.

Get up early

The quality of the light will be better in the few hours after sunrise and again before sunset – especially in the tropics when the sun will be harsh and unforgiving in the middle of the day. Sometimes seeing the sunrise is a part of the whole travel experience: sleep in and you will miss more than just photographs.

Stop and think

Don't just click away without any thought. Pause for a few seconds before raising the camera and ask yourself what you are trying to show with your photograph. Think about what things you need to include in the frame to convey this meaning. Be prepared to move around your subject to get the best angle. Knowing the point of your picture is the first step to making sure that the person looking at the picture will know it too.

Compose your picture

Avoid simply dumping your subject in the centre of the frame every time you take a picture. If you move it to one side, then your picture can look more balanced. This will also allow you to show a significant background and make the picture more meaningful. A good rule of thumb is to place your subject or any significant detail a third of the way into the frame; facing into the frame not out of it.

This rule also works for landscapes. Compose with the horizon two-thirds of the way up the frame if the foreground is the most interesting part of the picture; one-third of the way up if the sky is more striking.

Fill the frame

If you are going to focus on a detail or even a person's face in a close-up portrait, then be bold and make sure that you fill the frame. This is often a case of physically getting in close. You can use a telephoto setting on a zoom lens when photographing people or piles of colourful produce at a market, but this can lead to pictures looking quite flat: moving in close is a lot more fun!

Interact with people

If you want to shoot evocative portraits then it is vital to approach people and seek permission in some way, even if it is just by smiling at someone. Spend a little time with them and they are likely to relax and look less stiff and formal. Action portraits where people are doing something, or environmental portraits, where they are set against a significant background, are a good way to achieve relaxed portraits. Interacting is a good way to find out more about people and their lives, creating memories as well as photographs.

Focus carefully

Your camera can focus quicker than you, but it doesn't know which part of the picture you want to be in focus. If your camera is using the centre focus sensor then move the camera so it is over the subject and half press the button, then, holding it down, recompose the picture. This will lock the focus. Take the now correctly focused picture when you are ready.

Another technique for accurate focusing is to move the active sensor over your subject. Some cameras with touch-sensitive screens allow you to do this by simply clicking on the subject.

Leave light in the sky

Most good night photography is actually taken at dusk when there is some light and colour left in the sky; any lit portions of the picture will balance with the sky and any ambient lighting. There is only a very small window when this will happen, so get into position early, be prepared and keep shooting and reviewing the results. You can take pictures after this time, but avoid shots of tall towers in an inky black sky; crop in close on lit areas to fill the frame.

Bring it home safely

Digital images are inherently ephemeral: they can be deleted or corrupted in a heartbeat. The good news though is they can be copied just as easily. Wherever you travel, you should have a backup strategy. Cloud backups are popular, but make sure that you will have access to fast enough Wi-Fi. If you use RAW format, then you will need some sort of physical back-up. If you don't travel with a laptop or tablet, then you can buy a backup drive that will copy directly from memory cards.

Recently updated and available in both digital and print formats, Footprint's Travel Photography by Steve Davey covers everything you need to know about travelling with a camera, including simple post-processing. More information is available at www.footprinttravelguides.com

Where to stay

from bed and breakfast hotels to rustic lodges

Accommodation options cover all styles and budgets and in Costa Rica the variety and diversity is spectacular. Eccentric and purist designs perched on a hillside providing respite for mind and body, quiet hotels in secluded private reserves, beachfront properties and glorious romantic hideaways, down through steady steps of luxury, comforts and services to the simplest, most basic rooms.

Accommodation in Costa Rica favours couples and groups – the price of a single room is often the same as a double, and the price of a room for four is often less than double the price for two. So if you can get in a group, the cost per person falls considerably. Accommodation prices during the 'green' season (May to November), are generally much lower. A 13% sales tax plus 3.39% tourism tax (total 16.39%) are added to the basic price of hotel rooms. A deposit is advised at the more expensive hotels in San José, especially in the high season (December to April), to guarantee reservations. If you arrive late at night in the high season, even a guaranteed reservation may not be kept.

The **Costa Rica Bed & Breakfast Group**, which has 300 bed and breakfast inns and small hotels around the country in its membership, helps with reservations. The **Costa Rican Chamber of Hotels** ① *T2220-0575, www.costaricanhotels.com*, provides information about its members (mostly larger hotels) and an online reservation system.

The **Costa Rican Tourist Board** ① *T800-TOURISM, www.visitcostarica.com*, has an eco-rating system for hotels, an encouraging indicator of progress.

Price codes

Where to stay	Restaurants
$$$$ over US$150	$$$ over US$12
$$$ US$66-150	$$ US$7-12
$$ US$30-65	$ US$6 and under
$ under US$30	

Price of a double room in high season, including taxes.

Price for a two-course meal for one person, excluding drinks or service charge.

At the rustic end of the scale **Cooprena** heads a network of co-operatively owned lodges and houses that provide accommodation throughout the country in rural settings. Conditions are normally basic, but are in excellent positions for experiencing rural Costa Rican home life and with opportunities for activities nearby. Close to the ideals of ecotourism, the impact of visitors is minimal; sustainable use of the environment primary, and the money goes to the local community. Contact **Simbiosis Tours** ⓘ *San José, T2248-2538, www.turismoruralcr.com*.

Camping opportunities in Costa Rica are limited with few official campsites. It is possible to camp in some national parks. Contact the Fundación de Parques Nacionales in San José (T2257-2239, www.fpn-cr.org).

Food
& drink

from Costa Rican *casado* to *chan* drinks

Food

Costa Rican food is simple, relying heavily on the staples of rice and beans. Mixed with shredded beef, chicken or sometimes fish, served with a couple of warmed tortillas and you have the dish of *casado* that fuels the majority of the country's workers. One way of spicing up the food is with liberal helpings of Salsa Lizano which is always somewhere near the dinner table. *Sodas* (small restaurants) serve local food, which is worth trying.

In general, eating out in Costa Rica is more expensive than elsewhere in Central America. A sales tax of 13% plus 10% service charge are added to restaurant bills.

An excellent general rule when looking for somewhere to eat is to ask locally. Most restaurants serve a daily special meal, usually at lunchtime called a *comida corrida* or *comida corriente*, which works out much cheaper and is usually filling and nutritious. Vegetarians should list all the foods they cannot eat; saying '*Soy vegetariano/a*' (I'm a vegetarian) or '*No como carne*' (I don't eat meat) is often not enough. Street stalls are by far the cheapest – although not always the safest – option; another inexpensive place to eat is the local market. The best value is undoubtedly in small, family-run places. If self-catering, markets are cheaper than supermarkets.

Safety The golden rule is boil it, cook it, peel it or forget it, but if you did that every day, every meal, you'd never eat anywhere. A more practicable rule is that if large numbers of people are eating in a regularly popular place, it's more than likely going to be OK.

Drink

There are always plenty of non-alcoholic *refrescos* (soft drinks) and mineral water. *Agua fresca* – fresh fruit juices mixed with water or mineral water – and *licuados* (milk shakes) are good and usually safe. Milk should be pasteurized. Water should be filtered or bottled. Herbal teas – for example chamomile (*manzanilla*) and mint (*hierba buena*) – are readily available. All imported food and drink is expensive.

There are many types of cold drink made either from fresh fruit or milk drinks with fruit (*batidos*) or cereal flour whisked with ice cubes. Drinks are often sugared well beyond North American or European tastes (ask for *poco azúcar*). The fruits range from the familiar to the exotic; others include *cebada* (barley flour), *pinolillo* (roasted corn), *horchata* (rice flour with cinnamon), *chan*, which according to Michael Brisco is "perhaps the most unusual, looking like mouldy frogspawn and tasting of penicillin". All these drinks cost the same as, or less than, bottled fizzy products. The coffee is excellent. Local beers are Bavaria, Pilsen, Imperial, Rock Ice and Kaiser (which is non-alcoholic).

FOOD AND DRINK
Menu reader

A
aguacate avocado
ajillo garlic butter sauce
a la plancha food cooked on a sizzling plate or flat grill
al horno baked
arreglados bread filled with vegetables
arroz con pollo chicken and rice
asado roasted or grilled meat or fish

B
bistec encebollado steak bathed in onions
bocadillo sandwich
¡buen provecho! enjoy your meal

C
cajeta de coco coconut fudge
cajeta de leche milk sweet
cajetas traditional sweets, candied fruit
caliente hot
camarones de río freshwater prawns
camote yam
carimanolas stuffed yucca fritters
carne asada grilled beef
cerdo asado grilled pork
ceviche raw fish marinated in onions and lime juice
chorreados corn pancakes
churrasco grilled steak
comida corriente/comida casera set menu
comida económica cheap food/menu
comidas meals
cuajada lightly salted, soft feta-type cheese
curvina sea bass
curvina a la plancha grilled sea bass

D
desayuno breakfast
dorado a la parilla grilled dorado fish

E
elote corn on the cob
empanadas pastries filled with meat or chicken

G
gallo filled tortilla
gallo pinto fried white rice and kidney beans, with onions and sweet pepper, often served for breakfast
garbanzos chick peas
gaseosas fizzy drinks

H
huevos fritos fried eggs

I
indio viejo cornmeal and shredded beef porridge with garlic and spices

J
jugo pure fruit juice

L
langosta lobster
langosta blanca 'white lobster' ie cocaine
lomo relleno stuffed beef

M
mahi mahi grilled dorado fish
mar y tierra surf and turf
mariscos seafood
melocotón star fruit/peach
mojarra carp
mole chocolate, chilli sauce

N
nacatamales cornmeal, pork or chicken and rice, achote (similar to paprika), peppers, potatoes, onions and cooking oil, all wrapped in a big green banana leaf and boiled
natilla a slightly sour cream
níspero brown sugar fruit

O
Olla de carne soup of beef, plantain, corn, yucca, ñampi and chayote (local vegetables)

P

paca large, nocturnal rodent
palmitos palm hearts, popular in salads
pan bread
pargo al vapor steamed snapper
pargo rojo/blanco red/white snapper
para llevar to take away
parrillada Argentine-style grill
patacones deep-fried plantain slices, popular on the Caribbean coast
pescado fish
pescado a la suyapa fresh snapper in a tomato, sweet pepper and onion sauce
picadillo meat and vegetable stew
picante hot, spicy
piniona thin strips of candied green papaya
Pío V corn cake topped with light cream and bathed in rum sauce
pitaya cactus fruit, blended with lime and sugar
plátano plantain
plato típico typical Costa Rican food
pollo chicken
pollo asado grilled chicken
pupusas tortillas filled with beans, cheese and/or pork, traditionally from El Salvador but also available in Costa Rica

Q

quesadillas fried tortilla with cheese, chilli and peppers
quesillos mozzarella cheese in a hot tortilla with salt and bathed in cream
queso crema moist bland cheese, good fried
queso seco slightly bitter dry cheese

R

refresco/fresco fruit juice or grains and spices mixed with water and sugar
robalo snook
rosquillas baked corn and cheese biscuits

S

sábalo/sábalo real tarpon/giant tarpon
sopa de mondongo tripe soup
sopa negra soup with black beans and a poached egg
sorbete ice cream
surtido sampler or mixed dish

T

tacos fried tortilla stuffed with chicken, beef or pork
tacos chinos egg rolls
tamales cornmeal parcels, filled with pork or chicken, and cooked in a banana leaf
tiste grainy indigenous drinks served in an original jícaro gourd cup
tipitapa tomato sauce
tres leches very sweet cake made with three kinds of milk (fresh and tinned)

Y

yuca frita fried yucca

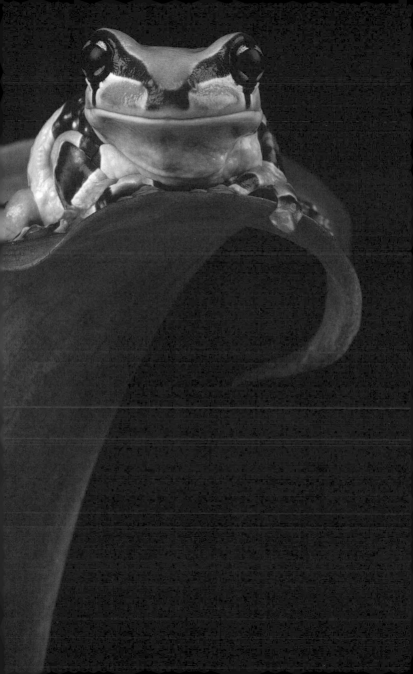

San José
& around

Home to one-third of the country's population, San José is the gritty capital of Costa Rica: a modern, sprawling, high-charged city jammed with traffic and frenetic crowds of pedestrians. It is not so much aesthetic as intriguing – the place to see a nation on the move.

The city was founded in 1737 with the expansion of lucrative tobacco plantations in the fertile valley of Aserrí. In 1823, it emerged as the capital of a newly independent Costa Rica after turbulent wars with the competing regional powers of Alajuela, Heredia and Cartago. Earthquakes have since destroyed much of the city's original architecture, but a smattering of historic mansions and churches remain.

Although it fails to charm most visitors, San José is one of the most friendly and accessible capitals in Central America, home to a thriving arts scene, fine restaurants, galleries, museums and nightclubs, as well as numerous shady plazas and parks, which are oases from the overheated mayhem outside.

Essential San José

Finding your feet

Most of the city conforms to a grid layout – *avenidas* run east–west; *calles* north–south. Avenidas to the north of Avenida Central are given odd numbers; those to the south even numbers. Calles to the west of Calle Central are even-numbered; those to the east are odd-numbered. Despite this semblance of order, neither *avenidas* nor *calles* are very well-marked beyond the downtown area and many locals give directions based on archaic points of reference (eg 'three blocks south of the gas station'). The length of a single city block is usually given as *'cien metros'* (100 m), regardless of its actual measurement.

Getting around

Walking is the best way to get around downtown San José with an increasing number of streets now fully or partly pedestrianized. Driving in San José is not recommended. Rush hour is officially 0700-0900 and 1700-1900, but the streets are often congested at all waking hours. If you do decide to drive, note that restrictions are in place for all local vehicles, including rental cars. The last digit of your licence plate assigns a no-drive day, applicable 0600-1900: 1 and 2 Monday; 3 and 4 Tuesday; 5 and 6 Wednesday; 7 and 8 Thursday; 9 and 0 Friday. Taxis can be ordered by phone or hailed in the street. They are red and are legally required to have and use meters (known as *marías*). Commuter trains now link the city centre with some of the suburbs and a few cities in the Meseta Central (see Transport, page 46).

Safety

The downtown area is generally safe in the day, but big city rules apply. As ever, speak to your hotelier about the safety of the local area. Most of the bus stations are in dicey neighbourhoods and you should use taxis to get in and out, especially at night. If you run into any trouble at all, tourist police are available. Note some taxi drivers are looking to make commissions from hotels and may try to deceive you about the safety or availability of your chosen lodging.

Immigration

The immigration office is on the airport highway, opposite Hospital México. You need to go here for visas extensions, etc. Queues can take all day. To get there, take bus No 10 or 10A Uruca, marked 'México', then cross over highway at the bridge and walk 200 m along highway – just look for the queue or ask the driver. Better to find a travel agent who can obtain what you need for a fee, say US$5. Make sure you get a receipt if you give up your passport.

Weather San José

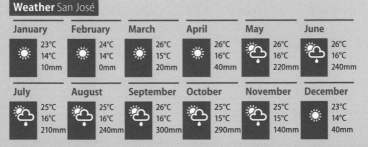

January	February	March	April	May	June
23°C 14°C 10mm	24°C 14°C 0mm	26°C 15°C 20mm	26°C 16°C 40mm	26°C 16°C 220mm	26°C 16°C 240mm

July	August	September	October	November	December
25°C 16°C 210mm	25°C 16°C 240mm	26°C 16°C 300mm	25°C 15°C 290mm	25°C 15°C 140mm	23°C 14°C 40mm

Around Avenida Central and Calle Central

Many of the most interesting public buildings in San José (altitude 1150 m) are near the intersection of Avenida Central and Calle Central. The **Teatro Nacional** ⓘ *just off Av 2, on Calle 3, T2010-1100, Mon-Sat 0900-1800, www.teatronacional.go.cr, from US$5*, built in 1897, has marble staircases, statues, frescoes and foyer decorated in gold with Venetian plate mirrors. Nearby is **Plaza de la Cultura** ⓘ *Av Central, Calle 3-5*, which, in addition to being a great place for people-watching, hosts occasional public concerts. The **Museo de Oro Precolombino** ⓘ *entrance is off Calle 5, T2243-4221, www.museosdelbancocentral.org, daily 0915-1700, US$10*, has a booty of golden treasure buried beneath the Plaza de la Cultura. Fine golden figures of frogs, spiders, raptors and other creatures glisten in this spectacular pre-Columbian gold museum sponsored by the **Banco Central**.

Four blocks east of the plaza, it's worth checking out the **Museo del Jade y Arte Precolombino** ⓘ *Av Central and Calle 13, T2287 6034, www.portal.ins-cr.com, daily 1000-1700, US$10*, which hosts the largest collection of jade carvings in Central America, as well as pre-Columbian pottery and sculpture.

Also east from the Plaza de la Cultura, the **Museo Nacional** ⓘ *Calle 17, Av Central-2, T2257-1433, www.museocostarica.go.cr, Tue-Sat 0830-1630, Sun 0900-1630, US$8, children*

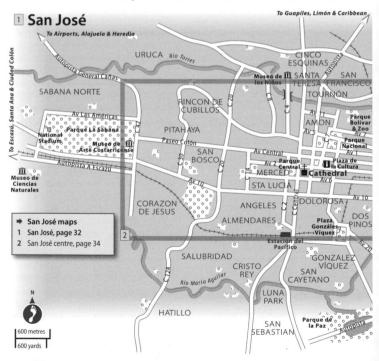

➡ San José maps
1 San José, page 32
2 San José centre, page 34

and students with ID free, has interesting displays on archaeology, anthropology, and national history. Facing it is the **Plaza de la Democracia**, a concrete cascade built to mark the November 1989 centenary of Costa Rican democracy. The **Palacio Nacional** ⓘ *Av Central, Calle 15*, is home of the Legislative Assembly; any visitor can attend debates, sessions start at 1600.

Two blocks north of the Museo Nacional is the **Parque Nacional**, with a grandiloquent bronze monument representing the five Central American republics ousting the filibuster William Walker. To the north of the park is the **Biblioteca Nacional**. In the old liquor factory west of the Biblioteca Nacional, now the Centro Nacional de la Cultura, is the **Museo de Arte y Diseño Contemporáneo** ⓘ *Av 3, Calle 15-17, T2257-7202, www. ww.madc.cr, Mon-Sat 0930-1700, US$3, students with ID US$1*.

Along Calle Central, west of the Teatro Nacional, is **Parque Central**, with a bandstand among trees. East of the park is the monumental architecture of the **Catedral Metropolitana**; to the north is the **Teatro Melico Salazar** ⓘ *see press for details or call T2295-6000, www. teatromelico.go.cr*, which has a good mix of performances throughout the year.

Further west, in **Parque Braulio Carrillo**, opposite the eclectic neo-Gothic design of La Merced church, is a huge carved granite ball brought from the Diquis archaeological site near Palmar Norte. There are other such designs at the entrance to the Museo de Ciencias Naturales.

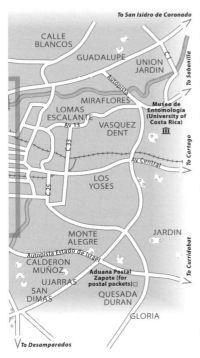

Parque La Sabana

At the end of Paseo Colón, at Calle 42, **Parque La Sabana** was converted from the former city airport in the 1950s; the old airport building on the east side is now the **Museo de Arte Costarricense** ⓘ *T2256-1281, Tue-Sun 0900-1600, www.musarco.go.cr, free*, with a small but interesting display of paintings and sculptures. At the west end of the park is the **Estadio Nacional**, with seating for 20,000 spectators at (mainly) football matches.

Opposite the southwest corner of Parque Sabana are the impressive natural displays of the **Museo de Ciencias Naturales** ⓘ *Colegio La Salle, T2232-5179, www.lasalle. ed.cr, Mon-Sat 0730-1600, Sun 0900-1700, US$1.50, children US$1*, next to the Ministry of Agriculture; take 'Sabana Estadio' bus from Avenida 2, Calle 1 to the gate.

North of Avenida Central

On Calle 2, is the **Unión Club**, the principal social centre of the country. Opposite is the **Correo Central**, general post and telegraph office which also houses an internet café, pastry shop and the **Museo Postal, Telegráfico y Filatélico** ⓘ *upstairs, Mon-Fri 0800-1700, free*.

A couple of blocks to the west is the hustle and bustle of the **Mercado Central**, dating back to 1881, rich with the shouts, cries, smells and chaos of a fresh produce market. Good cheap meals for sale as well as some interesting nick-nacks for the passing tourist. Often crowded; watch for thieves.

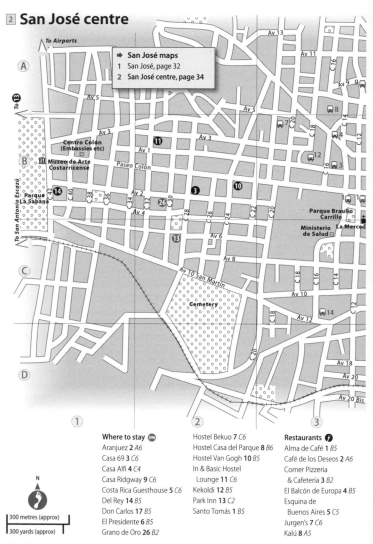

② **San José centre**

➡ **San José maps**
1 San José, page 32
2 San José centre, page 34

Where to stay 🛏
Aranjuez **2** A6
Casa 69 **3** C6
Casa Alfi **4** C4
Casa Ridgway **9** C6
Costa Rica Guesthouse **5** C6
Del Rey **14** B5
Don Carlos **17** B5
El Presidente **6** B5
Grano de Oro **26** B2

Hostel Bekuo **7** C6
Hostel Casa del Parque **8** B6
Hostel Van Gogh **10** B5
In & Basic Hostel
  Lounge **11** C6
Kekoldi **12** B5
Park Inn **13** C2
Santo Tomás **1** B5

Restaurants 🍽
Alma de Café **1** B5
Café de los Deseos **2** A6
Corner Pizzeria
  & Cafeteria **3** B2
El Balcón de Europa **4** B5
Esquina de
  Buenos Aires **5** C5
Jurgen's **7** C6
Kalú **8** A5

N

300 metres (approx)
300 yards (approx)

The Disneyesque building on the horizon to the north of the city is the **Centro Costarricense de Ciencias y Cultura** (Scientific and Cultural Centre) in the old city penitentiary with the **Galería Nacional, Biblioteca Carlos Luis Sáenz**, the **Auditorio Nacional** and **Museo de Los Niños** ① *Calle 4, Av 9, T2258-4929, www.museocr.org, Tue-Fri*

La Criollita **9** *B5*
Lubnan **10** *B2*
Machu Picchu **11** *B2*
Park Café **13** *A1*
Sapore Trattoria **17** *C5*
Shakti **18** *C5*
Soda Tapia **14** *B1*
Tin Jo **15** *C5*
Vishnu **16** *B5*

Buses 🚌
Alajuela & Airport
  Buses **1** *B3*
Heredia Buses **2** *B3/B4*
Liberia Buses **3** *B3*
Panaline Bus **4** *B3*
San Isidro Buses **5** *D4*
Ticabus **6** *C5*
Transnica Bus **7** *B3*
Terminal Alfaro **8** *A3*

Terminal Atlántico
  Norte **9** *A3*
Terminal Caribe
  (Sixaola) **10** *A4*
Terminal Cartago **11** *D5*
Terminal Coca Cola **12** *B3*
Terminal Los Santos **13** *D6*
Terminal Puntarenas **14** *C3*
Terminal Turrialba **15** *C5*

0800-1630, Sat-Sun 0930-1700, US$3, children US$2.50. Interesting as much for the well-restored building as for the exhibits using former prison cells and spaces to good effect.

Along Avenida 3, north of the Plaza de la Cultura, are the four gardens of the remodelled **Parque Morazán**. A little to the northeast, **Parque España**, cool, quiet and intimate, is home to the **Casa Amarilla** (Yellow House), seat of the Ministry of Foreign Affairs, and the **Edificio Metálico**, imported from Europe to become one of the country's first schools.

To the north of Parque Morazán is **Parque Simón Bolívar**, now a recreation area, with **Simón Bolívar National Zoo and Botanical Gardens** ⓘ *Av 11, just east of Calle 7 (go down Calle 7 about 3 blocks from Av 7), T2233-6701, www.fundazoo.org, Mon-Fri 0800-1530, Sat-Sun 0900-1630, US$4.30, children US$3*. It's been remodelled and much improved, with all native plants numbered and listed in a brochure; although the animal cages are small.

To the north of the city, a reasonable walk or a short taxi ride away, is **Spirogyra** ⓘ *100 m east, 150 m south of Centro Comercial El Pueblo (near Hotel Villa Tournón), T2222-937, Mon-Fri 0900-1400, Sat-Sun 0900-1500, guided tours for more than 10 people (reservations required), US$8, US$6 students, US$4 children*, a fascinating butterfly farm. To get there, take 'Calle Blancos' bus from Calle 3 and Avenida 5 to El Pueblo.

Around San José

fashionable, relaxed well-heeled suburbs

East of the centre

Extending east of the downtown core, the youthful town of **San Pedro** is home to the University of Costa Rica. Avenida Central enters this de facto suburb of San José at the well-to-do residential neighbourhood of **Los Yoses**, framed by Calle 33 in the west, Río Ocloro in the south and traffic-plied Cicunvalación in the east. Los Yoses is liberally endowed with chic guesthouses and bohemian restaurants, a chilled-out alternative to the grime and grind of the city centre. Beyond Circunvalación, San Pedro caters to its feisty student population with the best bars and clubs in the city.

Escazú

Fancying itself a cut above San José, Escazú is a fashionable enclave for wealthy Ticos and, as time goes on, soft-bellied expats seeking the convenience, cleanliness and comfort that can only come with US-style shopping malls and heavily air-conditioned condos. Located 20 minutes west of San José, Escazú is in fact three separate settlements climbing a hillside, each with its own church, each increasingly authentic: San Rafael, San Antonio and, at the top of the hill, San Miguel. If you're in town on the second weekend of March, don't miss the **Día del Boyero** (National Day of the Oxcart Driver), hosted by San Antonio. Festivities culminate on the Sunday in a colourful oxcart parade from the school to the centre, accompanied by typical *payasos* (clowns). See Festivals, below.

Tourist information

Instituto Costarricense de Turismo (ICT)
*East side of Juan Pablo II Bridge, over the
General Cañas Highway, T2299-5800,
www.visitcostarica.com. Mon-Fri 0700-1500.*
The central offices of ICT are inconveniently
located in the northwest of the city. Instead,
the helpful downtown branch (Av Central,
between Calles 1 and 3, T2222-1090),
is recommended for casual enquiries.
An **ICT kiosk** can also be found at Juan
Santamaría airport.

Where to stay

Central San José
For hotels near the airport, see Alajuela,
page 51.

$$$$-$$$ Grano de Oro
*Calle 30, Av 2-4, T2255-3322,
www.hotelgrano deoro.com.*
A sumptuous converted early 20th-century
tropical mansion with 40 rooms and suites,
beautiful terrace gardens, renowned
restaurant, jacuzzi and massage services.
A stylish blend of tradition and modernity.
Recommended.

$$$$-$$$ Park Inn
*Av 6 y Calle 28, T2257-1011,
www.parkinn.com/hotel-sanjose.*
A business hotel from Radisson, the Park Inn
boasts 117 rooms and all modern amenities
including pool, gym, business centre, meeting
rooms, and bar-restaurant. Decor is sleek and
contemporary. Good service, reliable.

$$$ Don Carlos
*Calle 9, Av 7-9, T2221-6707,
www.doncarloshotel.com.*
A slightly eccentric traditional city house
adorned with interesting artwork, antiques,
and statuary. They offer a variety of tasteful
rooms and suites, free coffee, sun deck, Wi-Fi,
gift shop, airport shuttle, car hire and tours.
Breakfast included.

$$$ El Presidente
*Av Central, Calle 7, T2010-0000,
www.hotel-presidente.com.*
A landmark business hotel with 91 plush
rooms and suites, stylish contemporary
furnishings, and all modern amenities
including LCD TVs with premium channels,
Wi-Fi, safes, gym, spa, casino, restaurant,
jacuzzi and business services.

$$$ Hotel del Rey
*Av 1, Calle 9, T2257-7800,
www.hoteldelrey.com.*
At the heart of the upmarket red-light
district, the landmark Hotel del Rey is home
to the most famous (legal) brothel in Costa
Rica, the **Blue Marlin** bar. It's an interesting
place for people-watching, popular with
couples out for a drink as much as lonely
'Sexpats' in search of company. The rooms
are quite comfortable, but the walls are a bit
thin. There's also a restaurant and casino.

$$$ Santo Tomás
*Av 7, Calle 3-5, T2255-0448,
www.hotelsantotomas.com.*
Don't be put off by the plain exterior, Santo
Tomás is a well-recommended boutique
lodging set in a converted French Victorian
mansion. It boasts 20 comfortable rooms,
restful and enticing common areas, and
helpful, friendly, professional staff. Amenities
include garden, pool, jacuzzi, Wi-Fi, secure
parking and restaurant. Tours available.

$$ Casa 69
*Calle 25bis No 69, T2256-8879,
www.casa69.com.*
An award-winning B&B, centrally located
with an emphasis on hospitality and service.
Rooms are comfortable and stylish; common
areas include living room, dining room,
sundeck and a leafy courtyard. Lots of bars
on the same street. Recommended.

$$ Casa Alfi
Calle 3 No 459, Av 4-6, T2221-2102,
www.casaalfihotel.com.
Near the Teatro Nacional, an old-school
B&B with no-frills single rooms, spacious
standards and suites, all fully equipped with
orthopaedic mattresses, hot water, Wi-Fi and
cable TV. 1 wheelchair-accessible room is
also available. Friendly, comfortable, simple
and quiet.

$$ Costa Rica Guesthouse
Av 6, Calles 21-23, T2223-7034,
www.costa-rica-guesthouse.com.
A restored 1904 Victorian townhouse with
23 private rooms (cheaper with shared bath),
each with TV, Wi-Fi and semi-orthopaedic
mattress. Amenities include parking, bar-
lounge, disabled access, free tea and coffee.
Decor is simple, tasteful and calm.

$$ Hotel Aranjuez
Calle 19, Av 11-13, T2256-1825,
www.hotelaranjuez.com.
A well-established wood-built hotel
composed of 9 houses faithful to their
1930s architectural heritage. Rooms are
comfortable and cosy with lots of original
details like double doors, French windows,
clapboard walls and wooden floors. Studios
and apartments are also available for weekly
or monthly rental. Recommended.

$$ Hotel Kekoldi
Av 9, Calle 5-7, T2248-0804, www.kekoldi.com.
A 1920s art deco building nestled among
the former mansions of coffee barons in the
historic Barrio Amón. They have 10 well-
appointed rooms and a shady garden replete
with tropical plants and birds. Clean, friendly,
bright and comfortable. Recommended.

$$-$ Casa Ridgway
Calle 15, Av 6-8, T2233-6168,
www.casaridgwayhostel.com.
A friendly non-profit guesthouse run
by the Quaker Peace Center. They offer
dorms ($) and private rooms ($$) with

or without bath, all named after peace
activists like Mother Teresa and Gandhi.
A good place to engage with others on
human rights and social justice issues.
Group rates and facilities available.

$$-$ Hostel Casa del Parque
Calle 19, Av 1-3, T2233-3437,
www.hostelcasadelparque.com.
A very clean and presentable family-run
hostel, not a party place, complete with a
pleasant patio, shared kitchen, common
areas, free coffee, Wi-Fi, a 10-bed dorm
and 4 private rooms, all with orthopaedic
mattresses. Relaxed and friendly.
Recommended.

$$-$ Hostel Van Gogh
Calle 7, Av 7-9, 150 m from Parque Morazán,
T8399-3879, www.hostelvangogh.hostel.com.
Small, friendly, helpful hostel with dorms ($)
and private rooms ($$). Amenities include
Wi-Fi, pool table, shared kitchen (basic), book
exchange, satellite TV, DVDs and garden.
Relaxed place, hospitable, professional,
well maintained and recommended.

East of the centre

$$-$ Hostel Bekuo
325 m west of Spoon, Los Yoses, T2234-1091,
www.hostelbekuo.com.
An intimate, laid-back, friendly, homely
hostel with a range of private rooms ($$) and
dorms ($), as well as a small garden complete
with a rabbit. Services include Wi-Fi, kitchen,
movies, luggage store, phone, info.

$$-$ In & Basic Hostel Lounge
200 m south and 75 m west of Spoon, north
side of Fatima's chuch, Los Yoses, T2232-2998,
www.inbasic.com.
A very hip and stylish hostel with glamorous
1950s decor. They have 8 private rooms ($$)
and dorm beds ($), a fully equipped kitchen,
3 lounge areas, a backyard and a barbecue
area. Recommended.

Escazú

$$$ Tierra Mágica
Calle San Miguel, T2289-9154,
www.tierramagica-costarica.com.
Doubling up as the art studio of Barbara
Odio Ygelsias, Tierra Mágica is a very cosy
and beautifully presented B&B with great
tile work, artistic concrete floors and a lush
garden. Rooms are spacious and relaxing.
Art workshops are also available here.

$$$-$$ Costa Verde Inn
300 m south of the 2nd San Antonio
de Escazú cemetery, T2228-4080,
www.costaverdeinn.com.
A secluded and charming country home
with 14 imaginatively decorated rooms – a
popular choice away from the town centre.

Restaurants

Central San José
At lunchtime, cheaper restaurants offer a set
meal called a *casado*, US$5-10, which is often
good value.

$$$ El Balcón de Europa
Calle 9, between Av Central and Av 1,
25 m al norte de Chelles, T2221-4841.
This old-school Italian trattoria is a
convenient and reliable dinner spot in the
heart of the downtown area. They serve
good home-cooked pasta, lasagne, soups,
and seafood. A cosy interior adorned with
historic photos of the neighbourhood.

$$$ Esquina de Buenos Aires
Calle 11 esquina Av 4, T2223-1909,
www.laesquinadebuenosaires.com.
Highly popular and full of character, this
stylish Argentine steak house cooks up
some of the most flavourful cuts in the city,
including succulent rib eye, striploin and
tenderloin steak. Vegetarians can enjoy a
range of home-made pastas.

$$$ Kalú
Calle 7 y Av 11, 300 m al norte del Parque
Morazán, Barrio Amón, T2221-2081,
www.kalu.co.cr.

Kalú is a young and trendy place, a welcome
oasis in the urban grind. The owner, Chef
Camille Ratton, was trained in France and
offers an eclectic range of international
dishes including Thai chicken, falafels,
gourmet sandwiches and burgers.

$$$ Lubnan
Paseo Colón, Calle 22-24, T2257-6071,
www.lubnancr.com.
A long-standing Lebanese restaurant serving
authentic cuisine from the homeland,
including shwarma, kafta and shish kebab.
Vegetarian selections too, including falafel
and hummus, great service, and belly
dancing on Thu.

$$$ Park Café
Sabana Norte, 75 m north of Rosti Pollos,
T2290-6324, www.parkcafecostarica.
blogspot.com. Tue-Sat 1730-2100.
Chef Richard Neat has won multiple Michelin
stars in Europe and now brings his culinary
mastery to Costa Rica with this prestigious
restaurant set in the garden of an intriguing
antique store. Dress code applies, no small
children, reservations a must.

$$$ Tin Jo
Calle 11, Av 6-8, T2221-7605, www.tinjo.com.
Established more than 3 decades ago,
Tin Jo is a San José institution. It serves
probably the best Asian cuisine in town with
authentic dishes from China, India, Japan,
Thailand, Vietnam and the Philippines. Great
setting in a converted historic mansion.
Recommended.

$$$-$$ The Corner Pizzeria and Cafeteria
Calle 28 y Av 2, T2255-3333.
A casual joint serving tasty artisan-style
pizzas with traditional Italian crusts. Friendly
staff, good ambience and occasional live
music on Fri night. A great option for couples
and families.

$$$-$$ Machu Picchu
Calle 32, Av 1-3, T2222-7384,
www.restaurantemachu picchu.com.
Mon-Sat 1000-2200, Sun 1100-1800.

As the name might suggest, excellent Peruvian food, including tasty ceviche starters and succulent seafood mains such as spicy prawns, garlic octopus, and lemon sea bass. Good service and a homely atmosphere.

$$$-$$ Sapore Trattoria
Av 2a, 75 m west of Plaza de la Democracia, T2222-8906.
A small but graceful Italian restaurant serving home-made pastas, pizzas and other traditional dishes, all lovingly made with genuine Italian ingredients. Good wines and desserts.

$$-$ La Criollita
Av 7, Calle 7-9, T2256-6511.
If you're hankering after a wholesome plate of good old-fashioned *comida típica*, La Criollita is a classic downtown option. At lunchtime they dish up massive and reasonably priced *casados*, hugely popular with local business men. Recommended.

$$-$ Shakti
Av 8 y Calle 13, T2222-4475, www.restauranteshakti.com.
A host of health-conscious options including tasty salads, pastas, soups, soya burgers and fruit juices are on the menu at this bright and airy vegetarian restaurant, established in 1987.

$$-$ Vishnu
Av 1, Calle 1-3, also on Calle 14, Av 2. Daily 0800-2000.
Best known vegetarian place in town, always bustling at lunchtime. Try their cheap and good *plato del día*, their soya cheese sandwiches and ice cream, or their wholemeal bread.

$ Soda Tapia
Calle 42, Av 2-4, east side of Parque Sabana, www.sodatapia.com.
On the park, a classic stopping place for Josefinos. They serve wholesome *comida típica*. Cheap, cheerful, and quick.

Cafés

Alma de Café
Av 2, Calle 3-5, in foyer of National Theatre, www.almadecafe.net. Mon-Sat.
This stylish café inside the national theatre is reminiscent of old Europe with its lofty ceiling and marble floor. In addition to good coffee, they serve crêpes, sandwiches and quiches. Pricey but worth it for the sheer style and sophistication of the belle époque interior.

Café de los Deseos
Calle 15, Av 11, T2222-0496, www. cafedelosdeseos.com. Closed Mon.
Buzzing and bohemian, Café de los Deseos is a fun place to hang out, popular with local hipsters. In addition to coffee and craft beer, they serve international comfort food like fish tacos, chicken wings, pizza, quesadillas and burgers.

East of the centre

$$$ Jurgen's
Calle 41 and Paseo Rubén Darío, Barrio Dent in Los Yoses, T2224-2455. Closed Sun.
Adjoining **Boutique Hotel** Jade, Jurgen's is a smart and sophisticated place, good for a business lunch or a romantic evening meal. It boasts an excellent and creative international menu. First-class service.

Bars and clubs

Central San José
There are dark and interesting bars around Parque Morazán, many of them populated by wastrel gringo expats and ladies of ill repute. The **Centro Comercial El Pueblo**, north of town in Barrio Tournón, is a mall with a cluster of restaurants, bars and discos. This is where many young Ticos party the night away until dawn, but it is now in decline, increasingly insalubrious and unsafe; better entertainment can be had in San Pedro (see below).

East of the centre

North of Av Central, Calle de la Armagua (aka Calle 3) is the swinging epicentre of the student drinking scene, home to scores of bars and nightclubs, a great place to wander in a group. The action really gets going after 2300 and one of the most popular joints is **Terra U** (www.terrau.com). For live music, you could try:

Jazz Café

Paralela a la Autopista Próspero Fernández 1st exit after the toll, next to Comfort Suizo, opposite Hospital Cima, www.jazzcafecostarica.com. As the name suggests, this is the place to soak up some syncopated rhythms. Check the website for the live music schedule. Also a branch in Escazú.

Entertainment

Cinemas

Modern cinemas showing latest releases are located throughout the metropolitan area, see *La Nación* for listings.

Cine Universitario, *at the UCR's Abelardo Bonilla law school auditorium in San Pedro, T2511-5323, www.accionsocial.ucr.ac.cr/web/ec/cine-universitario.* Shows good films Thu-Fri, 1830, US$5.

Sala Garbo, *Av 2, Calle 28, T2222-1034, www.salagarbocr.com.* Shows independent art house movies.

Variedades, *Calle 5, Av Central-1, T2222-6108.* Others can be found in **Los Yoses** (T2223-0085), **San Pedro** (T2283-5716), **Rohrmoser** (T2232-3271) and **Heredia** (T2293-3300).

Theatre

More than 20 theatres offer live productions in the San José area; check the *Tiempo Libre* entertainment supplement every Thu in *La Nación* for show times, mostly weekends.

Teatro del Angel, *Av Central, Calle 13-15, T2222-8258.* Has 3 modern dance companies.

Teatro Melico Salazar, *Parque Central, T2295-6000, www.teatromelico.go.cr.* For popular, folkloric shows.

Teatro Nacional, *Av 2, Calle 3-5, T2221-5341, T2010-1100, www.teatronacional.go.cr.* Recommended for the productions, the architecture and the bar/café. Behind it is La Plaza de la Cultura, a large complex.

Festivals

Dec-Jan Christmas/New Year. Festivities last from mid-Dec to the 1st week of Jan, with dances, horse shows and much confetti throwing in the crowded streets. The annual **El Tope** horse parade starts at noon on 26 Dec and travels along the principal avenues of San José with a **carnival** the next day.

Mar The **International Festival of Culture** assembles musicians from throughout Central America in a week of performances in the Plaza de la Cultura around the 2nd week of Mar, although concern over the future of the event exists due to lack of funding.

2nd weekend in Mar Día del Boyero (Day of the Oxcart Driver) is celebrated in San Antonio de Escazú. Parades of ox-drawn carts, with music, dancing and blessings from the priesthood. Festivities culminate on the Sun in a colourful oxcart parade. Dancing in the evening to marimba music.

Mar/Apr Street parades during **Easter week**.

Sep 15 Independence Day. Bands and dance troupes move through the streets, although activities start to kick-off the night before with the traditional nationwide singing of the National Anthem at 1800.

Shopping

Crafts and markets

Canapi, *Calle 11, Av 1.* An *artesanía* cooperative, cheaper than most.

Centro Comercial El Pueblo, *near the Villa Tournón Hotel.* Has a number of stalls but is mainly upmarket, built in a traditional *pueblo* style.

La Casona, *Calle Central, Av Central-1. Daily 0900-1900.* A market of small *artesanía* shops, full of interesting little stalls.

Galería Namu, *opposite the Alianza Francesa building on Av 7 and Calle 5-7, T2256-3412, www.galerianamu.com. Mon-Sat 0900-1630.* The best one-stop shop for home-grown and indigenous art, with the distinctly bright-coloured ceramics of Cecilia Figueres. Items can be shipped if required and online shopping is possible.

Mercado Nacional de Artesanía, *Calle 11, Av 4, T2221-5012. Mon-Fri 0900-1800, Sat 0900-1700.* A good one-stop shop with a wide variety of goods.

Plaza de la Democracia, *in front of the National Museum.* Tented stalls run the length of a city block, a great place to buy hammocks, arts and crafts at competitive prices. Don't be afraid to negotiate.

What to do

Bungee jumping

After Rafael Iglesias Bridge (Río Colorado), continue on Pan-American Highway 1.5 km, turn right at Salón Los Alfaro, down the track to Puente Colorado.

Tropical Bungee, *T2248-2212, www.bungee.co.cr.* Operates daily 0900-1600 in high season, US$75 1st jump, US$45 for the 2nd (same day only) includes transport from San José, reservations required.

Cycling

Coast to Coast Adventures, *T2280-8054, www.ctocadventures.com.* Run trips in the local area.

Language schools

The number of schools has increased rapidly. Listed below are just a selection recommended by readers. Generally, schools offer tuition in groups of 2-5 for 2-4 weeks. Lectures, films, outings and social occasions are usually included and accommodation with families is encouraged. Many schools are linked to the university and can offer credits towards a US course. Rates, including lodging, are around US$1000-1100 a month.

Academia Tica de Español, *in San Rafael de Coronado, 10 km north of San José, T2229-0013, www.academiatica.com.*

AmeriSpan, *1334 Walnut St, 6th floor, Philadelphia, PA 19107, T215-751-1100, www.amerispan.com.* Has affiliated schools in Alajuela, Heredia, San José and 6 others locations.

Costa Rican Language Academy, *Barrio California, T2280-5834, www.spanishandmore.com.* Run by Aída Chávez, offers language study and accommodation with local families, and instruction in Latin American music and dancing as well.

Costa Rica Spanish Institute, *Zapote in San Pedro district, T2234-1001, www.cosi.co.cr.* Also branch in Manuel Antonio.

Universal de Idiomas, *in Moravia, T2223-9662, www.universal-edu.com.* Emphasis is on conversational Spanish.

Nature tours

ACTUAR, *T2290-7514, www.actuarcostarica.com.* An association of 26 community-based rural tourism groups.

Aguas Bravas, *T2292-2072, www.aguas-bravas.co.cr.* Whitewater rafting on rivers around the Central Valley, also horse riding, biking, hiking and camping.

Bay Island Cruises, *Paseo Colón, 275 m north of Pizza Hut, opposite Policía Municipal, T2258-3536, www.bayislandcruises.com.* One of several companies focusing on trips to Tortuga Island. Daily tours (US$115) include lunch and transport from San José area.

Costa Rica Expeditions, *Av 3, Calles 25 y 29, T2521-6099, www.costaricaexpeditions.com.* Upmarket wildlife adventures include whitewater rafting (US$99-169 for 1-day trip on Río Pacuare, includes lunch and transport) and further options. They own **Tortuga Lodge**, **Corcovado Lodge Tent Camp** and **Monteverde Lodge**. Daily trips, highly recommended.

Ecole Travel, *Barrio Escalante, del Centro Cultural Costarricense Norteamericano, 50 m norte y 25 m oeste, T2253-8884, www.ecole travel.com.* Chilean-Dutch, highly recommended for budget tours to Tortuguero, Corcovado and tailor-made excursions off the beaten track.

Horizontes, *Calle 28, Av 1-3, T2222-2022, www.horizontes.com*. A big operator in Costa Rica, high standards, educational and special interest, advice given and arrangements made for groups and individuals.

Ríos Tropicales, *Calle 38, between Paseo Colón and Av 2, 50 m south of Subway, T2233-6455, www.riostropicales.com*. Specialists in whitewater rafting and kayaking, good selection, careful to assess your abilities, good food, excellent guides, from US$225 for 2-day trip on Río Pacuare, waterfalls, rapids, including camping and food. Many other options throughout the country.

Night tours

Costa Rican Nights Tour, *La Uruca, T2242-9200, www.puebloantiguo.co.cr*. Takes place Wed, Fri, Sat 1900-2200. This 3-hr dinner show incorporates fireworks, marimba music, a show and a guided tour through San José in Pueblo Antiguo.

Tour operators

Aventuras Naturales, *Av 5, Calle 33-35, T2225-3939, www.adventurecostarica.com*. Specialists in whitewater rafting with their own lodge on the Pacuare, which has a canopy adventure tour. Also several other trips.

COOPRENA (Simbiosis Tours), *San José, T2290-8646, www.turismoruralcr.com*. A group supporting small farmers, broadly working to the principle of sustainable tourism. Offers tours and accommodation around the country.

Costa Rican Trails, *325 Curridabat de la Pops, 300 m al sur y 250 m al este, T1 888-803-3344 (USA), T1866-865-7013 (Canada), www.costaricantrails.com*. Travel agency and tour operator, offering 1-day and multi-day tours and packages, selected and resorts, reliable local ground and air transport.

Swiss Travel Service, *T2282-4898, www.swisstravelcr.com*. One of the biggest tour operators with branches in many

of the smarter hotels. Can provide any standard tour, plus several specialist tours for birdwatchers. Good guides and warmly recommended.

Transport

San José
Air
The **Aeropuerto Internacional Juan Santamaría (SJO)**, T2437-2400, www. fly2sanjose.com, is at El Coco, 16 km from San José along the Autopista General Cañas. All international departures are subject to US$29 departure tax, payable at the **Bancrédito** counter prior to check-in. A 2nd airport, **Aeropuerto Tobias Bolaños**, 8 km west of San José, in Pavas, is a hub for charter and some domestic flights.

Efficient **Tuasa** buses to city centre from the highway outside the ground-floor terminal, every 10 mins, 35 mins, US$1; also services to **Alajuela**, every 15 mins, 15 mins, US$1; and **Heredia**, every 20 mins, 20 mins, US$1. In San José, buses to **airport** (continuing on to Alajuela) leave from Av Central-2, Calle 10, every 10 mins from 0500-2100; 45 mins, US$1 (good service, plenty of luggage space).

Bright orange airport taxis (T2222-6865, www.taxiaeropuerto.com) cost around US$25, tickets available from pre-payment kiosks. Taxis run all night from the main square. For early flights you can reserve a taxi from any San José hotel the night before. All taxi companies run a 24-hr service.

Domestic flights 2 airlines operate domestic flights: **Sansa**, T2290-4400, www. flysansa.com, and **Nature Air**, T2299-6000, www.natureair.com. The Sansa terminal is next to the main terminal at SJO and they run a free bus service for passengers. If you made reservations before arriving in Costa Rica, confirm and collect tickets as soon as possible after arrival. Book ahead, especially for the beaches. In Feb and Mar, planes can be fully booked 3 weeks ahead. On all internal scheduled and charter flights there is a baggage allowance of 1 checked and 1 carry-on bag, 7-18 kg depending on carrier and fare class; fees for excess weight approximately US$2-3 per kg. Oversized items such as surfboards or bicycles are charged at US$30 if there is room in the cargo hold. Departure and arrival taxes applicable if travelling to Arenal, Quepos and Tambor; total US$5-14. For more information, see Getting around, page 175.

Bus

Local Urban routes in San José cost US$0.50 or less. A cheap tour of San José can be made on the bus marked *periférico* from Paseo Colón in front of the Cine Colón, or at La Sabana bus stop, a 45-min circuit of the city. A smaller circuit is made by the 'Sabana/Cementerio' bus; pick it up at Av 2, Calle 8-10.

Long distance Buses have their terminals scattered round town (see map, page 34) but the majority are close to the Coca Cola Terminal, in the central west of the city.

There are several shuttle bus companies including **Interbus**, T2283-5573, www.interbusonline.com, and **Fantasy Tours/GrayLine**, T2220-2126, www.graylinecostarica.com, offer transport from the capital to dozens of beach and tourism destinations in comfortable a/c minibuses, with bilingual drivers and hotel pickup. Tickets US$30-80 one-way, with a good weekly pass.

Meseta Central To the **Aeropuerto Internacional Juan Santamaría** and onwards to **Alajuela**, every 10 mins, 0400-2200, 20-40 mins, US$1, departing from the TUASA Terminal, Av 2, Calle 12-14. To **Cartago**, every 10 mins, 0500-0000, 45 mins, US$1.10, departing from Calle 5 and Av 10 with **Empresa Lumaca**, T2537-2320. To **Heredia**, every 10 mins, 0500-2300, 30 mins, US$0.90, departing from Calle 1, Av 7-9. To **Turrialba**, hourly (direct service), 0500-2100, 2 hrs, US$2.90, departing from the Transtusa terminal, Calle 13 and Av 6, T2222-4464, indirect services are slower

but more frequent. To **Volcán Irazú**, 2 daily, 0800, 1230, 2hrs, US$4.20, departing from Av 2, Calle 1-3.

Northern Costa Rica To **Ciudad Quesada (San Carlos)**, every 40 mins (direct service), 0730-1730, 2-3 hrs, US$3.60; to **La Fortuna**, 3 daily, 0615, 0840, 1130, 5 hrs, US$4.50; to **Los Chiles**, 2 daily, 0530, 1500, 5 hrs, US$5.40; all departing from the San Carlos Terminal, Calle 12, Av 7-9 with **Autotransportes San José-San Carlos**, T2255-0567. To **Tilarán**, 5 daily, 0730-1830, 4 hrs, US$7.20, departing from Calle 20 y Av 3, T2695-5611. To **Cañas**, 5 daily, 3½ hrs, US$5.40, departing from Calle 14, Av 1-3 with **Empresa La Cañera**, T2258-5792. To **Liberia**, hourly, 0600-2000, 4½ hrs, US$6, departing from Calle 24, Av 5-7, Pulmitan de Liberia, T2222-1650. To **Monteverde/Santa Elena**, 2 daily, 0630, 1430, 5 hrs, US$5.10, departing from Calle 12, Av 7-9, with **Transportes Tilarán**, T2222-3854. To **Peñas Blancas** on the Nicaraguan border, hourly, 0330-1900, 6 hrs, US$8.40, departing from Calle 14, Av 3-5, 1 block north of the Coca Cola Terminal with **Transportes Deldú**, T2256-9072; for more on the crossing to Nicaragua, see Nicaragua–Costa Rica box, page 173. To **Puntarenas**, hourly (direct), 0600-1900, 2½ hrs, US$3, departing from Calle 16 y Av 12 with **Empresarios Unidos**, T2222-8231.

Península de Nicoya To **Montezuma** and **Malpaís**, 2 daily, 0600, 1400, 5 hrs, US$9.20, including ferry connection; to **Playa Bejuco**, 2 daily, 0530, 1400, 4 hrs, US$10; all departing from the San Carlos Terminal, Calle 12, Av 7-9, T2221-7479. To **Nicoya**, 6 daily, 0530-1700, 5 hrs, US$5; to **Playa Sámara**, 2 daily, 1200, 1700 (only in high season), 5 hrs, US$8.10; to **Playa Tamarindo**, 2 daily, 1130 via Liberia, 1530 via Tempisque, 5½ hrs, US$10.20; to **Santa Cruz**, 7 daily, 0700-1900, 5 hrs, US$5.20, all departing from the Alfaro Terminal, Calle 14, Av 5, T2222-2666. To **Playa del Coco**, 3 daily, 0800, 1400, 1600, 5 hrs, US$7.50, departing from Calle 24, Av 5-7, Pulmitan, T2222-0458. To **Playa Flamingo**, 3 daily,

0800, 1030, 1500, 6 hrs, US$11, departing from Calle 20, Av 1-3, with **Tralapa**, T2221-7202.

Central Pacific Coast To **Dominical** and **Uvita**, 2 daily, 0600, 1500, 7 hrs, US$9.50; to **Quepos** and **Manuel Antonio**, 6 daily, 0600-1930, 4 hrs, US$6.30, all departing from the Terminal Tracopa, Calle 5, Av 18-20, T2221-4214. To **Jacó**, 7 daily, 0600-1900, 1½ hrs, US$4.30, departing from the Terminal Coca-Cola, Calle 16, Av 1-3, T2290-7920.

Southern Costa Rica To **Ciudad Neily**, 4 daily, 0500-1830, 8 hrs, US$13.30; to **Golfito**, 3 daily, 0700, 1530, 2215, 8 hrs, US$13.30; to **Palmar Norte**, 8 daily, 0500-1630, 7 hrs, US$10.50; to **Paso Canoas**, 8 daily, 0500-2200, 7 hrs, US$13.40; to **San Isidro**, 14 daily, 0500-1830, 3 hrs, US$6.30; to **San Vito**, 4 daily, 0600-1600, 7½ hrs, US$12.70; all departing from the Tracopa terminal, Calle 5, Av 18-20, T2221-4214. To **Puerto Jiménez**, 2 daily, 0800, 1200, 8 hrs, US$13.60, departing from Calle 14, Av 9-11 with **Transportes Blanco**, T2257-4121.

Caribbean coast To **Cahuita**, 4 daily, 0600-1600, 4 hrs, US$8.50; to **Puerto Viejo de Talamanca**, 4 daily, 0600-1600, 4½ hrs, US$9.90; and to **Sixaola** (on the Panamanian border), 4 daily, 0600-1600, 6 hrs, US$12.10, all departing from Terminal Atlántico Norte (also known as Terminal San Carlos), Calle 12, Av 7-9, T2750-0023; for more on crossing the border to Panama, see the Costa Rica– Panama box, page 174. To **Cariari**, 9 daily, 0630-2030, 2 hrs, US$4; to **Puerto Limón**, hourly, 0500-1900, 3 hrs, US$5.75; to **Puerto Viejo de Sarapiquí**, 10 daily, 0630-1830, 2 hrs, US$5; and to **Siquirres**, 11 daily, 0630-1800, 1½ hrs, US$3.45, all departing from the Terminal del Caribe, Calle Central and Av 15, with **Transporte Caribeños**, T2222-0610.

International In Dec and Jan, buses are often booked 2 weeks ahead. Before departure, have your ticket confirmed on arrival at the terminal. When buying and confirming your ticket, you must show your passport. If luggage is light, it is often faster to hop between local buses and cross the border on foot.

Ticabus terminal at Paseo Colón, 200 m north and 100 m west of Torre Mercedes, T2221-0006, www.ticabus.com; downtown ticket agent at Calle 9-11, Av 4, T2221-8954, office open Mon-Sun 0600-1700. **Ticabus** to **Guatemala City**, 3 daily, 60 hrs, US$78 tourist class, US$99 tourist-executive class, with overnight stay in Managua and San Salvador. To **Tegucigalpa**, 3 daily, 48 hrs, US$48 tourist class, US$61 tourist-executive class, overnight in Managua. To **Managua** 3 daily, US$27 tourist class, US$40 executive class, 10 hrs including 1 hr at Costa Rican side of border and up to another 2 hrs on Nicaraguan side while they search bags. To **Panama City** 1200 daily, US$42 tourist class, US$58 executive class, 18 hrs (book in advance). **Transnica**, Calle 22, Av 3-5, T2223-4242, www.transnica.com, runs buses with TV, video, a/c, snacks, toilet, to **Managua** 4 daily, US$27. **Expreso Panaline** goes to **Panama City** daily at 1200 from the Terminal de Empresarios Unidos de Puntarenas Calle 16, Av 10-12, T2221-7694, www.expresopanama.com, US$40 1 way, US$80 return, reduction for students, arrives 0300; a/c, payment by Visa/MasterCard accepted. A bus to **Changuinola** via the Sixaola– Guabito border post leaves San José at 1000 daily, 8 hrs, from opposite Terminal Alfaro, T2556-1432 for info, best to arrive 1 hr before departure; the bus goes via Siquirres and is the quick route to **Limón**. For more on crossing the border to Panama, see also the Costa Rica–Panama border crossing box, page 174.

Car hire
Most local agencies are on or close to Paseo Colón, with a branch or drop-off site at or close to the airport and other locations around the country.

International companies with services include **Adobe, Alamo, Avis, Budget, Dollar, Economy, Hertz, Hola, National, Payless, Thrifty, Toyota** and **Tricolor**.

Rent-a-car Costa Rica, T2442-6000, www.rentacarcostarica.com, is a local company with several offices around town including Hostal Toruma, most competitively priced in town; **Wild Rider Motorcycles**, also rents cheap 4WD vehicles (see below).

Cycle repairs
Cyclo Quiros, Apartado 1366, Pavas, 300 m west of US Embassy. The brothers Quiros have been repairing bikes for 25 years, highly recommended.

Motorcycle and bike rental
Wild Rider Motorcycles, Paseo Colón, Calle 32 diagonal Kentucky, next to **Aventuras Backpackers**, T2258-4604, www.wild-rider.com, Honda XR250s, Yamaha XT600s and Suzuki DR650SE available for rent from US$55-80 a day, US$700-1200 deposit required. 4WD vehicles also available, US$240-410 per week, monthly discounts.

Taxi
Minimum fare US$1 for 1 km, US$1.10 additional kilometre. Taxis used to charge more after 2200, but that rule has been rescinded. Taxis are red and have electronic meters called *marías*, if yours doesn't, get out and take another cab. For journeys over 12 km, price should be negotiated between driver and passenger. Radio cabs can be booked in advance. To order a taxi, call **Coopeguaria**, T2226-1366, **Coopeirazu**, T2254-3211, **Coopemoravia**, T2229-8882, **Coopetaxi**, T2235-9966, **Taxi San Jorge**, T2221-3434, **Taxis Guaria**, T2226-1366, **Taxis Unidos SA**, which are the official taxis of the Juan Santamaría International Airport and are orange instead of red, T2222-6865.

Train
Costa Rica has revived its train services between the capital and some nearby destinations in the Meseta Central, although they are intended more for commuters than tourists. The Terminal Atlántico, Av 3 and Calle 21, serves **Cartago** and **Heredia** with departures every 30-45 mins, Mon-Fri, in the early morning and early evening only. For more information, see www.trenurbano.co.cr.

Meseta Central

Hilly and fertile with a temperate climate, the Meseta Central is a major coffee-growing area where fairly heavily populated, picturesque and prosperous settlements sit in the shadows of active volcanoes. Exploring the towns and villages of the region – each with its own character and style – gives a good insight into the very heart of Costa Rica. Although it's easier to explore the region in a private vehicle, frequent public buses and short journeys make hopping between towns fairly straightforward. If stepping out from San José it's probably worth dumping most of your luggage in the city and travelling light.

Alajuela and around

relaxed provincial capital famous for its flowers and market days

Despite being the second largest city in the country, Alajuela is a mild place, far removed from the chaos of neighbouring San José. Located five minutes from the airport, it is a popular pit-stop for those on early flights and late arrivals, and a good base for exploring the surrounding countryside, including down-to-earth villages, verdant hills, vertiginous waterfalls and nature reserves full of brightly feathered avian life.

Sights
The social and spiritual heart of Alajuela is the shady Parque Central, home to the 19th-century neoclassical cathedral with its red metal dome. Five blocks east, the unusual church of La Agonía exhibits an interesting mix of architectural styles. One block south of the Parque Central, a monument commemorates Juan Santamaría, the drummer boy and national hero who set ablaze the building in Rivas (Nicaragua) where William Walker's filibusters were entrenched in 1856. The **Museo Histórico Juan Santamaría** ⓘ *on the north side of the Parque Central, T2441-4775, www.museojuansantamaria.go.cr, Tue-Sun 1000-1800,* tells, somewhat confusingly, the story of this war.

Most tour operators listed in this guide will offer nature-oriented tours. There are many well-kept and well-guarded national parks and nature reserves that protect some samples of the extraordinarily varied Costa Rican ecosystems. In the north the variety is daunting and includes some of the last patches of dry tropical forest in the Parque Nacional Santa Rosa, the cloudforest of Monteverde and the Talamanca Mountains, and nine active volcanoes including Rincón de la Vieja, Poás, Irazú and of course Arenal. For volunteering opportunities, see ASVO and FPN below and Volunteering, Costa Rica, page 185.

Birdwatchers and butterfly lovers have long flocked to Costa Rica to see some of the 850 or so species of bird and untold varieties of butterfly. All of these can best be seen in the parks, together with monkeys, deer, coyotes, armadillos, anteaters, turtles, coatis, raccoons, snakes, and, more rarely, wild pigs, wild cats and tapirs.

Although the national parks and other privately owned reserves are a main tourist attraction, many are in remote areas and not easy to get to on public transport; buses or coaches that do go tend to stay for a short time. There is a tendency for tour companies to dominate the National Park 'market' to the exclusion of other public transport. For tight budgets, try making up a party with others and sharing taxis or hiring a car.

Asociación de Voluntarios (ASVO), T2258-4430, www.asvocr.org. Contact if you want to work as a volunteer in the parks, with a small daily fee for lodging and food.
Fundación de Parques Nacionales (FPN), T2257-2239, www.fpn-cr.org. Contact for information and permits to visit and/or camp, conduct research or volunteer in the parks. Check in advance if your trip depends on gaining entrance.
Sistema Nacional de Areas de Conservación (SINAC), T2283-8004, www.costarica-nationalparks.com, administers the national park system. Contact them for information, maps and permits.

On the southeastern outskirts of Alajuela, the **Ara Project** ⓘ *Desamparados, T8389-5811, www.thearaproject.org*, is a breeding and release centre for endangered great green and scarlet macaws. To tour the facilities and meet some of the cheeky parrots in person, contact the administrators through their website.

Parque Nacional Volcán Poás
Tue-Sun, 0700-1600, US$15, good café next door, and toilets further along the road to the crater. If you wish to get in earlier you can leave your car/taxi at the gates, walk the 3 km up the hill and pay on your way out. The volcano is very crowded on Sun so go in the week if possible. Arrive early as clouds often hang low over the crater after 1000, obstructing the view. Wear good shoes, a hat and suncream.

Volcán Poás (2708 m) sits in the centre of the Parque Nacional Volcán Poás (6506 ha), where the still-smoking volcano and bubbling turquoise sulphur pool are set within a beautiful forest. The crater is almost 1.5 km across – the second largest in the world. The park is rich with abundant birdlife, given the altitude and barren nature of the terrain, and home to the only true dwarf cloudforest in Costa Rica. Trails are well marked to help guide you from the visitor centre to the geysers, lake and other places of interest. The main crater is 1 km along a road from the car park. There is a visitor centre by the car park with explanations of the recent changes in the volcano. There is also a good café run by **Café Britt**; alternatively, bring your own food and water.

La Paz Waterfall Gardens
6 km north of Vara Blanca, T2482-2720, www.waterfallgardens.com. Daily 0800-1700, US$38 (buffet lunch US$13), children US$22 (buffet lunch US$7).

La Paz Waterfall Gardens, 32 km north of Alajuela on Highway 126, has forest trails, five huge waterfalls, one of the world's largest butterfly and hummingbird gardens, a restaurant with buffet lunch and the **Peace Lodge Hotel ($$$$)**. The road is twisty, winding through lush forest down to the lowlands at **San Miguel**. Here the road leads either northeast heading to La Virgen and eventually Puerto Viejo de Sarapiquí (see page 141), or northwest to Venecia (see below).

La Virgen
Some 10 km northeast of San Miguel is La Virgen, near the Río Sarapiquí, a good spot for Grade I, II and III rafting, which is organized by the hotel **Rancho Leona**. From San José, take the Río Frío bus which passes through San Miguel, or a bus from Ciudad Quesada (San Carlos), and ask to get off at **Rancho Leona**. Juan Carlos in La Virgen has been recommended as a guide for rafting, T2761-1148, from US$30 per person.

Venecia and around
Heading west from San Miguel, Venecia (two buses daily from San José, 4½ hours, US$3) has an interesting church. Near Venecia are the pre-Columbian tumuli of **Ciudad Cutris**. A good road goes to within 2 km of Cutris, from where you can walk or take a 4WD vehicle; get a permit to visit from the local finca owner.

West of Venecia is Aguas Zarcas, where the road splits. Heading directly north, the roads descends into the jungle lowlands, following the Río San Carlos towards the Nicaraguan border, passing through several small towns. After about 40 km, in Boca Tapada, is **La Laguna del Lagarto Lodge ($$,** www.lagarto-lodge-costa-rica.com).

Grecia
The road from Alajuela northwest to Ciudad Quesada (San Carlos) (see page 65) passes through Grecia and several towns, the surrounding hills covered with green coffee bushes. Grecia is also a major pineapple producer, and has an interesting church made entirely of metal. A short distance along the road to Alajuela is **El Mundo de las Serpientes** ① *T2494-3700, www.theworldofsnakes.com, 0800-1600, US$11, children US$6, reductions for biology students*, a snake farm with more than 50 species. On the old road about 10 km towards Tacares is **Los Chorros Recreational Park** ① *US$4*, with two massive waterfalls and picnic spots.

Sarchí and around
Heading west from Grecia is the town of Sarchí, the country's artisan centre, where you can visit the *fábricas* that produce the intricately geometric and floral designs painted on ox-carts, which are almost a national emblem. The town is divided in two, Sarchí Norte and Sarchí Sur, separated by some 4 km. The green church (until they paint it again) in Sarchí is especially attractive at sunset. Travel agents in San José charge around US$75 for a day trip to Sarchí usually combined with a trip to Volcán Poás and a coffee finca.

The road continues north to **Naranjo**, a quiet agricultural town with an exquisite bright white church and a shocking post-modern pyramidal structure in the main square.

Zarcero

Frequent bus services from San José/Alajuela pass through Zarcero, on the lip of the continental divide, en route to Ciudad Quesada (San Carlos). The town is famous for vegetable farming, dairy products and notable for the topiary creations of Evangelista Blanco Breves that fill the main plaza. Bushes are clipped, trimmed and shaped into arches leading up to the white church with twin towers, with shapes of animals, dancing couples, a helicopter, many designs of Henry Moore-like sculptures and a small grotto. The interior of the quaint church, overshadowed somewhat by the plaza, is made entirely of wood.

Bajos del Toro and around

Encompassing a reasonably remote and loosely defined area on Highway 708, Bajos del Toro is enviably positioned between Poás volcano, Parque Nacional Castro Blanco and the Bosque de Paz biological reserve. With such stunning natural scenery in every direction, it's no surprise that a slew of upscale eco-lodges have opened their doors here, but ideally you'll need your own vehicle to explore the area.

San Ramón and around

West of Naranjo along the Pan-American Highway is the town of San Ramón, known locally as the City of Poets, with an attractive Parque Central and a street market on Saturday mornings. The **Museo de San Ramón** ⓘ *opposite the park, Tue-Sat 1000-1800, T2447-7137, www.so.ucr.ac.cr, voluntary donation,* records the history and culture of the local community. There's good walking in the surrounding area. You can visit the coffee-processing plant (in season) at the **Cooperativa de Café** ⓘ *US$15-39,* in San Ramón. The local fiesta is around the day of San Ramón, 30 August, when local saints are carried on litters to the town's church.

Palmares, 7 km southeast of San Ramón, has a pretty central park with lovely tall trees, where sloths are occasionally spotted. The quiet town comes alive in January for the annual Fiestas de Palmares, with food, carnival rides, concerts and parades.

Atenas

After Palmares you can return to the Pan-American Highway and head to the coast, or go back to San José via Atenas. The church and main plaza in Atenas lie on an earthquake fault. The local speciality, *toronja rellena*, is a sweet-filled grapefruit. Atenas is reputed to have the best climate in the world, with stable temperatures of between 17 and 32°C year round.

Los Angeles Cloud Forest Reserve

Heading north from San Ramón the road forks, left to Zarcero. The right fork heads north to La Tigra and La Fortuna, passing the Los Angeles Cloud Forest Reserve (20 km from San Ramón). The private 800-ha reserve (see **Hotel Villablanca**, Where to stay, below) offers hiking, guided tours, horse riding and canopy ascents.

Where to stay

Alajuela

Hotel prices in Alajuela are generally higher than those of San José, and an 'economical' room for 2 will set you back US$40-50. Business-class lodgings within walking distance of the airport include **Hampton Inn & Suites** and the **Holiday Inn Express**.

$$$$ Xandari

T2443-2020, www.xandari.com.

Once an old coffee finca overlooking the Central Valley, this architectural treasure has 24 individually designed private villas nestled in its rambling estate. One of the best hotels in Costa Rica, complete with organic gardens, trails and waterfalls, and spa treatments. Sumptuous and sublime.

$$$ Hotel 1915

Calle 2, Av 5-7, 300 m north of Parque Central, T2440-7163, www.1915hotel.com.

An old family home, smartly refurbished with stylish decor and tasteful rooms. There's also a pleasant terrace and garden patio for chilling out. One of the best in town.

$$ Hotel Casa Tago

Del Seguro Social Antiguo, 75 m al este, Av de Las Provincias, T2431-3121, www.hotelcasatago.com.

A welcoming little hotel with simple but spacious rooms, some with windows, others without. Breakfast is included. No frills, friendly and family run. Recommended.

$$ Hotel Pacandé

T2443-8481, del Parque Central, 200 m al norte, 50 m oeste, www.hotelpacande.com.

An excellent downtown option with a mix of economical quarters with shared bath and 'superior' suites for those seeking extra comfort. A fresh fruit breakfast is served every morning in a lovely patio-garden. Very helpful staff and friendly management. Recommended.

$$-$ Cortez Azul

Av 5, Calle 2-4, T2443-6145, www.hotelcortezazul.com.

Funky backpacker joint with a range of dorms ($) and private rooms, with ($$) or without ($) private bath. The quality varies, so check before accepting. Sociable, bohemian vibe.

$$-$ Maleku Hostel

Del Hospital Nuevo, 50 m al oeste, T2430-4304, www.malekuhostel.com.

Friendly, low-key, down-to-earth hostel with a mix of private rooms ($$) and dorms ($), all with shared bath. Clean and efficient, with good service and helpful staff. Near the bus station.

Parque Nacional Volcán Poás

Camping in the park is not permitted but there are several places advertising cabins on the road up to Poás and nearby.

$$$$-$$$ Poás Volcano Lodge

West of Poasito, 500 m from Vara Blanca junction on road to Poasito, at El Cortijo farm, sign on gate, 1 km to house, T2482-2194, www.poasvolcanolodge.com.

A superb luxury mountain lodge steeped in rolling pastures and expansive views of Poás, the mountains and the northern Caribbean plains. The estate is criss-crossed by hiking trails with some rooms opening onto the edge of the cloudforest. Recommended.

$$$ Altura Hotel

Access road on the left after the 3rd bridge past the gas station in Poasito, T2482-1124, www.alturahotelcr.com.

An excellent small hotel located 5 mins from Poás volcano. Modern rooms are fully equipped with electric stoves, coffee-makers, fridges and cable TVs. Extras include great views of the Meseta, walking trails, and a roaring fireplace that's brought to life every evening. Breakfast included.

Grecia

$$ B&B Grecia
150 m south of Parque Central, T2444-5326, www.bandbgrecia.com.
This centrally located, low-key B&B has just 4 rooms, all light and breezy, simple, comfortable and clean. There's a small back garden with soft seats and hammocks for chilling out. Helpful and knowledgeable.

Sarchí and around

$$ Cabinas Daniel Zamora
Sarchí, T2454-4596.
Basic rooms with bath, fan, hot water, very clean and extra blankets if cold at night. Also owns **Hotel Villa Sarchí**, 800 m west of town.

$$ Hotel Paraíso Río Verde
San Pedro de Sarchí, de la Iglesia Católica, 200 m al sur, T2454-3003, www.hotelparaisorioverde.com.
Pleasant little bungalows and a couple of private rooms overlooking the rolling countryside. Services include Wi-Fi, breakfast and parking. You'll need your own vehicle to get here.

Zarcero

$$-$ Don Beto
By the church, T2463-3137, www.hoteldonbeto.com.
A friendly little guesthouse with a whitewashed exterior. They have a handful of simple, homely, peaceful rooms with (**$$**) or without (**$**) private bath. Amenities include Wi-Fi, hot water, cable TV.

Bajos del Toro

$$$$ El Silencio
T2231-6122, www.elsilenciolodge.com.
A top-tier eco-lodge nestled in the forested hills. Lodging is in luxury suites and villas, some equipped with outdoor whirlpools and viewing decks. Amenities include an excellent restaurant with a mirador, spa facilities and yoga deck. Romantic and secluded.

$$$$-$$$ Bosque de Paz
T2234-6676, www.bosquedepaz.com.
Highly recommended for birdwatchers and nature photographers, Bosque de Paz is an intimate and ethically managed eco-lodge set inside a 1000-ha private nature reserve. The grounds extend into lush cloudforests and boast their own hummingbird and butterfly gardens. Rates are per person.

$$ Catarata del Toro
6 km north of the church, T2476-0800, www.catarata-del-toro.com.
A 100-ha private nature reserve and biological corridor bordering both Juan Castro Blanco and Poás national parks. Activities include wildlife observation, extreme hiking, rappelling and a hummingbird photo shoot.

San Ramón and around

$$$ Casa Amanecer
North of San Ramón, turn off before Concepción, T2445-2100, www.casa-amanecer-cr.com.
Nestled amid rambling coffee plantations, this tasteful teak and stone-built lodging featured in *Su Casa* architecture magazine. Along with 5 well-appointed rooms, it boasts verdant gardens and fine views. Costa Rican-style breakfast included.

$$ La Posada
400 m north of the cathedral, T2445-7359, www.posadahotel.net.
Locally owned and well-established, a reliable mid-range option with 34 rooms in typical Tico style. Amenities include Wi-Fi, kitchen, garden, mini-gym, laundry, parking.

$$-$ Hostel Sabana
Del Hospital, 700 m al oeste, opposite the transit police, T2445-8105, www.hostelsabana.com.
A friendly, family-run hostel with an ultra-clean dorm (**$**) and guestrooms (**$$**). Very friendly and helpful, the best budget option in town. Recommended.

Atenas

$$$ Orchid Tree
Calle Oratorio, T2446-0852,
www.orchidtreecostarica.com.
An excellent, intimate B&B, conveniently
located in the village. The property boasts
a lush garden, popular with local birdlife, a
small pool, hammocks and restful enclaves. A
romantic option for couples. Recommended.

$$$-$$ El Cafetal Inn
Out of Atenas, in St Eulalia, 4.7 km towards
Grecia, T2446-5785, www.cafetal.com.
A rural B&B with an appealing setting on
a rambling coffee plantation. They have
14 tranquil rooms and suites, bungalows,
a lush garden, fine views, and a large pool.
Airport transfer available. Recommended.

Los Angeles Cloud Forest Reserve

$$$$ Hotel Villablanca
North of town set in the 800-ha Los
Angeles Cloud Forest Reserve, T2461-0300,
www.villablanca-costarica.com.
Boutique mountain hotel and spa with
luxury *casitas* and suites, a sublime setting,
one of the best in Central America, very
romantic and popular with honeymooners.
Lots of outdoor activities and tours available.

Restaurants

Alajuela
Finding a casual meal in Alajuela is not
difficult, most restaurants, cafés and *sodas*
are within 1 or 2 blocks of the Parque Central
and down Calle Central.

$$$-$$ El Chante Vegano
25 m oeste de la Oficina de Correos, www.
elchantevegano.com. Tue-Sun 1100-2000.
This fantastic vegan restaurant offers a
delicious array of healthy options that includes
portobello mushroom burgers, vegetable
pizza, quesadillas, vegan sushi, and fantastic
fresh fruit smoothies (try the watermelon and
mint). Casual outdoor seating, lovely owners
and attentive service. Recommended.

$$$-$$ Jalapeños Central
Calle 1, Av 3-5, T2430-4027, 50 m south of the
Post Office.
A very popular family restaurant that's often
buzzing with locals and tourists alike. They
serve reliable Tex Mex, including hearty
burritos, enchiladas, quesadillas and nachos.
Fun and friendly.

$$ La Sandwichería
100 m north of the Iglesia Agonía.
Interesting and creative sandwiches served
on tasty ciabatta bread with a side of home-
made vegetable crisps. There are also stuffed
pittas, wraps, and mainly Italian *platos fuertes*.
Take-away available.

$$-$ Cevichitos
Calle Central and Av 3, 100 m north of
Heladería Pops, Parque Central.
A very casual little seafood eatery on the
corner with fast service and good-value
grub. The *ceviche de corvina*, breaded fish
fillet, and *licuado de guanábana* (milkshake);
are all delicious. Recommended.

Cafés

Coffee Dreams
Calle 1 and Av 3.
The coffee and desserts are very good, but
the food is average. Good for a quick stop or
a morning buzz.

Zarcero
The town is known for cheese and
fruit preserves.

$ Soda/Restaurant El Jardín
1st floor, overlooking the plaza.
Local lunches and breakfasts.
Good view of topiary.

San Ramón

$$$ Musashi
Opposite the Banco de Costa Rica.
Something different: good, fresh, authentic
sushi in San Ramón. Sake and Japanese beers
too. Pleasant interior, good for a romantic meal.

$$-$ Mi Choza
Opposite the cemetery.
Also known as **Los Negritos**, they serve
hearty *bocas* on cooking boards, including
tacos, whole fish and omelettes. A fun place
for groups. Simple and unpretentious.

Festivals

Alajuela
11 Apr Juan Santamaría Day, a week of
bands, concerts and dancing in celebration
of the life of the town's most famous son.
Mid-Jul The fruitful heritage comes to
the fore with a **Mango Festival** of parades,
concerts and an arts and crafts fair.

Shopping

Alajuela
Goodlight Books, *Calle 1-3, T2430-4083.*
Quality used books, mostly English, as well
as espresso and pastries. Internet available.

Sarchí and around
One of the largest *artesanías* is **Fábrica de
Chaverri** in Sarchí Sur. **Taller Lalo Alfaro**,
the oldest workshop, is in Sarchí Norte
and worth a visit to see more traditional
production methods. Both sell handmade
furniture, cowhide rocking chairs and
wooden products as well as ox-carts,
which come in all sizes.

Transport

Alajuela
Bus Service to **San José**. Depart Alajuela
from main bus terminal Calle 8, Av Central-1,
or Av 4, Calle 2-4 every 10 mins, 30 mins,
US$0.90, with both services arriving on Av 2
in the capital. To **Heredia** from 0400 until
2200, 30 mins, US$0.70. 1 block south of
the terminal buses depart for several small
villages in the area including **Laguna de
Fraijanes** and **Volcán Poás**.

Parque Nacional Volcán Poás
The volcano can be reached by car from **San
José**. A taxi for 6 hrs with a side trip will cost
about US$50-60. There is a daily excursion
bus from the main square of Alajuela right up
to the crater, leaving at 0915 (or before if full),
connecting with 0830 bus from San José
(from Av 2, Calle 12-14); be there early for a
seat, although extra buses run if necessary;
the area gets very crowded, US$4 return.
The bus waits at the top with time to see
everything (clouds permitting), returning
1430. For **Poasito** organize a taxi, hitch or
take the 0600 or 1600 bus from Alajuela to
San Pedro de Poás, hitch/ taxi to Poasito
and stay overnight, hiking or hitching up the
mountain next morning.

Sarchí and around
Express bus from **San José** to Sarchí, Calle
16, Av 1-3, 1215, 1730 and 1755, Mon-Fri,
returning 0530, 0615, 1345, Sat 1200, 1½
hrs, US$1.80. **Tuan**, T2441-3781, buses every
30 mins, 0500-2200 from Alajuela bus
station, 1½ hrs, US$1.30.
  Transportes Naranjo, T2451-3655, run
buses to/from **San José**'s Coca Cola terminal
every 40 mins, US$1.25. Buses connect other
towns and villages in the area.

San Ramón and Los Angeles Cloud Forest Reserve
San Ramón is a transport hub. A regular
service from **San José Empresarios Unidos**,
T2222-0064, at Calle 16, Av 10-12, go to
Puntarenas, 10 a day, every 45 mins or
so, US$2.30. There is also a regular service
to **La Fortuna** and **Alajuela**. Buses run to
surrounding villages and towns.

Atenas
The library on the plaza in Atenas also serves
as the bus office, **Cooptransatenas**, T2446-
5767. Many daily buses to **San José**, either
direct or via **Alajuela**, US$1.40.

Some 10 km north of San José, Heredia is capital of the province of the same name and an important coffee centre. It is away from the pollution of San José but close to the capital and the airport, and with good public transport. The central area is laid out in a grid, relatively compact and easily explored on foot.

Sights

The town is mostly new with only the main square maintaining a colonial atmosphere in its architecture. The short squat **Basílica de la Inmaculada Concepción**, built in 1797, has survived countless earthquakes. To the north of the central plaza, with a statue to the poet Aquileo Echeverría (1866-1909), is the solitary defensive structure of **El Fortín**. Across the street the **Casa de la Cultura** is a fine colonial home that now hosts concerts and exhibitions. The School of Marine Biology at the Universidad Nacional campus has a **Museo Zoológico Marino**.

Britt's Coffee Farm

US$22, tours 1100, 1½ hrs, includes lunch and show, T2277-1500, www.coffeetour.com.

One of the region's largest coffee *beneficios* is Café Britt's coffee farm, near Barva de Heredia, where you can see the processing factory, tasting room and a multimedia presentation of the story of coffee. You can be picked up from Heredia or at various points in San José. The **Teatro Dionisio Chaverría** at Café Britt hosts weekend theatre and a children's show on Sunday afternoons.

Barva and around

North of Heredia is the historic town of Barva, on the slopes of Volcán Barva; there are frequent buses to/from Heredia. At Barva, the **Huetar Gallery** is recommended for arts, crafts and delicious food. There is also a **Museo de Cultura Popular** ⓘ *Mon-Fri 0900-1600, US$3,* 500 m east of the Salón Comunal de Santa Lucía de Barva. North of Heredia through San Rafael, above Los Angeles, is **Galería Octágono** ⓘ *T2267-6325 www.galeriaoctagono. com*, an arts gallery with textiles handmade by a women's community cooperative, and also a B&B (see Where to stay, below). Beyond Barva, to the west, is **Santa Bárbara**, where you can find good seafood at the **Banco de los Mariscos** (T2269-9090), 500 m west from the central plaza. Five kilometres west of Heredia is **San Joaquín de Flores**, a small rural town with views of Barva and Poás volcanoes.

INBio Parque

South of Heredia on the road to Santo Domingo, T2507-8107, www.inbio.ac.cr, Fri 0800-1700, Sat-Sun 0900-1730, US$44.

INBio Parque is an educational and recreational centre that explains and gives insight into Costa Rica's biological diversity. In a small area you can visit the ecosystems of central highland forest, dry forest and humid forest, with trails set out for bromelias and *guarumo*.

Volcán Barva

Parque Nacional Braulio Carrillo ⓘ *park entry US$15, no permit needed (see page 140)*, to the north of Heredia, includes Volcán Barva, at 2906 m. This section of the park is ideal for hiking with a good trail leading up to the summit with three lagoons nearby, and excellent views and wildlife encounters for the few that make the effort. The really enthusiastic can hike all the way down to the lowlands arriving close to La Selva Biological Station near Puerto Viejo de Sarapaqui, but careful planning is required. There is a ranger station and campsite near the entrance, 4 km north of Sacramento, from where it's a 3-km easy climb to the top – still a treasure and, amazingly, a well-kept secret from the hordes.

Aserrí to San Pable de Turrubares

Some 10 km south of San José is Aserrí, a village with a beautiful white church. On Friday and Saturday evenings, street bands begin the fiesta with music from 2000, followed by marimbas. Extremely popular among locals, the dancing is fabulous, with *chicharrones*, tortillas and plenty of other things to eat and drink. Further along the same road is **Mirador Ram Luna**, a restaurant with a fine panoramic view. At the end of the road is **San Ignacio de Acosta**, again with a good church containing life-size Nativity figures. Buses go there from San José (Calle 8, Avenida 12-14 in front of the Baptist church) via Aserrí hourly from 0500 to 2230, return 0430 to 2100, one hour. The unpaved road continues to **Santiago de Puriscal**, which was the epicentre for many earthquakes in 1990. Although the church is now closed as a result, there are excellent views from the town and the road. From here it is possible to take a dirt road to the Pacific coast, joining the coastal road near Parrita (see page 114). Alternatively, take the road to **San Pablo de Turrubares**, from where you can either head west for Orotina, via an unpaved road through San Pedro and San Juan de Mata, or for Atenas (see page 50) via Quebradas, then east to Escobal, next stop on railway, then 4WD necessary to Atenas.

Where to stay

Heredia

$$$ Valladolid
Calle 7, Av 7, T2260-2905,
www.hotelvalladolid.net.
A smart and long-standing business hotel with 11 spacious rooms and suites, all with a/c, private bath, telephone and cable TV. 5th floor has sauna, jacuzzi and **Bonavista Bar** with fine views overlooking the Central Valley.

$$$-$$ Hotel and Boutique Hojarascas
Av 8, Calle 4-6, opposite Mas x Menos car park, T2261-3649, www.hotelhojarascas.com.
A very professional, comfortable, family-run hotel with good service and attention to detail. Rooms are tasteful, restful and immaculately clean, with solid wooden furniture, fast Wi-Fi, hot water, cable TV. Breakfast included, but cheaper without. Recommended.

$$ Apartotel Vargas
800 m north of Colegio Santa Cecilia and San Francisco Church, T2237-8526, www.apartotelvargas.com.
9 large, well-furnished apartments with cooking facilities, hot water, laundry facilities, TV, internet. Sr Vargas will collect you from the airport. Excellent choice if taking language classes and in a group. Best option in town.

$ Las Flores
Av 12, Calle 12-14, T2261-8147.
Quiet, low-key, family-run guesthouse with cheap, clean rooms with private bath. Friendly and helpful. Recommended.

Barva and around

$$$$ Finca Rosa Blanca
1.6 km from Santa Bárbara de Heredia, T2269-9392, www.fincarosablanca.com.
Deluxe suites in an architectural explosion of style and eloquence. Romance and exclusivity at the extremes of imagination.

Spa facilities for comfort. Quality restaurant and bar.

$$$$-$$$ Bougainvillea de Santo Domingo
just west of Santo Domingo, T2244-1414, www.hb.co.cr.
An award-winning mountain lodge with a commitment to sustainability and acres of dazzling landscaped tropical gardens. Excellent service, pool, sauna, spectacular setting, free shuttle bus to San José. Highly recommended.

$$$ Galería Octágono
T2267-6325, www.galeriaoctagono.com.
An arts gallery and B&B; other meals and transport available at additional cost, wonderful cypress cabin, hikes, and friendly and informative owners.

$$$ Hotel Chalet Tirol
3 km north of Castillo Country Club, T2267-6222, www.hotelchaleteltirol.com.
Colourful Alpine-style chalets and well-appointed suites set in flowery gardens and pine trees. This intriguing lodge is also home to a very reputable restaurant serving French fusion and international gourmet.

Restaurants

Heredia
There are lots of cheap *sodas* and food stalls inside the market, Calle 4 and Av 8, where you can pick up a carb-rich breakfast or set lunch (**$$-$**). On the eastern outskirts of town, Calle 9 is a small 'Zona Rosa' with several fun restaurants and a few bars.

$$$ Baalbek Bar & Grill
San Rafael de Heredia on the road to Monte de la Cruz, T2267-6482, www.baalbekbaryrestaurante.com.
A well-established Lebanese restaurant recommended chiefly for its romantic views of the Central Valley. A good place for a date. Belly dancing on Fri, live music on Sat.

$$$-$$ L'Antica Roma
Calle 7 and Av 7.
The best Italian restaurant in town, serving good wood-fired pizzas, various pastas, and cold beer. Seating indoors or out. Recommended.

$$-$ Las Espigas
Corner of Parque Central.
A convenient central location. Drop in for a cheap set lunch, coffee or pastries. There's also a fruit smoothie stand by the main door offering takeaway.

What to do

Language schools
Centro Panamericano de Idiomas, *San Joaquín de Flores, T2265-6306, www.cpi-edu. com.* Accommodation with local families.
Intercultura Language and Cultural Center, *Heredia city campus, T2260-8480, www.interculturacostarica.com.* Intensive Spanish course for adults of all ages, free cultural activities and excursions to beaches, volcanoes, rainforest. Family and kids' classes too.

Transport

Heredia
Buses from **San José**, from Av 2, Calle 12-14, every 10 mins daily, 0500-0015, then every 30 mins to 0400, 25-min journey, US$0.70. Return buses from Av 6, Calle 2-1.
    Local buses leave from Av 8, Calle 2-4, by the market.

Volcán Barva
Accessible from **Heredia**, there is no route from the San José–Limón Highway. Buses leave from the market at 0630, 1230 and 1600, returning at 0730, 1300, 1700. Arriving at **Porrosati** (a town en route to Volcán Barva). Some continue as far as Sacramento, otherwise walk 6 km to park entrance, then 4 km to lagoon. Be careful if leaving a car; there are regular reports of theft from rental cars.

Encircled by mountains, Cartago (altitude 1439 m) is at the foot of the Irazú Volcano and 22.5 km from San José on a toll road (US$0.75). Founded in 1563, it was the capital of Costa Rica for almost 300 years until San José assumed the role in 1823. Since then the town has failed to grow significantly and remains small, though densely populated. Earthquakes in 1841 and 1910 destroyed many of the buildings and ash from Irazú engulfed the town in 1963. While colonial-style remnants exist in one or two buildings, the town feels as if it is still reeling from the impact of so much natural devastation and is keeping quiet, waiting for the next event.

Sights
The most important attraction in town, and the focal point for pilgrims from all over Central America, is the **Basílica de Nuestra Señora de Los Angeles**, the patroness of Costa Rica, on the eastern side of town. Rebuilt in 1926 in Byzantine style, it houses the diminutive **La Negrita**, an indigenous image of the Virgin under 15 cm high, worshipped for her miraculous healing powers. The basilica also houses a collection of finely made *milagros* (miracles) – silver and gold charms, no larger than 3 cm high, of various parts of the human anatomy, offered in the hope of being healed. The most important date in the pilgrims' calendar is 2 August, when the image of La Negrita is carried in procession to churches in Cártago with celebrations throughout Costa Rica.

Also worth seeing is **La Parroquia** (the old parish church), roughly 1 km west of the basilica, ruined by the 1910 earthquake and now converted into a delightful garden retreat with flowers, fish and hummingbirds.

Around Cartago
Aguas Calientes, 4 km southeast of Cartago and 90 m lower, has a warm-water *balneario* ideal for picnics. On the road to Paraíso, 8 km from Cartago, is an orchid garden, the **Jardín Botánico Lankester** ⓘ *10 mins' walk from the main road, T2552-3247, daily 0830-1630, US$7.50,* run by the University of Costa Rica. The best displays are between February and April. The Cartago–Paraíso bus departs every 30 minutes from the south side of central park in Cartago (15 minutes); ask the driver to drop you off at Campo Ayala. Taxi from Cartago, US$5.

Volcán Irazú
US$15, 0800-1530 most of the year.

The crater at the top of Irazú (altitude 3432 m) is an impressive half-mile cube dug out of the earth, surrounded by desolate grey sand, which looks like the surface of the moon. President Kennedy's visit in 1963 coincided with a major eruption and, in 1994 the north wall of the volcano was destroyed by another eruption that sent detritus down as far as the Río Sucio. The views of the valley are stupendous on a clear day, but the clouds normally move in, enveloping the lower peaks and slopes by 1300 (sometimes even by 0900 or 1000 between July and November); so get there as early. There's little wildlife other than the ubiquitous Volcano Junco bird and the few plants which survive in the barren landscape.

Orosí Valley

Further east from Cartago a trip round the Orosí Valley makes a beautiful circular trip, or a fine place to hang out for a while in a valley that is often overlooked as the crowds rush to the more popular spots on the coast. The centrepiece of the valley is the artificial Lake Cachí used for hydroelectric generation. Heading round the lake anti-clockwise, the road passes through Orosí, clips the edge of Parque Nacional Tapantí, continuing to the Cachí Dam and completes the circuit passing through Ujarrás. Along the way there are several miradors which offer excellent views of the Reventazón Valley. For transport, see each destination. Day trips can be easily arranged from San José.

In **Orosí** there is an 18th-century **mission** ① *Tue-Sun, closed Mon*, with colonial treasures, and just outside the town are two **balnearios** ① *US$2.50*, with restaurants serving tasty meals at fair prices. It's a good place to hang out, take some low-key language classes, mixed with mountain biking and trips to the national park and other sites of interest.

Parque Nacional Tapantí-Macizo de la Muerte
Daily 0700-1700, US$10.

Some 12 km beyond Orosí is the Parque Nacional Tapantí-Macizo de la Muerte, one of the wettest parts of the country (some parts reportedly receiving as much as 8 m of rain a year). From June to November/December it rains every afternoon. Approached from Orosí, and just 30 km from Cartago, the national park is surprisingly easy to reach and packs in the interest.

Covering 58,000 ha, Tapantí-Macizo includes the former Tapantí National Park and much of the Río Macho Forest Reserve. The park protects the Río Orosí basin which feeds the Cachí Dam hydro power plant. Strategically, the southern boundary of the park joins with Chirripó National Park, extending the continuous protected area that makes up La Amistad Biosphere Reserve. The park incorporates a wide range of life zones with altitudes rising from 1220 m to over 3000 m at the border with Chirripó. The diverse altitudes and relative seclusion of the park has given rise to an impressive variety of species including 260 bird species and 45 mammals. There are picnic areas, a nature centre with slide shows (ask to see them) and good swimming in the dry season (November-June), and trout fishing season (1 April-31 October).

Cachí

Continue around the lake to Cachí and the nearby **Casa del Soñador** (Dreamer's House), which sells wood carvings from the sculpture school of the late Macedonio Quesada. The road crosses the dam wall and follows the north shore to Ujarrás, then back to Cartago. The **Charrarra tourist complex**, 30 minutes' walk from Ujarrás, has a good campsite, restaurant, pool, boat rides on the lake and walks. It can be reached by direct bus on Sunday. Buses leave from Cartago, one block north of the Cartago ruins.

Ujarrás

Ujarrás (ruins of a colonial church and village) is 6.5 km east of Paraíso, on the shores of the artificial Lago Cachí. There is a bus every 1½ hours from Paraíso that continues to Cachí. Legend has it that in 1666 English pirates, including the youthful Henry Morgan, were seen off by the citizens of Ujarrás aided by the Virgin. The event is now celebrated annually in mid-March when the saint is carried in procession from Paraíso to the ruined church.

Tourist information

Cartago
Mercatur, *next to Fuji at Av 2, Calle 4-6.*
Provides local tourist information.

Where to stay

Cartago

$ Dinastia
Calle 3, Av 6-8, close to the old railway station, at the Las Ruinas end of town, T2551-7057.
Slightly more expensive with private bath. The rooms are small although better with a window.

$ Los Angeles Lodge B&B
Near the Basílica at Av 4, Calle 14-16, T2591-4169.
Clean, nice rooms, restaurant.

Around Cartago

$$$ Sanchirí Mirador and Lodge
2 km south of Parque Paraíso, Orosi road, T2574-5454, www.sanchiri.com.
Commanding views at this highland lodge where guests can rest up in pleasant wooden *cabañas* or modern rooms with balconies. A certified sustainable business with organically farmed produce and environmentally friendly technology.

Volcán Irazú

$$$ Grandpa's Hotel
7 km north of Cartago on the Irazú road, 500 m west of 'El Cristo' in the village of Cot, T2536-6666, www.grandpashotel.com.
A cosy Victorian house with fine views and a well-tended flower-filled garden. Lodging includes a range of pleasant rooms, suites, rustic log cabins and an apartment.

Orosí Valley

$$$ Chalet Orosí
1.5 km south of Orosí, turn west off the highway at Planta Santa María, T2533-3268, www.chaletorosi.com.
A French-run guesthouse near Tapantí National Park, close to a river and nestled amid coffee plantations and forests. Accommodation is in a range of well-appointed wooden chalets with amenities including solar-heated spa, barbecue and Wi-Fi.

$$ Orosí Lodge
T2533-3578, www.orosilodge.com.
6 rooms and a house with balcony overlooking the valley towards Volcán Irazú. Just about everything you could want: divine home-baked cookies, mountain bikes, kayaks and horses for rent, and internet service. Credit cards accepted. Excellent value.

$ Montaña Linda
T2533-3640, www.montanalinda.com.
A classic and well-run backpackers' place, with a range of options. Dormitory rooms, camping, and B&B service if you just can't get out of bed. There is also a language school, with package deals for lodgers. Great spot with a very friendly, knowledgeable team.

Parque Nacional Tapantí-Macizo de la Muerte

$$ Kiri Lodge
1.5 km from the park entrance, T2533-2272, www.kirilodge.net.
Excellent lodging and food, breakfast included. Peaceful, trout fishing, very friendly, good trails on 50-ha property.

Restaurants

Volcán Irazú

$$-$ Restaurante Linda Vista
Spectacular views, as you'd expect from
Costa Rica's highest restaurant, serving good
food and drinks. But most people stop to
post, stick, pin or glue a business card, or
some other personal item, to the wall.

What to do

Orosí Valley
Language schools
Montaña Linda Language School, *T2533-
3640, see Where to stay, above.* Uses local
teachers with a homestay option if you
want total submersion. Recommended.

Transport

Cartago
Bus To **San José** every 10 mins from Av 4,
Calle 2-4. Arrives and departs San José from
Calle 5, Av 18-20 for the 45-min journey,
US$0.90. After 2030 buses leave from Gran
Hotel Costa Rica, Av 2, Calle 3-5. **Orosí/Río
Macho**, for **Parque Nacional Tapantí** every
30 mins from Calle 6, Av 1-3, 35-55 mins,
US$0.95. **Turrialba**, every hour from Av 3,
Calle 8-10, 1 hr direct, US$1.40, 1 hr 20 mins
colectivo. **Cachí**, via **Ujarrá** and **Paraíso** from
Calle 6, Av 1-3, every 1½ hrs, 1 hr 20 mins.
Paraíso, every 5 mins from Av 5, Calle 4-6.
Aguacalientes, every 15 mins from Calle
1, Av 3-5. **Tierra Blancas** for **Irazú**, every
30 mins from Calle 4, Av 6-8, US$2.

Closest bus for **Irazú** rides to San Juan de
Chichua, still some 12 km from the summit.
The bus leaves Cartago from north of the
central market, Av 6, Calle 1-3, at 1730,
returning at 0500 the next day, so you have
to spend at least 2 nights on the volcano
or in a hotel if you can't get a ride. To visit
Volcán Turrialba take a bus from Calle 4 y
Av 6 to the village of San Gerardo.

Volcán Irazú
Bus It is possible to get a bus from Cartago
to Tierra Blanca (US$0.33) or San Juan de
Chicúa (which has 1 hotel) and hitch a ride in
a pickup truck. Or you can take a Cartago–
Sanatorio bus. Ask the driver to drop you at
the crossroads outside Tierra Blanca. From
there you walk 16 km to the summit. If you're
looking for a day trip from San José, a yellow
'school' express bus (**Buses Metropoli SA**,
T2530-1064), runs from Gran Hotel Costa
Rica, **San José**, daily 0800. It stops at Cartago
ruins 0830 to pick up more passengers,
returns 1230 with lunch stop at **Restaurant
Linda Vista**, US$3.90.

Taxi From **Cartago** is US$32 return. A taxi
tour from **Orosí** costs US$10 per person,
minimum 3 people, and stops at various
places on the return journey, eg Cachí dam
and Ujarrás ruins. Since it can be difficult
to find a decent hotel in Cartago, it may be
easier to take a guided tour leaving from **San
José**, about US$44, 5½ hrs includes lunch,
transport from San José. If driving from San
José, take the turn-off at the Ferretería San
Nicolás in Taras, which goes directly to Irazú,
avoiding Cartago.

Orosí Valley
Bus From **Cartago** to Orosí/Río Macho from
Calle 6, Av 1-3, every 30 mins, journey time of
35-55 mins, US$0.90.

Parque Nacional Tapantí-Macizo de la Muerte
Bus The 0600 bus from Cartago to Orosí gets
to Puricil by 0700, then walk (5 km), or take
any other Cartago–Orosí bus to Río Macho
and walk 9 km to the refuge. Alternatively
take a taxi from **Orosí** (US$7 round trip, up
to 6 passengers), or **San José**, US$50.

ecologically diverse zone with many fine coffee farms

Turrialba (altitude 646 m, 62 km from San José) connects the Central Valley highlands and Caribbean lowlands, and was once a stopping point on the old Atlantic railway between Cartago and Puerto Limón. The railway ran down to Limón on a narrow ledge poised between mountains on the left, and the river to the right, but no longer operates.

Sights
The **Centro Agronómico Tropical de Investigación y Enseñanza (CATIE)** ⓘ *about 4 km southeast of Turrialba, T2558-2000 ext 2275, www.catie.ac.cr, botanical garden open daily 0700-1600, T2556-2700, US$6,* covers more than 800 ha. It has one of the largest tropical fruit collections in the world and houses an important library on tropical agriculture; visitors and students are welcome for research or birdwatching. Past CATIE on the south side of the river, a large sugar mill makes for a conspicuous landmark in Atirro, the centre for macadamia nuts. Nearby, the 256-ha **Lake Angostura** has now flooded some of the whitewaters of the Río Reventazón.

Around Turrialba
Many whitewater rafting companies operate out of Turrialba, with trips to the **Río Reventazón and Río Pacuare**. The rafting is excellent; the Pascua section of the Reventazón can be Grade V at rainy times. The Pacuare is absolutely perfect with divine scenery. By contacting the guides in Turrialba you can save about 30% on a trip booked in San José, provided they are not already contracted.

Volcán Turrialba (3329 m) may be visited from Cartago by a bus from Calle 4 y Avenida 6 to the village of San Gerardo. From Turrialba take a bus to Santa Cruz. From both, an unpaved road meets at **Finca La Central**, on the saddle between Irazú and Turrialba.

Monumento Nacional Guayabo
T2559-1220, Tue-Sun 0800-1530, US$10, local guides available, water, toilets, no food.

About 19 km north of Turrialba, near Guayabo, is a 3000-year-old ceremonial centre excavated with paved streets and stone-lined water channels. The archaeological site, 232 ha and 4 km from the town of Guayabo, dates from the period 1000 BC-AD 1400. There are excellent walks in the park, where plenty of birds and wildlife can be seen. Worth a trip to see Costa Rica's most developed ancient archaeological site but small in comparison to the great sites of the Maya.

Listings Turrialba and around

Where to stay

Turrialba

$$$ Wagelia
Av 4, entrance to Turrialba, T2556-1566, www.hotelwageliaturrialba.com.
Comfortable lodging with 18 rooms, bath, some a/c, restaurant. Overpriced, but not much else to choose from at this level.

$$-$ Hostel Casa de Lis
Av Central, south of Bancrédito, next to ICE, T2556-4933, www.hostelcasadelis.com.
An excellent 'boutique' hostel offering comfort, style and service a cut above the rest. Accommodation options include economical dorms (**$**) and private rooms (**$$**), all kitted with orthopaedic mattresses and hot water. Recommended.

$$-$ Interamericano
Facing the old railway station on Av 1, T2556-0142, www.hotelinteramericano.com.
A basic but friendly place, family-run, home to a few dogs, popular with kayakers. Clean, private ($$) or shared bath ($). Safe for motorbikes. Communal area with TV and books.

Around Turrialba

$$$$ Casa Turire
14 km southeast of Turrialba, follow the signposts, T2531-1111, www.hotelcasaturire.com.
Overlooking Lake Angostura, 12 luxury rooms with bath, 4 suites, cable TV, phone, restaurant, pool, library, games room, in the middle of a 1620-ha sugar, coffee and macadamia nut plantation. Virgin rainforest nearby, trails, horses, bike rental, excursions.

$$$$ Pacuare Lodge
On the banks of the Pacuare river, T7016-3147, www.pacuareriverlodge.com.
An intriguing jungle lodge with a very solid reputation, popular with adventurers and honeymooners alike. Accommodation is in range of wooden cabins and luxury suites, all perched on a hillside overlooking the river. No drop-ins or independent visits, package stays only. Rafters can access the lodge as part of a whitewater trip.

$$$$ Rancho Naturalista
1.5 km south of Tuis, turn-off signed, T2100-1855, www.ranchonaturalista.net.
A premier birdwatching lodge surrounded by forests, family-run with 14 good rooms and a range of *casitas*. The main building has an observation balcony where 250 species have been recorded. Rates per person, guides cost extra.

$$$-$$ Turrialtico
On road to Siquirres, T2538-1111, www.turrialtico.com.
On top of hill with extensive views. Rooms are clean with private bath, comfortable, friendly. Going northeast from Turrialba, the main road follows the Río Reventazón down to Siquirres (see page 142).

Monumento Nacional Guayabo

$$$ Hotel Guayabo Lodge
300 m south of Santa Cruz cemetery, T2538-8492, www.guayabolodge.co.cr.
An airy mountain lodge with expansive views of the surrounding valleys and volcanic cones. They offer 22 standard rooms and 4 suites. Cooking classes, various tours and packages available.

What to do

Around Turrialba
See also the companies in San José (eg **Ríos Tropicales**, page 43).
Serendipity Adventures, *T2558-1000, www.serendipityadventures.com.* Canyoning, rappelling and hot-air ballooning. Recommended.
Tico's River Adventures, *T2556-1231, www.ticoriver.com.* With recommended local guides.

Transport

Turrialba
Bus From **San José** every hour 0530-2200 from Terminal Turrialba, Calle 13, Av 6-8, 1½ hrs, US$2.40 from **Cartago**, 1 hr, US$1.40, runs until about 2200. Service to **Siquirres**, for connections to Caribbean lowlands, hourly, 40 mins, US$2.

Monumento Nacional Guayabo
Bus From **Turrialba**, there are buses at 1100 (returning 1250) and 1710 (returning 1750), and on Sun at 0900, return 1700 (check times, if you miss it is quite difficult to hitch as there is little traffic), US$0.95 to Guayabo. Several daily buses pass the turn-off to Guayabo; the town is a 2-hr walk uphill (taxi US$10, easy to hitch back). **San José** tour operators offer day trips to Guayabo for about US$65 per person (minimum 4 people), cheaper from Turrialba.

Northern
Costa Rica

North of the Meseta Central, the land descends to languid tropical plains as far as the Nicaraguan border, a sweltering sprawl of fruit farms and cattle ranches framed by the teeming wetlands of the Caño Negro nature reserve in the north and two rugged mountain chains in the west: the Cordillera Tilarán and the Cordillera Guanacaste. At the heart of the region lies the iconic peak of Arenal volcano, rising above the waters of Costa Rica's largest lake. It continues to draw adventurers and eco-tourists despite falling dormant in 2011, its environs peppered with scores of protected areas, hiking trails, zip-lines, butterfly reserves and eternally soothing hot springs.

West of Arenal, the land climbs skyward to craggy peaks and gorges, a rolling patchwork of innumerable shades of green. Tempered by shifting veils of mist and sunshine, the region's remote rural villages are steeped in flowery meadows and cloaks of pine. Here, the primeval cloudforests of Monteverde are the principal draw, clothed in thick green mosses, lichens and fiery bromeliads.

In the far northwest, the land descends to Guanacaste, Costa Rica's macho Sabanero heartland. Dominated by rambling haciendas and wide open pastures, it could easily be the backdrop to a Hollywood Western.

Also known as San Carlos, Ciudad Quesada is the regional capital of Costa Rica's slow-paced northern lowlands, an area historically grounded in farming and ranching. True to form, it has a frontier feel with an air of bravado and a pinch of indifference. The huge church overlooking the main plaza stands out as the sole point of interest in Quesada, but its bus terminal, 1 km north of town, is seen by many travellers on their way to La Fortuna or Los Chiles.

Los Chiles

Heading north from Quesada, Highway 35 steers through rich red laterite soils in an almost straight line for 74 km, passing fragrant orange and citrus groves until finally arriving at the languid river port of Los Chiles. The days are hot and sluggish in this remote fishing outpost sprawled indolent on the banks of the Río Frío. There are two main reasons for visiting: one is to take a public boat onwards to the Río San Juan and the Nicaraguan border (see Nicaragua–Costa Rica border box, page 173); the other is to commission a private vessel to explore the humid wetlands of the Refugio Natural de Vida Silvestre Caño Negro.

Refugio Natural de Vida Silvestre Caño Negro

Caño Negro park administration, T2471-1309, for information and reservations for food and lodging; US$15 entrance to the park. The entrance to the park is via the village of Caño Negro on the road between Upala and Los Chiles.

Shrouded in dense tropical vegetation, the 10,171-ha Refugio Natural de Vida Silvestre Caño Negro encompasses a variety of watery habitats, including the 800-ha Caño Lake, which swells to life in the wet season. However, the drier months of January to March signal annual bird migrations and are the best time for observing the park's 365 avian species. You can join an organized expedition from La Fortuna (see page 67), but it is cheaper to commission a guide from the dock in Los Chiles. A three- to four-hour tour costs US$60-100 per group, depending on the size of the vessel, its engine, and the quantity of gasoline burned; Esteban, Oscar Rojas (T2471-1090) and Enrique have all been recommended. Fishing in the park is better than good with easily snagged giant snook and 2-m tarpon. Fully equipped sports fishing expeditions can be organized with professional tour operators in La Fortuna, starting at around US$100 per person for half a day.

Where to stay

Ciudad Quesada (San Carlos)

$$$ Hotel La Garza
Platanar de San Carlos, 8 km from Florencia,
north of Ciudad Quesada, T2475-5222,
www.hotellagarza.com.
12 charming bungalows with bath and
fan, overlooking river. Idyllic spot with
good views of Arenal, a 20-min drive from
La Fortuna. Guided tours, boat trips, fishing,
230 ha of forest and cattle ranch.

$$$ Tilajari Resort Hotel
Muelle San Carlos, 13 km north of Platanar
de San Carlos, T2462-1212, www.tilajari.com.
Resort-style lodge on the edge of the river.
Luxury rooms and suites, a/c, private bath,
tennis courts, 2 pools, sauna, bar, restaurant,
horses and excursions available. Popular
with groups.

$$ La Central
On west side of park, Ciudad Quesada,
T2460-0301, www.hotellacentral.net.
As the name suggests, a central option.
Private bath, hot water, fan, TV and phone
in room.

Los Chiles

$$ Hotel Wilson Tulipán
1 block west of the Parque Central opposite
the immigration offices, T2471-1414,
www.hoteleswilson.com.
10 clean well-appointed rooms with a/c,
TV, bath and hot water, breakfast and taxes
included. Can arrange a wide variety of tours
in the area including river safaris and fishing
trips. Restaurant-bar.

$ Hotel Carolina
Close to main highway, T2471-1151.
Clean and well maintained – the best of the
budgets. Accommodation ranges from small,
fairly dark rooms with shared bath to a/c
cabins with TV.

Restaurants

Ciudad Quesada (San Carlos)
Variety of *sodas* in the central market offer
casados, check out the great sword collection
displayed at **La Ponderosa**.

$$$ Coca Loca Steak House
Next to Hotel La Central, T2460-3208.
Complete with Wild West swing door.

$$ Los Geranios
Av 4 and Calle.
Popular bar and restaurant serving up good
bocas and other dishes.

$$ Restaurant Crystal
On the western side of the plaza.
Sells fast food, snacks, ice cream and good
fruit dishes.

Transport

Ciudad Quesada (San Carlos)
Bus To **La Fortuna**, 12 daily, 1½ hrs,
US$1.50; to **Los Chiles**, hourly, 3 hrs, US$4.30;
to **San José**, hourly, 0500-1930, 2½ hrs,
US$3.60; to **Tilarán** via La Fortuna and
Arenal, 0630, 1400, US$4. Regular buses also
travel northeast to towns on the Río San
Carlos and Río Sarapiquí, including **Puerto**
Viejo de Sarapiquí, 5 daily, 3 hrs and east to
the **Río Frío** district.

Los Chiles
Bus To **San José**, 2 daily, 0500, 1500,
5 hrs, US$4.20. Alternatively, travel to
Ciudad Quesada and take one of the more
frequent services. To get to Los Chiles from
La Fortuna, take the bus towards Ciudad
Quesada, get off at Muelle and wait for
a connection. For more information on
crossing from Los Chiles to Nicaragua, see
the Nicaragua–Costa Rica box, page 173.

With its perfectly proportioned conical peak rising 1633 m above the plains, Volcán Arenal forms an eternally aesthetic backdrop to the windswept waters of Arenal Lake, when it isn't completely obscured by clouds of course. Due to inclement weather, May to December are poor months to admire the volcano but the best times to avoid the hordes of package tourists, a ubiquitous presence in the dry season.

Historically, Arenal was not always so popular. Long thought to be little more than an innocuous hill, it was completely ignored by the Costa Rican institute of tourism – and almost everyone else – until one fateful day in July 1968 when it suddenly exploded to life and destroyed three villages. For more than four decades thereafter, constant volcanic drama ensued with perpetual roars and rumblings, ominous emissions of gas, steam and smoke, and earth-shuddering detonations accompanied by violent ribbons of blood-red lava weaving down its face. The 7500-year-old volcano was quickly dubbed one of the world's most active, and touristic infrastructure mushroomed at its base. Cavalcades of international travellers made their way to behold Arenal's eruptions, until suddenly, in 2011, for no explicable reason, the eruptions stopped.

Activity may or may not resume anytime soon, with or without the explosive violence of the 1968 eruption; but until then, Arenal remains set up for eco-tourism and outdoor adventures. Importantly, numerous mineral-rich therapeutic hot springs continue to bubble to the surface throughout the region – places where you can soak your weary bones and, if the weather is right, admire gently slumbering Arenal, the epitome of classic volcanic beauty.

La Fortuna See map, page 68.
The small town of La Fortuna (altitude 254 m) is a service, transport and tourism hub, and the conventional base for exploring the Arenal region. Once a humdrum village that shuddered in the shadow of the volcano's power, it has grown rapidly to accommodate visitors. The town's slew of modest hotels and *cabinas* best serve budget travellers, as well as those without independent transport. Those with the means may prefer to stay in one of the resort-style lodgings out of town. As a destination, La Fortuna lacks personality, but it is a convenient place to stage forays into the surrounding countryside: hiking, biking, windsurfing, canyoning, birdwatching, caving, canopy tours, kayaking, whitewater rafting and more can all be organized with the town's multitude of tour operators (for more information, see What to do, below).

Parque Nacional Volcán Arenal
Open 0800-1600, entrance US$15. Access is northwest of La Fortuna, follow the signs 14 km on the paved road towards Lago Arenal, then turn south 2 km on a gravel track; taxi US$25. Reception has maps and toilets.

Established in 1991, the Parque Nacional Volcán Arenal encompasses 12,124 ha of forested terrain, including the volcanic peaks of Arenal and Cerro Chato. Home to more than 450 avian species, it is one of Costa Rica's 21 Important Bird Areas – the three-wattled bell bird, the great curassow, the bare-necked umbrella bird, the keel-billed mot mot and the resplendent quetzal are all resident. From the reception area, hikers have a few options, all of them undemanding. The **Sendero Heliconias** is a flat, linear jaunt through early secondary forest, 1-km long. More interesting is the **Sendero Las Coladas**, flat for 1.5 km until it enters lava fields forged by Arenal's eruptions, whereupon it becomes steep and irregular for 500 m. The **Sendero El Ceibo**, 1.8 km, loops off Las Coladas throughout mature secondary forest and is 95% flat. A trail with vehicular access leads from the reception 1.3 km to a mirador with a parking area, benches and striking views. It is not permitted to climb to the summit of Arenal, but **Cerro Chato**, near Río Fortuna waterfall, can be scaled for expansive views of the surrounding area (see below).

Catarata Río Fortuna and Cerro Chato
Administered by ADIFORT, T2479-8338, www.arenaladifort.com, open 0800-1700, entrance US$10.

About 6 km southwest of La Fortuna is the numinous spectacle of Catarata Río Fortuna (**Río Fortuna Waterfall**) plunging 70 m into a cloud of swirling mist and spray. To get there, head south out of town for 2 km before turning west uphill through yucca and papaya plantations for another 4 km. From the entrance, a steep and slippery path leads 600 m down to the falls, so take shoes with a good tread. Bathing is possible, but it's safer 50 m downstream. If you don't want to walk, you can drive, but 4WD is necessary. Bicycle hire (US$3 per hour, US$15 per day) is another option and hard work, or you can hire a horse for the day at around US$55. Two- to three-hours' climb above the falls is the crater lake of Cerro Chato. The top (1100 m) is reached through mixed tropical/cloudforest, a demanding hike with a good view (if you're lucky); bring some cash to pay fees for crossing private land. Organized trips from La Fortuna US$75.

Hot springs
From rustic pools to luxury spas, there are scores of hot springs around Arenal. Almost 5 km north of La Fortuna is the **Baldi Thermae complex** ① *T2479-9651, daily 1000-2200, US$41*, with several thermal pools ranging from 37° up to 63°C – the limits of endurance

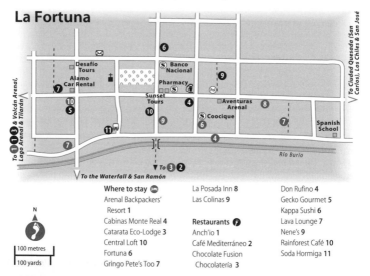

La Fortuna

To Ciudad Quesada (San Carlos), Los Chiles & San José

To Volcán Arenal, Lago Arenal & Tilarán

To ❶❸❸ & Volcán Arenal, Lago Arenal & Tilarán

Desafío Tours
Álamo Car Rental ❼
Banco Nacional ⓢ
Pharmacy
Sunset Tours
Aventuras Arenal ❽
Coocique ⓢ
Spanish School
Río Burío

▼ To ❶❸❷
∨ To the Waterfall & San Ramón

N

| 100 metres |
| 100 yards |

Where to stay 🛏
Arenal Backpackers' Resort **1**
Cabinas Monte Real **4**
Catarata Eco-Lodge **3**
Central Loft **10**
Fortuna **6**
Gringo Pete's Too **7**
La Posada Inn **8**
Las Colinas **9**

Restaurants 🍴
Anch'io **1**
Café Mediterráneo **2**
Chocolate Fusion Chocolatería **3**

Don Rufino **4**
Gecko Gourmet **5**
Kappa Sushi **6**
Lava Lounge **7**
Nene's **9**
Rainforest Café **10**
Soda Hormiga **11**

without being poached. It's a fun, popular place and there are slides and poolside drinks available. A taxi from town costs US$4, a bus is US$1. Around 5 km west of La Fortuna is **Eco Termales** ① *T2479-8787, www.ecotermalesfortuna.cr*, a much more intimate locale with six tastefully presented thermal pools. A limited number of guests are permitted entry, reserve in advance, around US$50 with a meal. Some 13 km northwest of La Fortuna, **The Springs Resort** ① *T2401-3313, www.thespringscostarica.com*, has five-star treatment in its immaculately landscaped grounds. It has numerous hot- and cold-water pools connected by a system of trails, all of them surrounded by fiery heliconias and other lush rainforest plants; a two-day pass costs US$50. Off the road to Lago Arenal, approximately 10 km northwest of La Fortuna, is **Balneario Tabacón** ① *T2519-1999, daily 1000-2200, day guests welcome but limited, reserve in advance, entry from US$75*, a kitsch complex of thermal pools, waterfalls and (for residents) beauty treatments, with three bars and a restaurant. The water is hot and stimulating; there are pools at descending heights and temperatures as well as water slides and a waterfall to sit under. A taxi from La Fortuna to Tabacón is US$6. Cheaper are the hot waters about 4 km further along the road at **Quebrada Cedeña**, which are clean and safe. There is no sign but look for local parked cars.

North to Upala
A quiet route north leads from La Fortuna to **San Rafael de Guatuso**. There is a 'voluntary' toll of US$1 between Jicarito and San Rafael. You can come back to the lake by turning off at **Venado**, where there are spooky caves filled with limestone stalactites and stalagmites, squeaky bats, spiders and other creepy crawlies; a day tour from La Fortuna including guide and transport costs US$75. Alternatively, you can return to La Fortuna via San Rafael, where there are a couple of basic hotels. If you continue along the road from San Rafael northwest towards the Nicaraguan border you come to unpretentious **Upala** and a poor road east to **Caño Negro** (see page 65). There is a direct bus from San José to Upala, T2221-3318 (from Avenida 3-5, Calle 10 at 1000 and 1700, four hours).

Around Lago Arenal
Lago Arenal, Costa Rica's largest lake, was artificially expanded by three times its original size with the construction of the Arenal dam on its eastern side in 1979. Today, stretching west from the foot of Volcán Arenal, it covers an area of approximately 85 sq km. It is a very blustery lake and both windsurfers and turbine builders exploit its gales and gusts. On its southeastern shore, 12 km by road from La Fortuna, the tiny community of El Castillo makes a viable low-key base for exploring the Arenal region, but only if you have your own transport. Here you'll find the **El Castillo Butterfly Conservatory** ① *T2479-1149, www.butterflyconservatory.org, daily 0800-1600*, offering popular educational tours of their laboratories, reproduction greenhouses, exotic frog habitats, host plant gardens and orchid collections. More ecological wonders can be discovered nearby at **Arenal Eco Zoo** ① *T2479-1058, www.arenalecozoo.com, 0800-1900*, home to some 70 reptile species, including a 5.5-m Burmese python called Eliza. On the northern side of Volcán Arenal, a paved road twists and winds from La Fortuna, passing scores of hotels and resorts until arriving at the lake and the dam, where boats making the 'jeep-bus-jeep' journey between Arenal and Santa Elena/Monteverde land. Further west, the road skirts the shore, soon arriving at **Nuevo Arenal**, a small town that was created to replace the one destroyed by the flooding of the lake. There is plenty of good accommodation in the area, much of it in the higher price brackets.

Continuing west towards Tilarán, the western side of the lake is popular with windsurfers throughout the year, and between December and April the conditions are world class. A batch of hotels cater for windsurfers of all levels; there are many other options in the area so take your pick if you want to stop. Whether travelling by bus or car, you can get from La Fortuna via Monteverde via Tilarán in a day, but set out early to make your connection with the 1230 bus in Tilarán or to avoid driving after dark.

Tilarán would not appear on the list of destinations for travellers were it not for its role as a small regional transport hub for people journeying between La Fortuna, Santa Elena/Monteverde and Cañas on the Pan-American Highway. In town there is pretty much nothing to do and, with luck, the connecting buses will be timed perfectly to avoid you having to wait too long. But if you do, there are several places to catch a bite to eat, and several good places to stay if you need a bed for the night.

Listings Volcán Arenal and around *map p68*

Where to stay

Volcán Arenal and around

La Fortuna (see below) is the easiest place to stay if you don't have your own transport, but the whole area west of the town is littered with decent hotels, far too many to mention here.

$$$$ The Springs Resort and Spa
12.9 km northwest of La Fortuna, T2401-3313, www.thespringscostarica.com.
A world class luxury resort with 18 artisan hot springs, 5 bars, 4 restaurants, and a range of sumptuous wood-built rooms, suites and bungalows. Very expensive, excellent service and highly romantic.

$$$$-$$$ Arenal Observatory Lodge
northwestern side of the volcano, 4 km after El Tabacón, a turn towards the lake down a (signposted) gravel road, T2290-7011, www.arenalobservatorylodge.com.
4WD recommended along this 9-km stretch. Set up in 1973, the observatory was purely a research station but it now has private rooms, suites and a villa. There are stunning views of the volcano, Lake Arenal and across the valley of Río Agua Caliente. Recommended.

$$$$-$$$ Los Lagos
T2479-1000, www.hotelloslagos.com.
98 comfortable cabin rooms sleeping up to 4, day visits US$20, excellent food and spectacular views of the volcano over the lake, good facilities and small café, spa, numerous spring-fed pools, canopy tour, trails and a frog farm.

$$$ Cabañas Brisas Arenal
1.6 km southwest of La Fortuna, T2479-9225, www.brisasarenal.com.
Family-run lodging committed to sustainability. Tasteful wood-built cabins set in a leafy garden, home to lots of colourful birdlife. Rustic chic, but very comfortable.

$$$-$$ Hotel Arenal Green
1 km south and 1 km west from La Fortuna, towards Río Fortuna waterfall, T2479-8585, www.arenalgreen.com.
6 modern cabins and 1 villa built with native wood, all equipped with a/c, hot water, cable TV, coffee-maker, mini-fridge and chill-out porch with volcano or garden views. Tranquil, leafy grounds.

$$ Vista del Cerro
3.5 km west of La Fortuna, T2479-7029, www.hotelvistadelcerro.com.
Simple, comfortable, affordable and unpretentious rooms with volcano views, as the name suggests. Amenities include restaurant, garden and pool. Very helpful, friendly and down-to-earth.

La Fortuna

As one of the most popular destinations in the country, accommodation tends to be quite pricey in high season. Conversely, generous discounts in the green/low season are common.

$$$ Catarata Eco-Lodge
2 km from town, T2479-9522, www.cataratalodge.com.
Reservations essential for the 21 rooms and cabins in this cooperative with organic garden. Home-made soaps and shampoos, good fresh food, butterfly farm, hot water, laundry and all meals. Run by community association and supported by WWF Canada and CIDA Canada.

$$$ Hotel Central Loft
100 m west of the Parque Central, T2479-9004, www.hotelcentralloft.com.
One of the best hotels in town, centrally located near the main plaza. Rooms are spacious and well-appointed with solid wood furniture – ask for one with views of the volcano. There's also a small pool for cooling off.

$$$ Hotel Fortuna
1 block east and 1 block south of the Parque Central, T2479-9197, www.lafortunahotel.com.
A popular downtown hotel with 44 comfortable rooms (12 wheelchair accessible), some have impressive views of the volcano. All comforts and amenities; price includes breakfast.

$$$-$$ Cabinas Monte Real
100 m south and 300 m east of the Parque Central, T2479-9357, www.monterealhotel.com.
Bordering the Burio river close to a small forest, Cabinas Monte Real is a quiet and friendly place, visited by sloths, iguanas and colourful birds fluttering about the garden. Rooms are large (premium rooms have volcano views). Pool and Wi-Fi. Helpful staff, parking available. Recommended.

$$$-$$ Las Colinas
Half a block south of the Parque Central, T2479-9305, www.lascolinasarenal.com.
A Rainforest Alliance-certified 'eco-friendly' option with 20 tidy rooms, some with incredible views. Family-run, friendly

management, good discounts in the low season. Breakfast included and served on an open-air terrace looking out to the volcano. Recommended.

$$-$ Arenal Backpacker's Resort
A short distance north of town on the main road, T2479-7000, www.arenalbackpackersresort.com.
Popular with 20-somethings, a resort-style hostel with a relaxing garden and pool, views of Arenal, hammocks, wet bar, comedy tight-rope, evening activities like ping-pong and twister. Lodging is in mixed or single-sex dorms ($), 'safari tents' ($$) or private rooms ($$).

$ Gringo Pete's Too
1½ blocks west of the bus station, T2479-8521, www.gringopetes.com.
Undoubtedly the cheapest option, very popular with thrifty backpackers, but also quite rule-orientated. Lodgings include basic dorms and private rooms with kitchen facilities and communal areas for relaxing.

$ La Posada Inn
250 m east of the Parque Central, opposite the Colegio, T2479-9793, www.posadainncr.com.
Simple, spartan and spotless rooms, with or without private bath, fans included but mosquitoes reported. Small communal area out front. Low-key, family-run and relaxed.

North to Upala

$$$$ Río Celeste Hideaway
2 km from the entrance of Tenorio National Park, beyond San Rafael, T2206-5114, www.riocelestehideaway.com.
Luxury rainforest *casitas* with wooden floors and bamboo ceilings. All comforts and amenities, and the chattering sounds of the jungle to lull you to sleep.

Around Lago Arenal
Hotels in El Castillo on the southern side of the lake are slightly cut off but have fantastic views.

$$$$ La Mansión Inn
Highway 142, T8763-2088,
www.lamansionarenal.com.
Luxury boutique villas set in 10 ha of tropical gardens. Overlooks the lake with a beautiful spring-fed infinity pool, jacuzzis, mirador. Well-appointed rooms with lovely hand-painted murals. Very relaxing.

$$$$ Toad Hall
Highway 142, T8534-3605,
www.toadhallarenal.com.
Nestled in the jungle and overlooking the lake, 4 superb stylish themed villas that will suit couples or families, all very tasteful and artistic. Great restaurant. Recommended.

$$$ Hotel Linda Vista
El Castillo, T2479-1551,
www.hotellindavista.com.
A well-established Castillo favourite owned by the Badilla Picado family. Nice views, several good, unspoilt trails in the area, horse-riding tours, restaurant, pool, attentive service. Recommended.

$$$-$$ Hotel Los Héroes (Pequeña Helvecia)
10 km from Arenal towards Tilarán,
T2692-8012, www.hotellosheroes.com.
Delightful Swiss owners with inspiring energy. A superb hotel, complete with Swiss train service.

$$$-$$ La Ceiba
6 km from Arenal, T2692-8050,
www.ceibatree-lodge.com.
Overlooking Lake Arenal, La Ceiba is set in a 15-ha private nature reserve with 5 bright, comfortable rooms. Tico-owned and run, good, helpful, great panoramic views, good breakfast. Recommended.

Tilarán

$ Cabiñas El Sueño
1 block north of bus terminal/Parque Central,
T2695-5347.
Clean rooms around central patio, hot water, fan, TV and free coffee. Good deal and friendly.

Restaurants

La Fortuna

$$$ Anch'io Restaurant
350 m west of the Catholic church.
Several restaurants in town serve pizza and this is possibly the best. Stone-baked, authentic and complemented by a menu of tasty pasta dishes. Open-air seating on a covered patio. Pleasant and romantic.

$$$ Don Rufino
1 block east of the Parque Central,
T2479-9997, www.donrufino.com.
A very presentable establishment with solid wood tables and a diverse international menu. Salads, steaks, chicken Kiev, risotto, seafood platter, lasagne and sandwiches are among the offerings. One of the better places in town, popular with the tourist crowd.

$$$ Kappa Sushi
Diagonally across from the Parque Central,
25 m north of the Banco Nacional.
This low-key and intimate little restaurant serves winning sushi – try the rolls. Modern decor, pleasant atmosphere and owners. Recommended.

$$$ Nene's
Calle 5, an alleyway east of Parque Central,
T2479-9192.
The best *comida típica* in town, including grilled meats, brocheta, chicken, pork ribs and prawns. Informal, but not downscale. Popular with local families and tourists. Try the ceviche.

$$$-$$ Café Mediterráneo
400 m south of the roundabout, T2479-7497.
Another strong contender for the best pizza joint in town, Café Mediterráneo serves as a coffee house in the daytime. In addition to delicious thin-crust Italian-style pizza, they serve tasty wraps, salads, panini, hot and cold coffee and cake.

$$$-$$ Lava Lounge
25 m west of the Catholic church,
www.lavaloungecostarica.com.

Funky bar and grill serving hearty international fare, including salads, wraps, pizza and pasta. House specialities include coconut chicken and grilled pork with 'tropical chutney'. Popular hangout with backpackers and other wandering souls.

$$ Gecko Gourmet
Across the street from Lava Lounge, www.geckogourmet.com.
La Fortuna's only deli-style eatery serves a variety of salads, wraps and sandwiches. Tempting fillings include Caprese chicken, meatloaf and barbecue pork. Also bagels, breakfasts, smoothies, ice coffee and sweet snacks.

$ Soda Hormiga
Next to the bus station.
Bustling and casual *soda* serving the best-value *casados* in town. Come with an appetite, the servings are on the large side.

Cafés

Chocolate Fusion Chocolatería
West of the Parque Central on the main road, next to Anch'io Restaurant.
The aroma of roasted cacao here is irresistible. As well as good coffee, they sell delicious artisan chocolates and ice cream. Tasty and extravagant.

Rainforest Café
125 m south of the Parque Central.
Travellers come here for the breakfasts, *casados*, coffees, smoothies, cakes and Wi-Fi. Casual Tico place.

Around Lago Arenal

$$$ Caballo Negro
A couple of kilometres west of (Nuevo) Arenal, T2694-4515, www.luckybugcr.net.
Overlooking a lush tropical garden, the best restaurant for miles, serving vegetarian, Swiss and German favourites, include *jaeger schnitzel*, *brawurst* and home-made *spaetzle*. Warm family atmosphere.

$$$ Gingerbread Restaurant
Nuevo Arenal, T2694-0039, www. gingerbreadarenal.com. Tue-Sun, 1700-2100, reservations essential.
Attached to the boutique **Gingerbread Hotel**, the most popular restaurant in the area, recommended by many. They serve eclectic international fusion cuisine by chef Eyal Ben-Menachem, including a changing daily menu and lots of fresh seafood. Recommended.

$$$-$$ Moya's place
Nuevo Arenal.
A funky and laid-back pizzeria with colourful murals. They also serve good wraps and salads. Good ambiance. Recommended.

$$$ $$ Tinajas Arenal
Rancho Las Tinajas, Highway 142.
Tasty and reasonably priced international fare, including vegan, fish and meat dishes. A verdant setting on an organic farm with fine views of the lake. Tricky to reach without your own transport; follow the signs on the highway. Great place. Recommended.

Tilarán

$$ Restaurant La Carreta
At the back of the church, T2695-6593.
The place to go and relax if you have time to kill. Excellent breakfast and lunch only, North American food, pancakes, coffee and good local information.

$ Stefanie's
Out of the bus station to the left on the corner of the main plaza.
Good and quick if you need a meal between buses.

What to do

La Fortuna
Boat tours
Available from several tour operators, safari river floats down the Río Peñas Blancas cost US$55 and offer the chance of glimpsing crocodiles, monkeys, sloths and birds

(kayaking is also an option). Day trips to Caño Negro reserve along the Río Frío involve travelling to Los Chiles and taking the boat from there, US$65. Prices include transport, guide and snacks as a minimum.

Canoeing, kayaking and whitewater rafting

The lake, Río Aguacate and Río Peñas Blancas are popular destinations for canoeing and kayaking. Whitewater rafting, best in the wet season, is available on several rivers, including:

Arenal Kayaks, *Nuevo Arenal, T2694-4336, www.arenalkayaks.com*. A range of 2- to 4-hr kayak tours, including a trip to a small island in the lake where you can see ancient artefacts. They can also manufacture kayaks by hand, if you're in the market.

Canoa Aventura, *Highway 142, 500 m west of downtown, T2479-8200, www. canoa-aventura.com*. Safari floats on kayak and canoe, whitewater rafting and hikes. Owned by a Costa Rican family with 25 years' experience in the industry.

Wave Expeditions, *behind the Catholic church, T2479-7262, www.waveexpeditions. com*. Wide range of whitewater trips, Class II-V, as well as local tours and longer tailored trips around the Meseta Central, Northern zone, Guanacaste and the Pacific.

Canopy tours

From high-speed zip-lines to high-altitude suspension bridges, there are many options for exploring the jungle canopy – more than can be listed here.

Arenal Hanging bridges, *access road off Highway 142, near Arenal dam, T2290-0469, www.hangingbridges.com*. No zip-line, but a complex network of trails and bridges snaking through 250 ha of tropical forest. Entrance US$24, children free; natural history/birdwatching packages, plus transport at extra cost.

Arenal Mundo Aventura, *2 km south of the Catholic church over the Río Fortuna, T2479-9762, www.arenalmundoaventura.com*.

The only zip-line to pass in front of the Río Fortuna waterfall. 10 cables, 200-800 m. Horse riding option. US$70, children US$50, transport included.

Ecoglide, *turn-off on Highway 142, 6 km west of La Fortuna, T2479-7120, www.arenal ecoglide.com*. Ecoglide's unique selling point is its Tarzan swing. 13 cables, 15 platforms, 10-430 m. US$55, transport included.

Sky Adventures Arenal, *access road off southeastern side of the lake, 2 km east of El Castillo, T2479-4100, www.skyadventures. travel*. Sky Adventures features a sky tram aerial tram ride and a suspension bridge tour (extra cost), as well as a complimentary butterfly and orchid garden. Their zip-line runs 10 cables, 200-750 m. US$77. Transport available at extra cost.

Horse riding

Horse riding to Río Fortuna waterfall is popular, US$55 per person. Riding through the forest to Monteverde costs around US$85 per person for the day trip; luggage is taken on pack animals or by vehicles. Some operators seem to change the route once underway due to some 'unforeseen problem', so agree the route and try to arrange compensation if there are major changes. Due to competition for business, many horses are overworked. Try not to bargain down the price and do ask to see the horses before beginning the journey.

Tour operators

Scores of tour operators are based in La Fortuna and they offer a broad range of local trips, including: hiking Arenal volcano, US$50; hiking and hot springs, from US$85; birdwatching, US$65; night tours, US$65; canyoning, US$95. Trips are flexible and can be combined with canopy tours.

Aventuras Arenal, *main street, T2479-9133, www.aventurasarenal.com*. Provides all tours in the area and has been around for many years. Can help with enquiries about other parts of Costa Rica.

Desafío, *behind the Catholic church, T2479-9464, www.desafiocostarica.com.* Reputable travel agency with an office also in Monteverde offering a full range of tours.

Tilarán
Kitesurfing and windsurfing
Tico Wind, *Highway 142, west side of Lake Arenal, T2692-2002, www.ticowind.com.* The country's foremost kitesurfing and windsurfing operation. Classes and equipment rental.

Transport

Volcán Arenal and around
Volcán Arenal is most easily reached on a paved road running west from Ciudad Quesada (San Carlos). Getting there from Santa Elena/Monteverde by bus demands an 8-hr haul on rough roads via Tilarán, where you must change. The so-called 'jeep-boat-jeep' service takes a short cut across Arenal Lake and cuts the journey time in half. Public transport arrives in La Fortuna, the region's main service town (see below).

La Fortuna
Bus To **Ciudad Quesada**, 14 daily, 1½ hrs, US$1.50. To **San José**, 2 daily, 1245, 1445, 4 hrs, US$4.50 (or go to Ciudad Quesada and change). To **Tilarán** there are 2 buses daily at 0800 (connecting to 1230 bus Tilarán–Santa Elena/Monteverde and 1300 bus Tilarán–Puntarenas) and 1630, US$2.90, 4 hrs.

Jeep-boat-jeep The service to **Santa Elena/Monteverde** can be booked with any tour operator (reserve 48 hrs in advance), 4 hrs, US$25-30; they should pick you up and drop you off at your chosen lodgings.

Tilarán
Bus To **Cañas**, 10 daily, 40 mins, US$1.50, from where buses head north and south of the Pan-American highway; to **La Fortuna**, 2 daily, 0700, 1230, 3 hrs, US$2.90; to **Puntarenas**, 2 daily, 0600, 1300, 3 hrs, US$3, or go to Cañas and change; to **Santa Elena/Monteverde**, 2 daily, 0700, 1600, 2½ hrs, US$2. For more information on getting to Monteverde, see page 83.

Monteverde and Santa Elena
plants, insects, birds and mammals in grand profusion

Monteverde Cloud Forest Reserve is one of the most precious natural jewels in Costa Rica's crown. Protected by law, this private preserve is also protected by appalling access roads on all sides (the nearest decent road is at least two hours from the town). Santa Elena and Monteverde, although separate, are often referred to as the same place; most sites of interest are between the town of Santa Elena at the bottom of the hillside and Monteverde Cloud Forest Reserve at the top.

Travelling between La Fortuna and Santa Elena, you can travel overland by horse, jeep, boat or combinations of the three. It's adventurous, challenging and enjoyable depending on the weather conditions at the time. Travel agents in either location can advise and organize. See also Transport, below.

Santa Elena and around
Santa Elena is a rugged and busy place, often packed with visitors exploring options or just passing time. It is cheaper to stay in town rather than along the single, unpaved road that twists and turns for 5 km through the village of Monteverde, with hotels and places of interest situated along the road almost to the reserve itself. **Santa Elena Reserve**, **Sky Trek** and **Sky Walk** are to the north of Santa Elena, all other places of interest are east, heading up the hill.

Very close to Santa Elena, at the start of the climb to Monteverde, is the **Herpetarium Adventures** ⓘ *T2645-6002, daily 0900-2000, US$13, children US$8*, with specimens of snakes and amphibians found in the nearby cloudforest. Other natural history places of interest include the **Frog Pond** ⓘ *T2645-6320, daily 0900-2030, US$12*, with 25 species of

Monteverde & Santa Elena

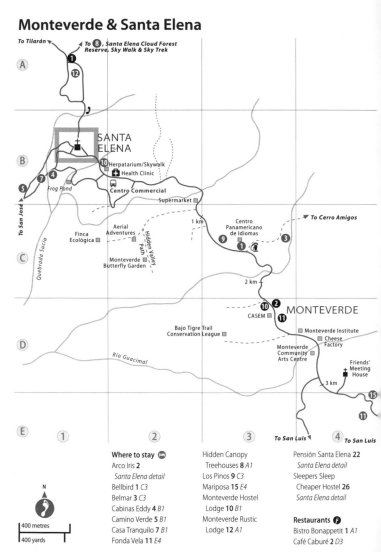

Where to stay ⌂
Arco Iris **2**
  Santa Elena detail
Bellbird **1** *C3*
Belmar **3** *C3*
Cabinas Eddy **4** *B1*
Camino Verde **5** *B1*
Casa Tranquilo **7** *B1*
Fonda Vela **11** *E4*

Hidden Canopy
Treehouses **8** *A1*
Los Pinos **9** *C3*
Mariposa **15** *E4*
Monteverde Hostel
Lodge **10** *B1*
Monteverde Rustic
Lodge **12** *A1*

Pensión Santa Elena **22**
  Santa Elena detail
Sleepers Sleep
Cheaper Hostel **26**
  Santa Elena detail

Restaurants ⓝ
Bistro Bonappetit **1** *A1*
Café Caburé **2** *D3*

frog, and the **Bat Jungle** ⓘ *daily 0900-2000, T2645-5052, www.batjungle.com, US$11*, where you can learn about the nocturnal habits of over 40 bats.

A dirt road opposite the **Hotel Heliconia** leads to the **Monteverde Butterfly Garden** ⓘ *T2645-5512, www.monteverdebutterflygarden.com, daily 0930-1600 (best time for a visit 1100-1300), US$15, US$10 students, including guided tour*, a beautifully presented large garden planted for breeding and researching butterflies. Near the Butterfly Garden is **Finca Ecológica** ⓘ *T2645-5869, www.santuarioecologico.com, daily 0700-1730, US$10, night tours US$15, free map, guides available*, with three trails totalling around 5 km with bird lists for birdwatching and varied wildlife in this transitional zone between cloud and tropical dry forest. Recommended for night tours as one of the few companies that does not lure the wildlife with food.

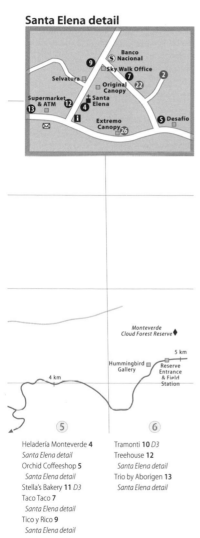

Santa Elena detail

Banco Nacional (S)
9
Sky Walk Office
Selvatura
7
2
Original Canopy
22
Supermarket & ATM
12
Santa Elena
13
i
Extremo Canopy
5 Desafío
26

Heladería Monteverde **4**
Santa Elena detail
Orchid Coffeeshop **5**
Santa Elena detail
Stella's Bakery **11** *D3*
Taco Taco **7**
Santa Elena detail
Tico y Rico **9**
Santa Elena detail

Tramonti **10** *D3*
Treehouse **12**
Santa Elena detail
Trio by Aborigen **13**
Santa Elena detail

Monteverde Cloud Forest Reserve ◆

Hummingbird Gallery
4 km
5 km
Reserve Entrance & Field Station

Santa Elena Cloud Forest Reserve

Offices are 200 m north of the Banco Nacional, T2645-5390, www.reservasantaelena.org, 0700-1600, entrance US$14, students US$7. It is a long, steep hike from the village; alternatively hire a taxi, US$6.50.

One kilometre along the road north from Santa Elena to Tilarán, a 5-km track is signposted to the reserve, managed by the **Centro Ecológico Bosque Nuboso de Monteverde**. It is 83% primary cloudforest and the rest is secondary forest at 1700 m, bordered by the Monteverde Cloud Forest Reserve and the Arenal Forest Reserve. There is a 12-km path network and several lookouts where, on a clear day, you can see Volcán Arenal. There are generally fewer visitors here than at Monteverde. The **Centro Ecológico Bosque Nuboso** is administered by the local community and profits go to five local schools. It was set up by the Costa Rican government in 1989 with collaboration from Canada. The rangers are very friendly and enthusiastic. There is a small information centre where rubber boots can be hired and a small café open at weekends. Hand-painted T-shirts are for sale.

★ Monteverde and around

Strung out along the road to the cloudforest, the settlement at Monteverde – between Santa Elena and the reserve – was founded by American Quakers in the 1950s. Without a centre as such, it started life as a group of dairy farms providing milk for a cooperative cheese factory. The **cheese factory** (shop closes at 1600), now privately owned, still operates selling excellent cheeses of various types, fresh milk, ice cream, milkshakes to die for and *cajeta* (a butterscotch spread).

Today, Monteverde maintains an air of pastoral charm, but tourism provides more revenue for the town than dairy produce ever could. It was the vision of the dairy farmers that led to the creation of the reserve to protect the community watershed. When George Powell and his wife spent time in the region studying birds they realized the importance of protecting the area. Working with local residents they created the reserve in 1972 – foresight that has spawned the creation of many other natural attractions locally and throughout the country.

The best way of getting the full low-down on the place is at the **Museum of Monteverde History** ① *daily 0930-1930, US$5*. This spacious museum records the history of Monteverde, from the creation of the Central American isthmus three million years ago to its settlement by indigenous people and then the arrival of the Ticos, followed by the Quaker settlers, and then biologists, conservationists and ecotourism.

Reserva Sendero Tranquilo ① *daily, T2645-5010, entry restricted to 12 people at any one time,* is a private 200-ha reserve near the Monteverde cheese factory. Reservations and guides should be arranged through **El Sapo Dorado** hotel, which also offers night tours for US$25 per person.

Just before the entrance to Monteverde Cloud Forest is the **Hummingbird Gallery** ① *T2645-5030, daily 0700-1700*, where masses of different hummingbirds can be seen darting around a glade, visiting feeding dispensers filled with sugared water. Outside the entrance is a small shop/photo gallery that sells pictures and gifts, as well as **Bromeliads Nature Bookstore and Café**. There is also a slide show at **Hotel Belmar**, *The Hidden Rainforest*, by Bobby Maxson (1930 daily except Friday).

Adjoining the Monteverde Cloud Forest is **El Bosque Eterno de los Niños (Children's Eternal Rainforest)** ① *T2645-5003, www.acmcr.org*, established in 1988 after an initiative by Swedish schoolchildren to save forests. Currently at 22,000 ha, the land has been bought and is maintained by the **Monteverde Conservation League** with children's donations from around the world. The **Bajo Tigre** trail takes 1½ hours, parking available with notice, a guide can be arranged, but no horses are allowed on the trail. Groups can arrange trips to the **San Gerardo** and **Poco Sol Field stations** ① *0800-1600, entrance US$6, students US$2, contact the Monteverde Conservation League for reservations at San Gerardo or Poco Sol, T2645-5003, www.acmcr.org, US$50 a night.*

★ Monteverde Cloud Forest Reserve

Straddling the continental divide, the 10,500-ha Monteverde Cloud Forest Reserve is privately owned and administered by the **Tropical Science Centre** – a non-profit research and educational association. The reserve is mainly primary cloudforest and spends much of the year shrouded in mist, creating stunted trees and abundant epiphytic growth. The best months to visit are January to May, especially February, March and April. The reserve contains more than 400 species of bird, including the resplendent quetzal, best seen in the dry months between January and May, especially near the start of the Nuboso

Essential Monteverde Cloud Forest Reserve

Park information

www.reservamonteverde.com. Office open daily 0700-1630; the park opens at 0700 and closes at 1700. Entrance fee US$18 (students with ID US$9) valid for multiple entry during the day, cannot be purchased in advance. The reserve entrance is at the field station at the top of the road. Bus from Santa Elena heads up the hill leaving at 0600 and 1100 returning at 1400 and 1700. The total number of visitors to the reserve at any one time is 150, so be there before 0700 to make sure of getting in during high season (hotels will book you a place for the following day). Tour buses come in from San José daily. A small shop at the office sells various checklists, postcards and APS film, gifts and excellent T-shirts, the proceeds of which help towards the conservation project.

Guides

Natural history walks with biologist guides leave every morning and afternoon, three to four hours, US$32; birdwatching tours, US$64; advance reservations at the office or through your hotel are strongly recommended. If you use a private (non-reserve) guide you must pay his entrance fee too. An experienced and recommended guide who also does night tours is **Gary Diller** (T2645-9916). There are 25 others operating, of varying specialization and experience. Excellent night tours in the reserve are available normally with **Ricardo Guindon** or call **Monteverde Reserve** (T2645-5112, US$17), at 1900 sharp. Day or night, a guide is recommended if you want to see wildlife, since the untrained eye misses a lot.

Donations and volunteer work

Donations are welcomed for purchasing additional land and maintaining and improving existing reserve areas. If you are interested in volunteer work, from non-skilled trail maintenance to skilled scientific assistance work, surveying, teaching or studying on a tropical biology programme, contact the reserve (US$14 per person, board and lodging, two weeks minimum). The Conservation League works with schools in the area on education regarding conservation. Donations can be made at the **Monteverde Cloud Forest Reserve office** (see above), **Tropical Science Centre** (San José, T2253-3267, www.cct.or.cr), or **Monteverde Conservation League** (Apdo Postal 124-5655, San José, Costa Rica, T2645-5003, www.acmcr.org).

trail; the three-wattled bellbird with its distinctive 'bonk' call; and the bare-necked umbrella bird. There are more than 100 species of mammal, including monkeys, Baird's tapir, six endangered cats (jaguar, jaguarundi, margay, ocelot, tigrillo and puma), reptiles and amphibians. But be warned, travellers frequently report there is little chance of seeing much wildlife. The reserve also includes an estimated 2500 species of plant and more than 6000 species of insect. The entrance is at 1500 m, but the maximum altitude in the reserve is over 1800 m. Mean temperature is between 16° and 18°C and average annual rainfall is 3000 mm. The weather changes quickly and wind and humidity often make the air feel cooler.

The commonly used trails are in good condition and there are easy, short and interesting walks for those who do not want to hike all day. Trail walks take from two hours but you could easily spend all day just wandering around. Trails may be restricted from time to time if they need protection. There is a trail northwards to the Arenal volcano that is increasingly used, but it is not easy. There are three refuges for people wishing to spend the night within the reserve boundaries, see Where to stay, below. Free maps of the reserve are available at the entrance. Follow the rules, stay on the paths, leave nothing behind, take no fauna or flora out; no radios/CD players/iPods, etc are allowed.

Listings Monteverde and Santa Elena *map p76*

Where to stay

Santa Elena

$$$ Arco Iris
Southeast of Banco Nacional, T2645-5067, www.arcoirislodge.com.
Stone- and wood-built cabins set among preserved forest fragments and landscaped gardens filled with ornamental and fruit trees. Verdant and tranquil. One of the best in Santa Elena.

$$$ Monteverde Rustic Lodge
1 km north of the church, T2645 6256, www.monteverderusticlodge.com.
A low-key Monteverde mountain lodge with a leafy garden, rustic wood finishes and spacious rooms equipped with Wi-Fi. Managed by the Badilla brothers. Breakfast included.

$$ Camino Verde
300 m southwest of SuperCompro supermarket, T2645-5641, www.hotelcaminoverde.com.
A friendly family-style B&B with a 'mi casa es tu casa' philosophy. Amenities include free tea and coffee all day, shared kitchen, maps, parking. Most rooms have TV and Wi-Fi. Helpful and hospitable.

$$-$ Cabinas Eddy
150 m south of SuperCompro supermarket, T2645-6635, www.cabinas-eddy.com.
This place has a great balcony for sipping morning coffee and enjoying the birdsong and sunshine. The owner, Eddy, is very helpful and friendly. He offers 14 rooms, some with kitchenette, cheaper without private bath. Breakfast included.

$$-$ Monteverde Hostel Lodge
100 m west of the Centro Comercial, T2645-5989, www.monteverdehostel lodge.com.

The only hostel in town that's perched right on the edge of the cloudforest. They have dorms (**$**), private rooms (**$$**), bungalows (**$$**), parking, internet, kitchen. Architecture is classic wood walls and floors.

$$-$ Pensión Santa Elena
250 m southeast of Banco Nacional, T2645-5051, www.pensionsantaelena.com.
Good range of rooms of varying standards and quality – all good value for the money. Very popular with backpackers, clean, good food, kitchen available.

$ Casa Tranquilo
200 m south of SuperCompro supermarket, next to Cabinas Eddy, T2645-6782, www.casatranquilohostel.wix.com/ tranquilobackpackers.
A funky, rustic little hostel, Tico-owned, just out of town and away from the hoi poloi. They have private rooms with or without private bath and an 8-bed mixed dorm. Relaxed, sociable and friendly, with breakfast included. Good reports.

$ Sleepers Sleep Cheaper Hostel
Main St, 150 m from the public bus stop, T2645-6204, www.sleeperssleepcheaperhostels.com.
Cheap budget accommodation with both private and dorm rooms. Top floor is best for the balcony and views. Kitchen and internet access too. Breakfast included, helpful, good value.

Monteverde

$$$$ Fonda Vela
T2645-5125, www.fondavela.com.
40 beautiful rooms and suites spread around 5 buildings. A 25-min walk, 5-min drive to the reserve, on a 14-ha farm with forest and trail system, good birding, 2 excellent

restaurants (open to public), bar, TV room, art gallery and conference room.

$$$$ Hidden Canopy Treehouses Boutique Hotel
300 m east of Camino Sky Trek crossroads, T2645-5447, www.hiddencanopy.com.
You'll enjoy impeccable views of the cloudforest canopy from these sumptuous treehouse chalets constructed with fine hardwoods and other natural materials. Blissful and romantic. Recommended.

$$$ Belmar
300 m behind service station, T2645-5201, www.hotelbelmar.net.
Established in Monteverde more than 30 years ago, Hotel Belmar has a proven commitment to the environment and sustainability. Lodging is in a fantastic Swiss-style chalet with astounding views of the canopy reaching out as far as Nicoya.

$$$-$$ Los Pinos
200 m east of Cerro Plano school, T2645-5252, www.lospinos.net.
Comfortable wood cabins (accommodates 2-6) with fully equipped own kitchen, Wi-Fi, hot water, cable TV; ask for one with a fireplace. Set on a private reserve with a mirador, hiking trails and hydroponic vegetable garden. Sustainable ethos. Recommended.

$$ Mariposa bed and breakfast
1 km past Monteverde cheese factory, T2645-5013, www.mariposabb.com.
Has 3 rooms in a single block sleeping up to 3 people, with private bath. A family atmosphere with breakfast included in the price. Cosy and down to earth.

$ Hotel Bellbird
Just before the gas station, T2645-5518, www.hotelbellbird.com.
Low-key and economical, Hotel Bellbird offers private rooms with wood-panelled walls, hot water and Wi-Fi. Built by Monteverde pioneers in 1958. Breakfast included.

Monteverde Cloud Forest Reserve
Shelter facilities throughout the reserve cost US$3.50-5 a night, reserve entry fee for each night spent in the park, plus key deposit of US$5. Bring sleeping bag and torch. You can make your own meals. Dormitory-style accommodation for up to 30 people at entrance, **Albergue Reserva Biológica de Monteverde** (T2645-5122, US$40 full board only, includes park entrance fee). Reservations only for all reserve accommodation (usually booked up by groups).

Restaurants

Santa Elena

$$$ Trio by Aborigen
25 m south of the SuperCompro supermarket, T2645-7254, www.aborigencr.com.
Creative offerings from a Costa Rican chef trained in the Basque Culinary Center in Spain. Try the pork spare ribs with guava, grits and barbecue sauce, and for dessert, the chocolate brownie with mint glaze.

$$$-$$ Bistro Bonapetit
Carretera a Tilarán, 10 mins' walk out of town, take a taxi at night.
A Tico-Italian restaurant serving good wood-fired pizzas and wholesome *casados*. Pleasant setting in an octagonal building; friendly and efficient service.

$$$-$$ El Marquez
On the northern edge of town, near the exit for the Carretera a Tilarán.
This modest eatery sells superb ceviche, shrimp, fish fillets and more – don't leave without trying the *mojitos*. Local, affordable and unpretentious.

$$$-$$ The Treehouse
Opposite the Catholic church, www.treehouse.cr.
The unique selling point of The Treehouse is the large ficus tree growing right through the dining area and the overall effect of sitting among the branches is somehow relaxing. They serve good international cuisine.

$$ Tico y Rico
50 m north of the Catholic church, opposite side of the road.
Reliable *comida típica*, including lunch time *casados*. Friendly service and unpretentious ambiance.

$$-$ Taco Taco
50 m southeast of the Banco Nacional, next to Pensión Santa Elena.
Popular hole in the wall selling a wide variety of tasty burritos and tacos, including slow-roasted beef, vegetarian and pork *al pastor*.

Coffee shops and ice cream parlours

Heladería Monteverde
Next to the Catholic church.
Owned by the cheese factory on the way to Monteverde, great locally produced ice cream.

Orchid coffeeshop
200 m west of the Centro Comercial.
Lovely little café selling excellent coffee, tasty sandwiches and pretty good *huevos rancheros* for breakfast. The best smoothies in town. Recommended.

Monteverde

$$$ Tramonti
3 km from Monteverde reserve before CASEM, T2645-6120, www.tramonticr.com.
Traditional Italian and completely authentic, including penne, fettuccini, spaghetti and other pastas, good wines and quite probably the best pizzas in the region. Beautiful setting on the edge of the forest.

$$$-$$ Café Caburé
Altos de Paseo, 150 m west of CASEM, T2645-5020, www.cabure.net.
An Argentine restaurant, coffee shop and chocolatier with a breezy veranda on top of a hill. They serve eclectic cuisine from Chinese soups to Mexican *moles*. Don't leave without trying the artisan chocolates.

$ Stella's Bakery
Opposite CASEM, T2645-5560.
Excellent wholemeal bread, cakes and good granola – there's a café if you want to eat in.

Festivals

Monteverde
Dec-Mar Monteverde Music Festival, T2645-5053. Classical and jazz concerts at sunset, local, national and international musicians. Programme available from local hotels.

Shopping

CASEM, *located just outside Monteverde on the road to the reserve next to El Bosque restaurant, T2645-5190.* A cooperative gift shop selling embroidered shirts, T-shirts, wooden and woven articles and baskets. Next door, there's a shop selling Costa Rican coffee.

What to do

Canopy tours
Monteverde is the canopy tour capital of Costa Rica. Thanks to the stiff competition for tourist dollars, every operator has at least 1 unique selling point. All cost US$45, except **Zip-line Monteverde**, US$35; 3-4 tours daily. Most companies have offices in Santa Elena (see map), advance booking essential.
100% Aventura, *3 km north of Santa Elena, T2645-6388, www.aventuracanopytour.com.* Home to the longest single zip-line in Latin America, 1590 m. Other attractions include a rope bridge, 2 'Superman'-style cables, a Tarzan swing (45 m), ATV tour, horse riding.
Extremo, *office in Calle Central, T2645-6058, www.monteverdeextremo.com.* Extremo is the longest canopy tour in Monteverde, covering a total of 4 km. It is a high-speed, high-altitude tour crossing farmland but no forest, 14 cables, 500-1000 m long. Options include the soaring 'Superman' harness, the biggest Tarzan swing in Costa Rica (60 m), a bungee jump of 143 m and horse riding. Recommended for all your adrenalin needs.

Selvatura, *office in Calle Central, T2645-5929, www.selvatura.com*. The only canopy tour in primary cloudforest, with 15 cables, 1 'Superman' cable and a Tarzan swing. A great option to see nature up close with 8 suspension bridges, the 3rd largest private insect collection in the world (fascinating, recommended), a dome butterfly garden with 50 live species, the biggest hummingbird garden in Monteverde and a reptile and amphibian exhibition, with 25 species from around Costa Rica. Transport included. Recommended.

Sky Adventure, *office in Calle Central, T2479-4100, www.skyadventures.travel*. The sister theme park to **Sky Adventure Arenal**, Sky Adventure Monteverde has 3 components. **Sky Trek** is the zip-line, with all cables and platforms interconnected, so there's no walking; the longest cable is 850 m. **Sky Tram** is a cable car ride over the cloudforest canopy and a part of the zip-line package. **Sky Walk** consists of suspension bridges and can be done independently of the zip-line or tram. They also manage the herpetarium downtown near the bus station.

The Original Canopy Tour, *office next to the Catholic church, T2645-5243, www.theoriginalcanopy.com*. As the name suggests, the first ones to set up in Monteverde, offering an exhilarating 40-m rappel down a strangulated fig tree and into the cloudforest. They have 15 cables, 60-800 m long, Tarzan swing, horseback and hot springs tours. Small groups, uncrowded and exclusive.

Zip-line Monteverde, *5 mins south of Santa Elena, T2645-6320, www.monteverdethemepark.com*. The cheapest option in town with 15 platforms, 9 cables, 2 rappels and a Tarzan swing. Short lines, undemanding and suitable for children and families.

Transport

Bus To get from Santa Elena to the Monteverde reserve, **Transmonteverde** operates 4 buses daily, 0615, 0730, 1320, 1500, US$1.50; returning 0645, 1130, 1400, 1600. Long-distance to **Puntarenas** via the Km 149 route, 3 daily, 0420, 0600, 1500, 3 hrs, US$2.50; to **San José**, 2 daily, 0630, 1430, 5 hrs, US$5.10, or take the Puntarenas bus and change on the Pan-American Highway; to **Tilarán**, 2 daily, 0400, 1230, 2½ hrs, you must catch the early bus to connect with the bus to La Fortuna. **Note**: if taking the regular bus to **San José**, keep your bag with you at all times; several cases of theft have been reported.

Car From the Pan-American Highway northwest to Km 149, turn right (just before the Río Lagarto). Continue for about 40 km on mostly gravel road (allow 2½ hrs) to Santa Elena. Parts of the road are quite good, but in wet weather 4WD is recommended for the rough parts. If driving, check that your car rental agreement allows you to visit Monteverde. A 33-km shorter route is to take the Pipasa/Sardinal turn-off from the Pan-American Highway shortly after the Río Aranjuez. At the park in Sardinal, turn left, then go via Guacimal to the Monteverde road.

There is a service station, Mon-Sat 0700-1800, Sun 0700-1200.

Horse Several places rent horses; look for signs between Santa Elena and Monteverde or ask at your hotel. Try not to hire horses that look overworked.

Jeep-boat-jeep The service to **La Fortuna** is faster, more convenient and comfortable than the bus, worth the extra dollars, 4 hrs, US$25; book with local tour operators (48 hrs' advance reservation).

Taxi Santa Elena to Monteverde, US$6, and Monteverde to the reserve, US$5.75 (hunt around for good prices). Not so easy to find a taxi for return trip, best to arrange in advance.

rolling plains of the northern ranches, home to the sabanero *cowboy*

North of Barranca, the Pan-American Highway heads towards the province of Guanacaste, the cultural heartland of Costa Rica. The province also includes the Peninsula of Nicoya and the lowlands at the head of the gulf. Rainfall is moderate; 1000-2000 mm per year. The long dry season makes irrigation important, but the lowlands are deep in mud during the rainy season.

Guanacaste, with its capital Liberia, has a distinctive people, way of life, flora and fauna. The smallholdings of the highlands give way here to large haciendas and great cattle estates. The rivers teem with fish and there are all kinds of wildlife in the uplands.

The people are open, hospitable and fun-loving, and are famed for their music and dancing; in fact, the *punto guanacasteco* has been officially declared the national dance. There are many fiestas in January and February in the local towns and villages, which are well worth seeing.

Heading northwest on the Pan-American Highway, turn right just after the Río Aranjuez at Rancho Grande (or just south of the Río Lagarto at Km 149) to access a dramatic and at times scenic route to Santa Elena-Monteverde.

Guanacaste Conservation Area

Some 43 km north of Barranca is the turn-off for **Las Juntas**, an alternative route to Monteverde for those using the Tempisque ferry or arriving from Guanacaste; a third of it is paved. After Las Juntas, there is a **mining ecomuseum** ⓘ *daily 0600-1800, US$1.80*, at **La Sierra de Abangares** with mining artefacts from a turn-of-the-20th-century gold mine.

Four kilometres north is a bridge crossing the Tempisque River. After about 6 km, a road to the right at San Joaquín leads to the **Hacienda Solimar Lodge** (see Where to stay, below), a 1300-ha cattle farm with dry tropical virgin forest bordering Parque Nacional Palo Verde (see below) near Porozal in the lower Tempisque River basin. The freshwater Madrigal estuary on the property is one of the most important areas for water birds in Costa Rica (only guests staying at the Hacienda can visit). Also surrounded by gallery forest, it is recommended for serious birdwatchers. Reservations are essential, contact **Birdwatch** ⓘ *T2228-4768, www.birdwatchcostarica.com*.

Some 67 km north of Barranca, Cañas has little to keep the visitor for long. There are a number of interesting sights nearby and, for the those arriving from the north, this is the cut-through to Tilarán and connecting buses to Arenal or La Fortuna. **Las Pumas** ⓘ *behind Safaris Corobicí, Cañas, free but donations welcome and encouraged*, is a small, private, Swiss-run animal rescue centre which specializes in looking after big cats, including jaguar. It's an unmissable if rather sad experience.

NICARAGUA

Santa Cecilia

Brasilia

Birmania

Pitilla Station

Volcán Cacao (1659m)
Cacao Station

Rincón Cacao Biological Corridor

Rincón Rainforest Reserve

Von Seebock (895m)

Volcán Rincón de la Vieja (1806m)

Parque Nacional Rincón de la Vieja

❷

Volcán Santa María (1916m)

Santa María

Colonia Blanca

Las Pailas ❶

Buenavista

Curubandé

❸ San Jorge

Liberia

◀ *To San José*

Parque Nacional Palo Verde

Administration offices, in Bagaces next to the service station, T2661-4717; park entrance US$15. There are 2 ranger stations, Palo Verde and Catalina. Check roads in wet season.

At the south of the neck of the Nicoya Peninsula is Parque Nacional Palo Verde, currently over 18,650 ha of marshes with many waterbirds. Indeed, more than 50,000 birds are considered resident in the *laguna*. The views from the limestone cliffs are fantastic. **Palo Verde Biological Station** ⓘ *T2661-4717, reservations on T2524-0607, www.ots.ac.cr*, is a research station run by the **Organization for Tropical Studies**. It organizes natural history walks and basic accommodation; US$89 with three meals and one guided walk per stay, cheaper for researchers; make advance reservations. Turn off the Pan-American Highway at **Bagaces**, halfway between Cañas and Liberia. There is no public transport.

Where to stay

$$ Hacienda Solimar Lodge
solimar@racsa.co.cr.
8 rooms with private or shared bathroom, includes meals, minimum 2 nights, transport on request, local guide, horse riding. Recommended for serious birdwatchers, contact **Birdwatch** (T2228-4768, www. birdwatchcostarica.com), see above. Reservations essential.

Restaurants

$$$ Rincón Corobicí
Next to La Pacífica, Cañas, T2669-6191.
Clean and pleasant, with a small zoo and offers rafting down Río Corobicí.

Transport

Bus The Cañas bus station is 500 m north of the centre, where all buses depart from except for those to San José, which leave from the terminal 300 m west of Parque Central on the Pan-American Highway.
To **San José**, 5 daily from 0400, 3½ hrs, US$5.40. To **Liberia**, hourly, 2 hrs, US$2.50. To **Puntarenas**, 8 daily from 0600. To **Upala**, for Bijagua and Volcán Tenorio, 7 daily from 0500, 1¾ hrs, US$1.50. To **Tilarán**, 7 daily from 0600. Buses to Tilarán for **Nuevo Arenal**, past the volcano and on to **La Fortuna**, or for connections to **Santa Elena** and **Monteverde**. If going by road, the turn-off for Tilarán is at the filling station, no signs.

Liberia and around

neat, clean cattle town

Known as the 'White City', Liberia (population 40,000) has a triangular, rather unattractive modern church, and single-storey colonial houses meticulously laid out in the streets surrounding the central plaza. The town is at the junction of the Pan-American Highway and a well-paved branch road leads southwest to the Nicoya Peninsula.

Parque Nacional Rincón de la Vieja
Park entry US$15. Day trips are possible to all areas, US$15 for Rincón de la Vieja, US$40 for Santa Rosa and US$50 for Palo Verde. Minimum of 4 required, prices per person. Park is closed Mon for maintenance.
....

Most easily visited from Liberia, Parque Nacional Rincón de la Vieja (14,161 ha) was created to preserve the area around the Volcán Rincón de la Vieja, to the northeast of the town. There are two ways into the park: the southern route, which has less traffic, goes from Puente La Victoria on the western side of Liberia and leads, in about 25 km, to the Santa María sector, closest to the hot springs. In this part, you can hike 8 km to the boiling mud pots (**Las Pailas**) and come back in the same day; the sulphur springs are on a different trail and only one hour away. The northern route turns right off the Pan-American Highway 5 km northwest of Liberia, through **Curubandé** (no public transport on this route). Beyond Curubandé, you cross the private property of **Hacienda Lodge Guachipelin** (US$2 to cross), beyond which is **Rincón de la Vieja Lodge**.

The park includes dry tropical forest, mud pots, hot sulphur springs and several other geothermal curiosities. The volcanic massif reaches to 1916 m and can be seen from a wide area around Liberia when not shrouded in clouds. The area is cool at night and subject to strong, gusty winds and violent rains; in the day it can be very hot, although always windy. These fluctuations mark all of the continental divide, of which the ridge is a part. From time to time the volcano erupts, the last eruption being in November 1995, when it tossed rocks and lava down its slopes.

The park is home to over 350 recorded species of bird, including toucans, parrots, three-wattled bellbirds and great curassows, along with howler monkeys, armadillos and coatis, ticks and other biting insects. It also has the largest density of Costa Rica's national flower the *guaria morada* or purple orchid. Horses can be rented in the park from some of the lodges. If you want to climb the volcano you will need to camp near the top, or at the warden's station, in order to ascend early in the morning before the clouds come in. Trails through the park lead to most sights of interest, including beautiful waterfalls and swimming holes. There are several accommodation options in or near the park, and shorter trips can easily be arranged from Liberia.

Parque Nacional Santa Rosa

About halfway to the Nicaraguan border from Liberia is Parque Nacional Santa Rosa (38,673 ha). Together with the **Murciélago Annex**, the peninsula to the north of the developed park, it preserves some of the last dry tropical forests in Costa Rica, and shelters abundant and relatively easy-to-see wildlife. During the dry season, the animals depend on the water holes and are thus easy to find until the holes dry up completely. Conservation work in the

Liberia

To Enrique Baltodano Hospital

To Nicaragua

To ⑤, Nicoya Perisula & Airport

To San José

To Parque Nacional Rincón de la Vieja

Río Liberia

Av 11
Av 9
Av 7
Av 5
Av 3
Av 1
Av Central
Av 2
Av 4
Av 6
Av 8
Av 10

Central
La Inmaculada
Mayorga Rivas
Rafael Iglesias

Regional Buses
Buses to San José
Ciberm@nia
Plaza
Supermarket
Toyota Car Rental
Sol Car Rental
25 de Julio

N
200 metres
200 yards

Where to stay	Wilson 5	Los Comales 3
Del Aserradero 2		Pizza Pronto 6
Garden Inn 3	**Restaurants**	Tierra Mar 5
Hospedaje Dodero 4	Café Liberia 1	Toro Negro 7
La Posada del Tope 9	Copa de Oro 4	
Liberia 12	El Mesón Liberiano 2	

area is also trying to reforest some cattle ranches in the area – helped by the fact that cattle have not been profitable in recent years.

Close to the park headquarters and research buildings, the historically important **La Casona** was where, in 1856, the patriots repelled the invasion of the filibuster William Walker, who had entrenched himself in the main building. The old hacienda building, once the Museo Histórico de Santa Rosa, was rebuilt in 2002 having been almost completely destroyed by fire the previous year. There are several good trails and lookouts in the park, the easiest of which is close to La Casona. Lasting a couple of hours, it leads through dry tropical forest with many Indio Desnudo (naked Indian) trees, which periodically shed their red flaky bark.

Deeper in the park, **Playa Naranjo** (12 km, three hours' walk or more, or use 4WD, park authorities permitting) and **Playa Nancite** (about the same distance from the entrance) are major nesting sites of **leatherback** and **olive ridley sea turtles**. The main nesting season is between August and October (although stragglers are regularly seen up to January) when flotillas of up to 10,000 ridley turtles arrive at night on the 7-km-long Playa Nancite. Females clumsily lurch up the beach, scoop out a deep hole, deposit and bury an average of 100 ping-pong-ball-sized eggs before returning exhausted to the sea. Playa Nancite is a restricted-access beach; you need a written permit to stay plus US$2 per day to camp, or US$15 in dormitories. Permits from SPN in San José, and the **Park Administration building** ① *Santa Rosa, T2666-5051, make sure you have permission before going*. Research has been done in the Playa Nancite area on howler monkeys, coatis and the complex interrelation between the fauna and the forest. Playa Naranjo is one of the most attractive beaches in the country. It is unspoilt, quiet and very good for surfing. There is good camping, drinking water (although occasionally salty) and barbecue facilities.

La Cruz and Isla Bolaños

The last town before Peñas Blancas and the border, La Cruz has a bank (for cash, traveller's cheques or credit card transactions), a handful of hotels and absolutely incredible sunsets from the hilltop overlooking the Bahía de Salinas. Down in the bay is the Islas Bolaños Wildlife Refuge and some of the best conditions for windsurfing in Costa Rica.

Isla Bolaños is a 25-ha National Wildlife Refuge protecting the nesting sites of the brown pelican, frigate bird and American oystercatcher. The island is covered with dry forest and you can only walk round it at low tide. The incoming tidal surge is very dangerous; make sure you're off the island before the tide comes in. No camping is allowed.

Listings Liberia and around *map p87*

Where to stay

Liberia

$$$ Hotel Garden Inn
Ruta 21, opposite the airport, T2690-8888, www.hiltongardeninn3.hilton.com.
The Hilton's contribution to Liberia is a charmless monstrosity on the outside but predictably comfortable on the inside. Located close to the airport.

$$ Hotel del Aserradero
Pan-American Highway and Av 3, T2666-1939, www.hoteldelaserradero.com.
A highway option, this one set back a short distance so you don't endure the noise of traffic. They have 16 large rooms with cable TV, Wi-Fi and hot water. The garden at the back is good for relaxing. Simple, spartan and quiet.

$$ Hotel Wilson
Calle 5, Av Central-2, T2666-4222,
www.hoteleswilson.com.
The colourfully illuminated plastic palms
out front add a touch of pazzaz to this
otherwise generic downtown option. Rooms
are small and well kept. Secure parking and
restaurant downstairs. Lacks personality, but
otherwise good.

$$-$ La Posada del Tope
Calle Real, 1½ blocks south from church,
T2666-3876, www.laposadadeltope.com.
A haphazard guesthouse adorned with
antique contraptions. They have basic rooms,
with or without private bath. The owner
Dennis also has a telescope for star gazing.
OK, would suit backpackers.

$$-$ Liberia
½ block south of main square, T2666-0161,
www.hotelliberiacr.com.
A lovely old house and long-standing
cheapie, almost a century old. Rooms are
simple, comfortable and quiet. Dorms are
also available ($) and there's an internal
garden and courtyard serving as a restaurant.
Recommended.

$ Hospedaje Dodero
Av 11, Calle 12-14, T2665-4326,
www.hospedajedodero.yolasite.com.
Close to the bus terminal, this intimate
and well-kept little guesthouse has simple
private rooms, a little garden at the back
and a basic shared kitchen. Very cheap,
relaxed and friendly. Similar options can
be found on the same street.

Parque Nacional Rincón de la Vieja

$$$$-$$$ Hacienda Lodge Guachipelin
Accessed through the northern route,
T2690-2900, www.guachipelin.com.
50 rooms, internet, meals available. Canopy
tour, naturalist guides, riding, hot springs,
sulphur springs, mud pools, waterfalls
(transport from Liberia arranged, US$50 per
person round trip).

$$$ Buena Vista Mountain Lodge
accessed through the Santa María sector,
T2690-1414, www.buenavistalodgecr.com.
Rooms, waterslide, canopy tour, spa, internet,
restaurant/bar.

$ Miravieja Lodge
Accessed through the Santa María sector,
T8383-6645, www.miravieja.co.cr.
Rustic lodge in citrus groves, meals, transport
and tours.

La Cruz and Isla Bolaños

$$$ Ecoplaya Beach Resort
Bahía Salinas, T2676-1010, www.ecoplaya.com.
All-inclusive resort, well maintained with
nice restaurant.

$$$ Hotel La Mirada
On road out to the Pan-American Highway,
T2679-9702, www.hotellamirada.com.
Clean, tidy rooms, ample parking.

$$ Amalia's Inn
100 m south of Parque Central.
Stunning views, small pool, very friendly
and excellent local knowledge. Extra person
US$5 and 1 room sleeps 6. Excellent value for
groups and recommended.

$ Cabinas Santa Rita
150 m south of Parque Central, T2679-9062.
Nice, clean, secure with good parking.
Cheaper with fan. Would be great in any
other town not competing with **Amalia's**.

Restaurants

Liberia

$$$ Toro Negro
Corner of Av Central and Calle 1, T2666-2456.
The best steakhouse in town, offering a
selection of succulent beef cuts grilled to
order, as well as some lighter fare, including
wood-fired pizzas and chicken cordon
bleu. A convivial family atmosphere.
Recommended for groups and carnivores.

$$$-$$ Café Liberia
Calle Real, 150 m sur de la Antigua Gobernación Casa Zúñiga-Clachar, T2665-1660, www.cafeliberia.com. Mon-Sat 1000-1800.
An intimate café-restaurant with a diverse menu of coffee, snacks and full meals, including sandwiches, *fajitas*, ceviche and not-to-be-missed lava cake. The setting is a handsome colonial building with an interesting ceiling fresco and a relaxed patio at the back. Lovely owner and staff, attentive service. Highly recommended.

$$$-$$ El Mesón Liberiano
Calle 3, Av 1-3, T2666-1819, www.elmeson liberiano.com. Mon-Sat 1100-2300.
Popular with local families, El Mesón Liberiano serves hearty ceviches, soup, steaks, chicken and seafood. Solid wooden tables and a pleasant open-air patio, very typical of traditional Guanacaste architecture.

$$$-$$ Pizza Pronto
Calle 1, Av 4.
Classier than the name might suggest, authentic stone-baked pizzas served in an atmospheric colonial house. Tasty, but servings are small for the price.

$$$-$$ Tierra Mar
Next to Parque El Pulmón.
An understated seafood restaurant with a tempting menu of finely prepared fish and shellfish, including snapper, clams, shrimp and ceviche. Open-air seating, good service and tasty cooking. Recommended.

$$ Copa de Oro
Calle Real, 100 m south of Parque Central, next to Hotel Liberia.
Good-value *comida típica*, including a range of wholesome meat, chicken and seafood *casados*. Think comfort food, not gourmet. Large portions, good service, friendly atmosphere and a pleasant setting in a colonial edifice.

$ Los Comales
Calle Central, Av 5-7. Open 0630-2100.
Traditional Guanacaste dishes prepared with maize, run by a women's cooperative. Bustling, low-key, economical.

La Cruz and Isla Bolaños

$ La Orqhídea
La Cruz, T2679-9316. Daily 0630-2200.
Seafood, cheap.

$ Restaurant Telma
La Cruz, T2679-9150.
Tico food, cheap.

$ Soda Marta
La Cruz, T2679-9347.
Cheap Tico fare.

Festivals

Liberia
25 Jul **Guanacaste Day** sees dancing, parades and cattle-related festivities.

Shopping

Liberia
Mini Galería Fulvia, *on the main plaza*. Sells English papers and books. English spoken and helpful.
Tiffany's, *Av C-2, Calle 2*. General gifts, cigars.

What to do

Liberia
Hotel Liberia and **La Posada del Tope** (see Where to stay, above) can organize tours, rent out bikes and assist with enquiries.

Transport

Liberia
Air The **Aeropuerto Daniel Oduber Quirós**, about 13 km from Liberia (LIR) on the road to the Nicoya Peninsula, was named after the former president who came from Guanacaste. The runway can

handle large jets and charter flights and has become a popular alternative entry point to the country.

Bus **San José** buses leave from Av 5, Calle 10-12, with 14 a day, US$4.25, 4 hrs. Other buses leave from the local terminal at Calle 12, Av 7-9. Liberia to **Playa del Coco**, hourly, 0500-1800, **Playa Hermosa** and **Panama**, 5 daily 0730-1730, 1½ hrs, **Puntarenas**, 7 a day, 0500-1530, **Bagaces/ Cañas**, 4 a day, 0545-1710, **Cañas Dulces**, 3 a day, 0600-1730, **La Cruz/Peñas Blanca**, 8 a day 0530-1800. **Filadelfia–Santa Cruz– Nicoya**, 0500-2020, 20 a day.

Car **Sol** and **Toyota** car rental agencies (see map) offer the same prices and allow you to leave the vehicle at San José airport for US$50.

Parque Nacional Rincón de la Vieja
A taxi costs US$30 1-way from Liberia. Most hotels will arrange transport for US$15 per person, minimum 6 passengers. Departure at 0700, 1 hr to entrance, return at 1700; take food and drink. You can also hitch; most tourist vehicles will pick you up. If you take your own transport a 4WD is best, although during the dry season a vehicle with high clearance is adequate.

Parque Nacional Santa Rosa
Parque Nacional Santa Rosa is easy to reach as it lies west of the Pan-American Highway, about 1 hr north of Liberia. Any bus going from Liberia to Peñas Blancas on the Nicaraguan border will drop you right at the entrance (US$0.70, 40 mins), from where it's a 7-km walk, but you may be able to hitch a ride. Last bus returns to Liberia about 1800. Coming from the border, any bus heading south will drop you off at the entrance.

La Cruz and Isla Bolaños
Bus Regular buses to **San José** from 0545 until 1630, 5½ hrs. To **Liberia**, 5 daily 0700-1730, 1½ hrs. To **Peñas Blancas on the Nicaraguan border**, 5 daily 0730-1730, 1 hr; for more on the crossing to Nicaragua, see the Nicaragua–Costa Rica box, page 173. To **Playa Jobo** in Bahía Solanos, at 0530, 1030 and 1500, from main plaza.

Península
de Nicoya

Fringed by idyllic white-sand beaches along most of the coastline, the Nicoya Peninsula is hilly and hot. There are few towns of any size and most of the roads not connecting the main communities are in poor condition. While several large hotel resorts are increasingly taking over what were once isolated coves, they are generally grouped together and there are still many remote beaches to explore. A few small areas of the peninsula are protected to preserve wildlife, marine ecosystems and the geological formations of Barra Honda.

Even in high season, you will be able to find a beautiful beach that is uncrowded. There are so many of them, you can just walk until you find what you want. You will see plenty of wildlife along the way, monkeys, iguanas and squirrels as well as many birds. There can be dangerous undertows on exposed beaches; the safest bathing is from those beaches where there is a protective headland, such as at Playa Panamá in the north.

Essential Península de Nicoya

Finding your feet

There are several ways of getting to the Nicoya Peninsula and most travellers use ferries from Puntarenas (see page 111). For the northern region, the car ferry crosses the Gulf of Nicoya to Playa Naranjo, where buses wait to take foot passengers to Nicoya (US$1.25, 2¼ hours), Sámara (US$1.30), Coyote, Bejuco and Jicaral. For the southern region, a ferry departs from Puntarenas to Paquera from the dock at Calle 35. On arrival, get on the bus as quickly as possible (to Cóbano, two to three hours, US$1.25, bad road, to Montezuma US$2.60, 1½ hours at least).

Drivers coming from Nicaragua have the option of entering the Peninsula overland. From Liberia, head west along the Highway 21 towards Santa Elena. The Taiwan Friendship Bridge over the Río Tempisque, leaving the Pan-American Highway roughly halfway between Puntarenas and Liberia, provides a short cut, saving time and gas money getting to the peninsula and eliminating the ferry. Just across the river is **Hotel Rancho Humo**, T2255-2463, www.ranchohumo.com, with boat trips on the Tempisque and Bebedero rivers, visits to Palo Verde and Barra Honda national parks. See also Transport, below.

Getting around

All the beaches on the Nicoya Peninsula are accessible by road in the dry season. Most places can be reached by bus from Nicoya. However, the stretch from Paquera to Montezuma and the Cabo Blanco Reserve is connected to Playa Naranjo and the north only by very poor roads. There is no bus connection between Playa Naranjo and Paquera and the road is appalling even in the dry season.

Santa Cruz and around

tranquil town famous for fiestas, dancing and regional food

Heading south from Liberia by road, the first town you reach is Santa Cruz, known as Costa Rica's National Folklore City. January is the month for the fiesta dedicated to Santo Cristo de Esquipulas, when it can be difficult to find accommodation. There is also a rodeo fiesta in January. But for the rest of the year, it's a quiet little town, with a charming modern church, providing supplies for the beach tourism industry. If you need to buy food, Santa Cruz is a good place to stock up.

In **Guaitil**, 9 km east of Santa Cruz and 19 km north of Nicoya, local artisans specialize in reproductions of indigenous Chorotegan pottery. They work with the same methods used by the indigenous long ago, with minimal or no use of a wheel and no artificial paints. Ceramics are displayed at the local *pulpería*, or outside houses. At **San Vicente**, 2 km southeast of Guaitil, local craftsmen work and sell their pottery.

Where to stay

Santa Cruz

If stuck, there are few cheap *pensiones* about town in addition to options below:

$$$ La Calle de la Alcalá
Av 7, Calle 1-3, 25 m east of the
Plaza de Los Mangos, T2680-0000,
www.hotellacalledealcala.com.
A reliable downtown option with clean, comfortable, spacious and generally decent rooms and suites, all with a/c, hot water, cable TV, Wi-Fi and wicker furniture. There's also a pool and restaurant.

$$ Hotel Diriá
On the highway, 3 km north of the Banco Nacional, www.hoteldiria.co.cr.
Bath, restaurant, pools.

Restaurants

Santa Cruz

$ Coopetortilla
3 blocks east of the church.
A local institution– a women's cooperative cooking local dishes. Cheap and enjoyable.

Transport

Santa Cruz
Bus Buses leave and arrive from terminals on Plaza de los Mangos. From **San José**, 9 daily, 0700-1800, 4½ hrs, US$8, Calle 18-20, Av 3, ½ block west of Terminal Coca Cola, return 0300-1700. To **Tamarindo**, 2030, return 0645, US$0.80, also to **Playa Flamingo** and nearby beaches, 0630, 1500, return 0900, 1700, 64 km. To **Liberia** every hour, US$1.60, 0530-1930. To **Nicoya** hourly 0630-2130, US$0.70.

Taxi To **Nicoya**, US$10.50 for 2 people.

★ West coast beaches

a series of beaches with nesting turtles, surfing and spectacular sunsets

A number of beaches are reached by unpaved roads from the Santa Cruz–Liberia road. Many can be accessed by bus from the Liberia bus station, others may require you to change buses at Santa Cruz. Each of the beaches has its appeal: Tamarindo and Playa del Coco for partying, Flamingo to the north and Junquillal for their greater seclusion and Grande for turtles and surfing.

Playa del Coco and around

After the town of **Comunidad**, a road leads east to Playa del Coco and Playa Hermosa and the ever-pending resort development of Playa Panamá, see below.

Playa del Coco is a popular resort some 8 km from the highway, set in an attractive islet-scattered bay hemmed in by rocky headlands. It's a good place to chill out, with a mix of good services without being too developed. The best beaches are to the south. All activities concentrate on the beach and fishing. Coco is the starting point for surf trips to Santa Rosa spots by boat, such as **Witch's Rock**. Snorkelling and diving are nothing special, but for a diving expedition to the **Islas Murciélago**, see What to do, below. Sightings of manta rays and bull sharks are common around Islas Catalinas and Islas Murciélago.

There are bars, restaurants and a few motels along the sandy beach. It is too small to get lost. To reach it, leave the road at Comunidad (road paved). Be wary of excursions to secluded Playa Verde, accessible by boat only, as some boatmen collaborate with thieves and reap the rewards later. A 2.5-km road heads southwest from Playa del Coco to **Playa Ocotal**.

Playa Hermosa and Playa Panamá

A spur road breaks from the main road to Playa del Coco heading north to Playa Hermosa. This is one of the best resorts and is served by a paved road. Accommodation is mixed, but it's a good quiet alternative to other beaches in the region. Walking either to the left or the right you can find isolated beaches with crystal-clear water. The big **Papagayo** tourist complex near Playa Panamá, which once planned to provide as many as 60,000 hotel rooms, started years ago.

Playa Tamarindo and around

South of Filadelfia, close to Belén, a mostly paved but poor road heads east to the beach and popular surf spot of Playa Tamarindo (www.tamarindobeach.net) and other beaches. The sunsets are incredible and while most people make their way to the beach for that magic moment, there's a strong beach culture and this is a popular place just to hang out.

Either side of the sunset, Tamarindo is a flurry of activity, easily the liveliest beach resort on the Nicoya Peninsula and development is quickly changing the place. The beach is attractive with strong tides in places so take care if swimming. Three good breaks provide a variety of options for the surf crowd. Beyond surf and sun, the most popular excursion is an evening trip to Playa Grande and the leatherback turtle nesting sights from October to March. There's a good blend of hotels and bars to make it a good beach stop – not too busy, but not dead.

Close to Tamarindo, to the south, **Playa Avellana** is a quiet beach with good surfing for those who want to get away from the service culture of Tamarindo. Shuttle buses run from Tamarindo and there are a handful of accommodation options.

Playa Grande

North of Playa Tamarindo is Playa Grande and the **Parque Nacional Marino Las Baulas de Guanacaste** (485 ha terrestrial, 22,000 ha marine), well known as a nesting site for **leatherback turtles** (October-February). Organized trips are only available from Tamarindo or from hotels in Playa Grande. Also in town is **El Mundo de La Tortuga** ⓘ *T2653-0471*, an unusual turtle museum. The road from the main highway at Belén leads directly to Playa Grande, a sleepy town with almost no transport and no way of getting around.

Playa Flamingo and beaches to the north

North of Tamarindo and Playa Grande are the beaches of Conchal, Brasilito, Flamingo and Potrero. It's a collection of beaches with subtle changes of atmosphere. **Conchal** is a beautiful 3-km beach full of shells, but with only luxury accommodation; most budget travellers stay at **Brasilito** and walk along the beach. Further north, the bay around **Playa Flamingo** has white sand, although the actual beach has some fairly intrusive developments with a grab-all approach to beachfront properties; in fact, the beach is now polluted and not as beautiful as it was. Several smaller beaches retain a relaxed atmosphere where life is governed by little more than the sunrise and beautiful sunsets. Further north is the isolated beach of **Potrero** with pockets of visitors.

Playa Junquillal

South of Tamarindo, Playa Junquillal is one of the cleanest beaches in Costa Rica and is still very empty. Completely off the beaten track with almost no tourist facilities, it does have a selection of stylish hotels, most of which are quite pricey, but there is also camping if you have a tent.

Where to stay

Playa del Coco and around

Good discounts (up to 40%) in green season. Playa Ocotal has only top-end accommodation, but good diving services.

$$$ Villa Casa Blanca
Playa Ocotal, T2670-0518,
www.hotelvillacasablanca.com.
15 idyllic rooms, with breakfast, friendly, informative, family atmosphere, small pool. Pricey but very good.

$$$-$$ Coco Palms
Next to the soccer field, Playa del Coco,
T2670-0367, www.sites.google.com/site/
hotelcocopalms.
Coco Palms has good location near the beach and downtown area. They offer a wide range of rooms, from simple economies to fully kitted apartments, all with a/c and cable TV. Amenities include large pool, computers, Wi-Fi, Sushi restaurant and bar, garden and supermarket.

$$$-$$ La Puerta del Sol
North of Playa del Coco, T2670-0195.
Great little family-run hotel. Good food in Italian restaurant, small pool and gym, friendly atmosphere and free scuba lesson in hotel pool.

$$ Cabinas Coco Azul
Playa del Coco, from the church, 100 m
northeast, 25 m south, T2670-0431,
www.cabinascocoazul.co.
Great hosts at this lovely little guesthouse, very homely, helpful and hospitable. Rooms are simple but immaculately clean and comfortable and there's a hot tub too. 2 mins from the beach. Recommended.

$$ Pato Loco Inn
Playa del Coco, T2670-0145.
Airy rooms, Italian restaurant, internet for guests.

$$ Villa del Sol
At northern end of Playa del Coco, T2670-
0085, www.villadelsol.com.
Canadian-owned (from Quebec), with pool, clean, friendly, safe, big garden with parrots. Recommended.

$$-$ Cabinas Chale
North of Playa del Coco, T2670-0036.
Double rooms and villas, with private bath. Pretty quiet, small resort-style spot, small pool, 50 m from beach. Good deal, especially villas, which sleep up to 6.

Playa Hermosa and Playa Panamá

Playa Panamá area has several all-inclusive resort-style hotels (**$$$$**).

$$$$-$$$ La Finisterra
Playa Hermosa, end of 1st beach road,
T2672-0227, www.lafinisterra.com.
Perched on a beachfront hill 100 m from the ocean, Hotel La Finisterra basks in expansive views and refreshing sea breezes, a comfortable option, in their own words, 'sophisticated but unpretentious'.

$$$ La Gaviota Tropical
Playa Hermosa, 2nd beach road to end,
then right 75 m to Roberto's, T2672-0011,
www.lagaviotatropical.com.
This boutique B&B offers 5 comfortable rooms, each tastefully decorated in its own tropical theme, including beach, bird and rainforest rooms. Great hosts, attentive service. Highly recommended.

$$-$ Congo's Hostel
Main street, 50 m before the beach,
T2672-1168, www.congoshostel.com.
Easy-going, friendly hostel with helpful owners and chilled-out vibe. Amenities include kitchen and leafy garden complete with a wooden deck. Simple rooms, family atmosphere. Camping is an option.

Playa Tamarindo and around

Plenty of accommodation – best in each price range listed. Book in advance at Christmas and New Year.

$$$$ Capitán Suizo
A long way south of the centre towards Playa Langosta, T2653-0075, www.hotelcapitansuizo.com.
8 bungalows, 22 rooms with patio or balcony, a/c, pool, restaurant, kayaking, scuba-diving, surfing and sport fishing available, riding on hotel's own horses, Swiss management. One of Costa Rica's distinctive hotels.

$$$$-$$$ Tamarindo Bay Boutique Hotel
100 m south of the Banco Nacional de Costa Rica, west of Hotel Arco Iris, T2653-2692, www.tamarindobayhotel.com.
Crisp minimalist design, with deluxe rooms being especially 'Zen' and boasting outdoor showers and mini espresso-makers. Swish, intimate and professional.

$$$ 15 Love
1 block behind the main road, 200 m before Hotel Jardín del Edén, T2653-0898, www.15lovebedandbreakfast.com.
15 Love is the hippest hotel in town, boasting spacious standard rooms and sumptuous suites with all modern conveniences and an ocean-view patio shaded by a native tree. Superb design, charming and stylish.

$$$ Witch's rock surf camp
Opposite Economy Rental Car, T2653-1238, www.witchsrocksurfcamp.com.
One of the most popular surf camps in Costa Rica, widely celebrated and built up over the years with a lot of hard work. Various packages and tours available and there's a beginners' break right on the doorstep.

$$ Hotel Mahayana
150 m northeast of Hotel Pasatiempo, T2653-1154, www.hotelmahayana.com.
Simple, tranquil and homely, rooms at Hotel Mahayana feature terracotta floor tiles, private terraces and solid wood beams.

Amenities include jacuzzi, kitchen, garden with hammocks, Wi-Fi, tours.

$$ Villas Macondo
1 block back from the beach, T2653-0812, www.villasmacondo.com.
Rooms with shared kitchen and apartments. Pool, washing machine, safety boxes, fridge and friendly people too.

$$-$ Chocolate Hotel and Hostel
*50 m east from **Stella** restaurant, T2653-1311, www.thechocolatehostel.com.*
The appetizingly named Chocolate Hotel and Hostel boasts 9 large apartment-style suites with private balconies and patios. For the thrifty, there's 'upscale' hostel-style lodging in shared dorms. Pool.

$ Blue Trailz
Main street, next to Alamo rent a car, T2653-1705, www.bluetrailz.com.
Good location near the beach and breaks, this highly popular surf school and hostel has cheap 6-bed dorm rooms (**$**) with a/c, shared kitchen, hot water, microwave and fridge. Surf-camp packages, board rental, lessons and tours available. For extra comfort, there are also studio apartments (**$$$**).

$ Botella de Leche
300 m from the beach, 2653-0189, www.labotelladeleche.com.
This self-described '5-star hostel' boasts funky cow decor and a bean bag common room, a 'paradise for the free spirit'. There are dorms and affordable private rooms, all the usual amenities including kitchen and pool. Cosy and sociable.

Playa Grande

$$$ La Marajeda
200 m sur de Minae, T2653-0594, www.hotelswell.com.
This cosy boutique hotel is a short 3-min walk from the beach. It has 8 crisp, clean, quiet and comfortable rooms with balconies and terraces overlooking a leafy garden and pool. A simple, tranquil spot.

$$$-$$ Hotel Las Tortugas
Right on the beach in the centre of town,
T2653-0423, www.lastortugashotel.com.
11 rooms with bathroom, pool, restaurant,
meals included, tours arranged.

$$$-$ Hotel El Manglar
Palm Beach Estates, T2653-0952,
www.hotel-manglar.com.
Beachside hostel-hotel, professionally
managed by 3 Costa Rican brothers and a
sister. Accommodations include dorms ($),
good-value split-level standards ($$) and,
for those seeking extra comfort, private
villas fully kitted with kitchen, living room,
hammocks and more ($$$). Recommended.

$$ Playa Grande Inn
T2653-0719, www.playagrandeinn.com.
Formerly **Rancho Diablo**. 10 rooms with fan,
good set up for surfers.

Playa Flamingo and beaches to the north

$$$$ Casa del Sol
Playa Portrero, T2296-0375,
www.resortcasadelsol.istemp.com.
Lavish condo units with 2 bedrooms,
2 bathrooms, fully equipped kitchen, washer-
dryer, private terrace and patio furniture.
Contemporary decor, very swish.

$$$ Conchal Hotel
Playa Brasilito, 200 m south of the school,
T2654-9125, www.conchalcr.com.
A 9-room boutique hotel a short walk from
Brasilito and Conchal beaches. Tastefully
decorated rooms with secluded patio areas,
views of the garden and pool.

$$$ Mariner Inn
Playa Flamingo, T2654-4081.
Has 12 rooms with bath, a/c, free camping
on the beach.

$$-$ Hotel Brasilito
Playa Brasilito, close to beach on plaza,
T2654-4237, www.brasilito.com. Closed Mon.
Good rooms. Horses, kayaks and bikes to
rent. **Los Arcades Restaurant**, run by Charlie
and Claire, mixes Thai and local dishes.

Playa Junquillal

$$$ Casas Pelicano
300 m north of the school, T2658-9010,
www.casaspelicano.cr.
Overlooking the Pacific Ocean, 2 villas with
private access to the beach. Well equipped
with hammocks, fans, kitchen, safe. Cooking
classes available from Sibyl, the owner, a
classically trained chef.

$$$ Mundo Milo Eco-lodge
Calle Mundo Milo, T2658-7010,
www.mundomilo.com.
Dutch-owned lodge with interesting
African, Mexican and Persian-style *cabinas*
built amidst the trees. Very comfortable
and creative with a solid sustainable ethos.
Breakfast included.

$$-$ El Castillo Divertido
T2658-8428, www.costarica-
adventureholidays.com.
Castle rooms, restaurant, gardens, rooftop
star-gazing deck, music.

$$-$ Guacamaya Lodge
T2658-8431, www.guacamayalodge.com.
Immaculate bungalows and 1 fully equipped
house with pool, ocean views, Swiss cuisine.

$ Hibiscus
Cose to the beach, T2658-8437.
Big rooms with big windows, seafood
restaurant with German specialities,
garden, 50 m to beach, German-run.

Restaurants

Playa del Coco and around

$$$ Mariscos la Guajira
On southern beach.
Popular and beautiful beachfront location.

$$$ Papagayo
Near the beach, T2670-0298.
Good seafood. Recommended.

$$ Bananas
On the road out of town.
The place to go drinking and dancing until
the early hours.

$$ Cocos
On the plaza, T2670-0235.
Bit flashy and pricey for the area, but
good seafood.

$$ El Roble
Beside the main plaza.
A popular bar/disco.

$$ Playa del Coco
On the beach.
Popular, open from 0600.

$ Jungle Bar
On the road into town.
Another lively, slightly rougher option.

Playa Tamarindo and around

$$$ Fiesta del Mar
On the loop at the end of town.
Large thatched open barn, good food,
good value.

$$$ Ginger
*At the northern end of town,
T2672-0041. Tue-Sun.*
Good Thai restaurant.

$$ Iguana Surf Restaurant
On road to Playa Langosta.
Good atmosphere and food.

$$ Coconut Café
On beach near Tamarindo Vista.
Pizzas, pastries and good fish. Check for
good breakfasts and cheap evening meals.

$$ El Arrecife
On roundabout.
Popular spot to hang out, with Tico fare,
good chicken and pizzas.

$$ The Lazy Wave
*On road leading away from the beach,
T2653-0737.*
Menu changes daily, interesting mix of
cuisine, seafood.

$$ Portofino
At end of road by roundabout.
Italian specialities and good ice cream

$$ Stellas
On road leading away from the beach.
Very good seafood, try *dorado* with mango
cream. Recommended.

$ Arco Iris
On road heading inland.
Cheap vegetarian, great atmosphere.

$ Frutas Tropicales
Near Tamarindo Vista.
Snacks and breakfast.

Playa Flamingo and beaches to the north

$$ La Casita del Pescado
Playa Brasilito.
Some reasonably priced fish dishes which
you have to eat quickly because the stools
are made of concrete.

$$ Marie's Restaurant
Playa Flamingo, T2654-4136.
Breakfast, seafood, *casados* and
international dishes.

$$ Pizzeria Il Forno
Playa Brasilito.
Serves a mean pizza.

$$ Restaurant La Boca de la Iguana
Playa Brasilito.
Good value.

$$-$ Las Brisas
At the northern end of Playa Potrero.
A great spot for a beer and a snack,
surprisingly popular for its cut-off location.

$ Costa Azul
Playa Potrero, by the football pitch.
One of several restaurants in the area,
popular with locals.

$ Cyber Shack
Playa Brasilito.
Internet, coffee, breakfast and UPS service.

Playa Junquillal

$$$ La Puesta del Sol
T2658-8442.
The only restaurant along the strip, but then
nothing could compete with the dishes from
this little piece of Italy. Spectacular setting.
Very popular so reservations required.

Entertainment

Playa Tamarindo and around
With a long beachside strip, it's a question of
exploring town until you find something that
works. Call it bar surfing if you like.

Shopping

Playa Tamarindo and around
The town is increasingly a retail outlet selling
everything you need for the beach. There are
also a couple of general stores in the centre.

What to do

Playa del Coco and around
Agua Rica Charters, *T2670-0473, or contact
them through the internet café.* Can arrange
transport to Witch's Rock for surfers,
approximately US$400 for up to 10.

Deep Blue Diving, *beside Hotel Coco Verde,
T2670-1004, www.deepblue-diving.com.*
Has diving trips to Islas Catalinas and Islas
Murciélago, where sightings of manta rays
and bull sharks are common. 2-tank dive
from US$79. Will also rent gear.
Rich Coast Diving, *T2670-0176,
www.richcoastdiving.com.*

Playa Hermosa and Playa Panamá
Diving Safari, *based at the Sol Playa Hermosa
Resort on Playa Hermosa, T2453-5044,
www.billbeardcostarica.com.* One of the
longest-running diving operations in the
country, offering a wide range of options
in the region.

Playa Tamarindo and around
Diving
Try the **Pacific Coast Dive Center** (T2653-
0267), or **Agua Rica Dive Center** (T2653-0094).

Surfing and yoga
Iguana Surf Tours, *T2653-0148.* Rent
surfboards, they have one outlet near the
beach, opposite the supermarket, the other
in the restaurant of the same name.
VOEC, *on the beach, T2653-0852, www.
voecretreats.com.* A women's retreat that
offers 6-night packages, which include surf
and yoga lessons.

Tour operators
There are many tours on offer to see the
turtles nesting at night in Playa Grande.
Hightide Adventures and Surfcamp,
T2653-0108, www.tamarindoadventures.net.
Offers a full range of tours.

Transport

Playa del Coco and around
Bus From **San José** from Calle 14,
Av 1-3, 0800, 1400, 5 hrs, return 0800,
1400 US$7. 6 buses daily from **Liberia**,
0530-1815, return 0530-1800.

Playa Hermosa and Playa Panamá
Bus From **Liberia**, Empresa Esquivel, 0730, 1130, 1530, 1730, 1900, return 0500, 0600, 1000, 1600, 1700, US$1.20.

Playa Tamarindo and around
Air Several daily flights from **San José** with Sansa (US$71, 1 way) and **NatureAir** (from US$83 to US$111) from **San José**. Daily flight from **La Fortuna** with Sansa.

Bus From **Santa Cruz**, 0410, 1330, 1500 daily. To Santa Cruz 1st bus at 0600, US$0.70. Express bus from **San José** daily from Terminal Alfaro, 1530, return 0600 Mon-Sat, 0600, Sun 1230, 5½ hrs. Bus back to San José,

can be booked through Hotel Tamarindo Diria, T2653 0032, US$9.60.

Playa Flamingo and beaches to the north
Bus From **San José** to Flamingo, Brasilito and Potrero, daily from Av 3, Calle 18-20, 0800, 1000, 6 hrs, from US$9.50, return 0900, 1400. From **Santa Cruz** daily 0630, 1500, return 0900, 1700, 64 km to Potrero.

Playa Junquillal
Bus Daily from **Santa Cruz** departs 1030, around US$9.80, returns to Santa Cruz at 1530.

Nicoya and around

pleasant little town at the heart of the peninsula

Nicoya is distinguished by possessing the country's second oldest church, the 17th-century church of San Blas. Damaged by an earthquake in 1822 it was restored in 1831 and is currently undergoing renovations. The Parque Central, on Avenida Central, is leafy and used for occasional concerts. Buses arrive at Avenida 1, Calle 3-5. Most hotels and banks are within a couple of blocks of the central park. The area Conservation Offices (ACT) are on the northern side of Parque Central. There is no general information for visitors, but they can assist with specific enquiries.

Parque Nacional Barra Honda
Entry US$10, no permit required.

A small park in the north of the Nicoya Peninsula, Barra Honda National Park (2295 ha) was created to protect a *mesa* with a few caves and the last remains of dry tropical forest in the region. The park office is near Barra Honda at **Santa Ana**, at the foot of the *mesa*, and there are two different trails to the top; two hours' hiking.

Sámara and Playa Carrillo
Sámara (www.samarabeach.com) is a smallish Tico village that has maintained some of its regular way of life alongside tourist development. The beautiful beach, 37 km from Nicoya on a paved road, is probably the safest and one of the best bathing beaches in Costa Rica. Playa Carrillo is 5 km away at the south end of the beach. The litter problem is being tackled with rubbish bins, warning signs, refuse collections and bottle banks. Both places have airstrips served by scheduled services from San José.

Nosara
Nosara (www.nosara.com) is a small village about 26 km north of Sámara without much to see or do in it – which makes it ideal if you like lying around on beaches. Indeed most come for the three unspoiled beaches which are not particularly close to the village.

Playa Nosara is north of the village across the Río Nosara where you may see turtles (see below); **Peladas** is the prettiest and smallest, south of the river, and **Guiones** is safe for swimming and good for surfing. Expatriates have formed the **Nosara Civic Association** to protect the area's wildlife and forests and prevent exploitation.

Playa Ostional

North of Nosara is Playa Ostional where olive ridley turtles lay eggs July-November along the coastal strip of the **Refugio Nacional de Vida Silvestre Ostional**. The turtles arrive for nesting at high tide. The villagers are allowed to harvest the eggs in a designated area of the beach, the rest are protected and monitored. Outside the egg-laying period it is very quiet. Contact the **MINAE (Ministry of Environment and Energy)** ① *T682-0470*, ranger station for details.

Listings Nicoya and around

Where to stay

Sámara

$$$$-$$$ El Pequeño Gecko Verde
600 m west and 100 m south of Hotel Samara Pacific Lodge, T2656-1176, www.gecko-verde.com.
Set in a lush tropical garden, 7 luxurious bungalows and 2 spacious rooms, all constructed using locally sourced wood. 5 mins by car from the village. Restful, recommended.

$$$ Lodge Las Ranas
800 m al oeste del Cruce de Cangrejal, T2656-0609, www.lodgelasranas.com.
A 10-room hotel set up on a hill to enjoy fine views of the mountains, ocean and jungle canopy below. Internet, kitchenette, breakfast, pool, private balconies.

$$$ Samara Tree House
Playa Sámara, T2656-0733, www.samaratreehouse.com.
6 luxury wood-built *casitas* on stilts, arranged in a neat row at the edge of the sand. Lush tropical gardens and an adults-only pool.

$$$-$$ Belvedere
Sloping up the hill, T2656-0213.
Very friendly German owners. A cosy hotel with 10 small rooms, very clean. Recommended.

$$$-$$ Hotel Giada
Main street, T2656-3232, www.hotelgiada.net.
24 rooms with a/c, cable TV, private bath and balcony. Amenities include pizza restaurant, Wi-Fi, jacuzzi, a smart green lawn and pools.

$$ Hotel Entre Dos Aguas
1st property in Sámara, T2656-0998, www.hoteldosaguas.com.
A tranquil 8-room hotel a short walk from the beach. Good-value rooms are spacious and include furniture crafted from local wood, stone and mosaic hot water showers. Lovely garden with a pool and hammocks.

$$-$ Hostel El Cactus
10 m south of Casa Coba, T2656-3224, www.samarabackpacker.com.
Located in the village, with good access to all the local services. A modern hostel with a large living room, TV, communal kitchen, garden and pool. Dorms, private rooms and bungalows available.

Nosara

$$$$ The Harmony Hotel
Playa Guiones, T2682-4114, www.harmonynosara.com.
Secluded and upscale surf lodge situated on a pristine break from any paved roads. Beautiful stylish rooms, suites and bungalows. Very tranquil. Recommended.

$$$ Lagarta Lodge
Reserva Biológica Nosara, Playa Pelada, T2682-0035, www.lagarta.com.
Situated on a commanding elevated bluff overlooking the ocean. Lodgings include 6 cosy standards and 6 superiors with views. Lots of wildlife in the area thanks to the adjacent nature reserve, including 270 bird species. Pool and restaurant.

$$$ Living Hotel
G-Section, Playa Guiones, T2682-5201, www.livinghotelnosara.com.
The epitome of rustic chic with boutique-styled wooden ranchos, spa treatments, yoga and surf retreats. Concierge service, saltwater pool, organic restaurant and Wi-Fi.

$$$-$$ Gilded Iguana Hotel
Playa Guiones, T2682-0259, www.thegildediguana.com.
Established in 1986, one of the oldest hotels in the area. Located 200 m from the beach with pool, Wi-Fi, free coffee, rooms with or without a/c. Family friendly.

$$-$ Almost Paradise
Playa Pelada, T2682-0172, www.almostparadise2012.com.
Fun, funky hostel with affordable dorms and private rooms, bar, restaurant, occasional spit-roasted pig.

$$-$ Jungle's Edge
200 m south of Nosara Yoga Institute then 200 m west, T2682-5314, www.jungles-edge.com.
A wide range of lodging from luxury suites to tents. Amenities include communal rancho with kitchen, juice bar, Wi-Fi and an open-air workout area for yoga, dance and martial arts.

$ Nosara Beach Hostel
200 m south of Harbor Reef Hotel, Punta Guiones, T2682-0238, www.nosarahostel.com.
Clean, sociable hostel with affordable bunk beds and 2 private rooms. Wi-Fi, board games and play station.

Playa Ostional
You can camp on the beach.

$ Cabinas Guacamaya
T2682-0430.
With bath, clean, good food on request. Price per person.

$ Cabinas Ostional
Next to the village shop.
Very cheap and basic accommodation in cabins with bath, clean, friendly.

Restaurants

Nicoya

$$ Café de Blita
2 km outside Nicoya towards Sámara.
Good.

$$ Soda El Triángulo
Opposite Chorotega.
Good juices and snacks, friendly owners.

$$ Teyet
Near Hotel Jenny.
Good, with quick service.

$ Daniela
1 block east of plaza.
Breakfast, lunches, coffee, *refrescos*, good.

Sámara
There are several cheap *sodas* around the football pitch in the centre of town.

$$$ Restaurant Delfín
On the beach.
Very good value and French-owned. They also rent out *cabinas*.

$$ El Ancla Restaurant
On the beach, T2656-0716.
Seafood.

$$ Las Brasas
By the football pitch, T2656-0546.
Spanish restaurant and bar.

$$ Restaurant Acuario
On the beach.
Serves Tico and other food.

$ Soda Sol y Mar
On the road to Nosara.
Costa Rican and international food.

Nosara

$$$ Gilded Iguana
Playas Guiones.
Gringo food and good company.

$$$ La Dolce Vita
South along the road out of town.
Good but pricey Italian food.

$$ Casa Romántica
Playas Guiones.
The European restaurant.

$$ Corky Carroll's Surf School
T2682-0385.
Surf lessons and a good Mexican/Thai restaurant (closed Sun).

$$ Giardino Tropicale
In the middle section.
Pizza.

$$ Hotel Almost Paradise
Playas Guiones, T2682-0173.
Good food with a great view.

$$ La Luna
Slightly up the hill.
Good food and ambience.

$$ Olga's
Playa Peladas.
Seafood on the beach.

$ Soda Vanessa
Playas Guiones.
One of several *sodas* in the village. Good, very cheap.

Playa Ostional

$$-$ Mirador de los Tortugueros
1 km south of Cabinas Guacamaya.
Good restaurant with coffee and pancakes. Great atmosphere. Recommended.

Entertainment

Sámara
Bar La Góndola is popular and has a dart board. Opposite is **Bar Colocho**. **Dos Lagartos** disco is on the beach near Al Manglar; and the disco at **Isla Chora** is the place to be during the season if you like resort discos.

Nosara
Some of the nightlife is in the village as well; **Bambú**, **Disco Tropicana** and various others line the football pitch.

What to do

Sámara
Language school
Intercultura Costa Rica, *Samara beachfront campus, T2656-3000, www.intercultura costarica.com.* Spanish classes right on the beach; immersion classes 18+, free cultural activities and weekend trips. Also classes for families and kids, and Spanish & Surf classes.

Tour operators
You can rent bikes from near the *ferretería* on the road to Cangrejal.
Tip Top Tours, *T2656-0650.* Run by a very nice French couple, offering dolphin tours (from US$45 per person), mangrove tours (US$43 per person) and waterfall tours (US$20 per person). Naturalist guided tours to Barra Honda and Isla Chora (US$70 per person), as well as slightly more unusual trips like *Journée Cowboy* where you spend a day on the ranch roping cattle and eat with a Tico family.
Wing Nuts Canopy Tour, *T2656-0153. US$40, kids US$25.* Family-run, friendly service, spectacular ocean views from the treetops, with 12 platforms, lots of wildlife close up, great photo opportunity, 1st-class equipment.

Nosara

Casa Río Nosara for horse or river tours and **Gilded Iguana** for kayaking and fishing. For turtle tours, try **Rancho Suizo** (T2682-0057), or **Lagarta Lodge** (T2682-0035), who are both sensitive to the turtles and don't exploit or bother them.

Transport

Nicoya

Bus From **San José**, 8 daily from Terminal Alfaro, 6 hrs, US$6.70-9; from **Liberia** every 30 mins from 0430-2200; from **Santa Cruz** hourly 0630-2130. To **Playa Naranjo** at 0500 and 1300, 2¼ hrs, US$3. 12 buses per day to **Sámara**, 37 km by paved road, 1 to **Nosara**.

Sámara

Air Daily flights from **San José**, Sansa US$71, **Nature Air**, US$83-111.

Bus From **Nicoya**, 45 km, 1½ hrs, US$2.20, 0800, 1500, 1600, return 0530, 0630, 1130,

1330, 1630. Express bus from Terminal Alfaro, **San José** daily at 1230, return Mon-Sat 0430, Sun 1300, 5-6 hrs. School bus to **Nosara** around 1600; ask locally for details. It is not possible to go from Sámara along the coast to Montezuma, except in 4WD vehicle; not enough traffic for hitching.

Taxi Official and others stop outside bus station (US$20 to **Nosara**, US$10 to **Nicoya**).

Nosara

Air Sansa has daily flights to **San José**, US$71, **Nature Air**, US$83-111.

Bus Daily from **Nicoya** to Nosara, **Garza, Guiones** daily from main station, 1300, return 0600, US$3, 2 hrs; from **San José** daily from Terminal Alfaro at 0600, 6 hrs, return 1245.

Playa Ostional

Bus 1 daily at 0500 to **Santa Cruz** and **Liberia**, returns 1230 from Santa Cruz, 3 hrs, US$1.75.

Southern Península de Nicoya

low-key coastal villages, waterfalls and wildlife reserves

The southern Nicoya Peninsula is almost completely cut off from the north. Roads are appalling and those that exist are frequently flooded in part. For this reason most access the region by ferry from Puntarenas. Beaches and stopping points are dotted along the southern shore of the peninsula, passing through Tambor, Montezuma, Cabuya, Mal País and Playa Santa Teresa.

Playa Naranjo and Paquera

Arriving at **Playa Naranjo** there are several expensive eating places by the dock and a gas station. **Paquera** is a small village 22 km along the coast from Playa Naranjo. There are a few shops and some simple lodgings; for example, **Cabinas Rosita** on the inland side of the village. It is separated from the quay by 1 km or so; apart from a good *soda*, a restaurant, a public telephone and a branch of **Banco de Costa Rica**, there are no facilities.

Tambor, Curú National Wildlife Refuge and Cóbano

The small village of **Tambor**, 19 km from Paquera, has a dark-sand beach, some shops and restaurants. The beach is beautiful, 6 km long with rolling surf, but 1½ hours on a bone-shaking road from the ferry. However, cruise ships from Puntarenas come here and part of the beach has been absorbed by the large and controversial **Hotel Playa Tambor**. Built around a cattle farm by the Barceló group of Spain, the resort is alleged to have encroached on the public beach and drained a swamp that was a wildfowl habitat. A second stage is planned at **Punta Piedra Amarilla**, with a 500-boat marina, villas and a total of 1100 rooms. Buses travelling from Paquera to Montezuma, pass through Tambor, connecting with the car ferry arriving from Puntarenas, US$2.60, two hours.

North of Playa Tambor is the **Curú National Wildlife Refuge** ⓘ *T2661-2392, in advance and ask for Doña Julieta*, which is only 84 ha, but has five different habitats and 110 species of bird. Access is through private land.

Cóbano, near Montezuma, can be reached by bus from Paquera ferry terminal and buses for Tambor, Cóbano and Montezuma meet the launches from Puntarenas (there is an airstrip with flights from San José). Roads north, west and south out of Cóbano, require 4WD. Cóbano has a petrol/gas station.

★ Montezuma

No longer a sleepy hamlet, Montezuma is a very popular small village on the sea. It is a well-liked backpacking destination and at busy periods hotels fill up every day, so check in early. Although it gets crowded, there are some wonderful beaches; many are rocky, with strong waves making it difficult to swim, but it's very scenic. There are beautiful walks along the beach – sometimes sandy, sometimes rocky, always lined with trees – that visit impressive waterfalls. The village can be reached in four hours from Puntarenas if you get the early launch. There is a tourist office at **Aventuras Montezuma**, which is very helpful and often knows which hotel has space; ask here first before looking around. The once-popular **Cabinas Karen** are now closed. Prior to her death in 1994, Doña Karen donated her land to the National Parks in memory of her late husband, creating what was to become Reserva Natural Absoluta Cabo Blanco (see below). **Cabinas Karen** now houses park guards.

Around Montezuma

Close to the village, 20 minutes up the Río Montezuma, is a beautiful, huge **waterfall** with a big, natural swimming hole, beyond which is a smaller waterfall. Intrepid walkers can carry on up to further waterfalls but it can be dangerous and accidents have been reported. There's another waterfall, 6 km north of Montezuma, with a pool right by the beach – follow the road out to the beach at the north end of town and keep going past three coves for about half an hour until you reach the trail off to the left (you can't miss it). See Tour operators, below.

You can use Montezuma as a base for exploring the **Reserva Natural Absoluta Cabo Blanco** ⓘ *Wed-Sun 0800-1600, US$6, jeep/taxi from Montezuma US$7, first at 0700, returns 1600*. The 1172-ha reserve is 11 km from Montezuma. The marine birds include frigate birds, pelicans and brown boobies; there are also monkeys, anteaters, kinkajou and collared peccary. You can bathe in the sea or under a waterfall. At the beautiful **Playa Balsitas**, 6 km from the entrance, there are pelicans and howler monkeys.

At **Cabuya**, 2 km from Cabo Blanco Reserve, the sea can be cloudy after rough weather. Cabuya Island can be visited on foot at low tide. On the road west out of Cabuya, **Cafetería El Coyote** specializes in local and Caribbean dishes. On the west coast of the peninsula is the fast-growing village of **Mal País**. The coast here is virtually unspoilt with long white beaches, creeks and natural pools, and the facilities stretch north up the beach to blend with **Santa Teresa**. The surfing appeal of the area is growing with Mal País best suited for beginners, with the more experienced crowd going up to Santa Teresa. It's a fast-changing area.

You can also arrange tours to **Isla Tortuga**. Many businesses rent horses; check that the horses are fit and properly cared for. Recommended for horses are **Cocozuma Traveller** and **Aventuras Montezuma**.

Where to stay

Playa Naranjo

$$ Oasis del Pacífico
On beach, T2661-0209.
A/c, old building, clean, quiet, with pool, good restaurant and free transport from ferry. Recommended.

$ Cabinas Maquinay
1.3 km towards Jicaral, T2661-1763.
Simple rooms with a pool and the attached **Disco Maquinay**.

$ El Paso
North of ferry, T2641-8133.
With bath, cheaper without, cold water, clean, restaurant and pool.

Tambor, Curú National Wildlife Refuge and Cóbano

$$$$ Tango Mar
3 km from Tambor, T2683-0001, www.tangomar.com.
All services including golf course and its own waterfall.

$ Cabinas Cristina
On the beach, Tambor, T2683-0028.
With bath, cheaper without, good food.

$ Dos Lagartos
Tambor, T2683-0236.
Cheap, clean, good value.

Montezuma

Montezuma is a very small place; hotels furthest from the centre are a 10-min walk.

$$$ El Tajalín
T2642-0061, www.tajalin.com.
Very smart hotel, spotlessly clean, rooms come with private hot water shower and a/c, located in a quiet out of the way spot and yet moments from the high street. Hammock terrace for relaxing.

$$$-$$ Amor de Mar
T2642-0262, www.amordemar.com.
This well-loved hotel has the feeling of a special place. Rooms are pristine with private bath and hot water. Breakfast and brunch is served on a very pretty terrace that joins well-manicured gardens, where visitors can recline in hammocks and gaze out to sea.

$$$-$$ El Jardín
T642 0074, www.hoteleljardin.com.
15 rooms and 2 fully equipped villas located on the hill overlooking the town and ocean beyond. Shower, hot water, a/c, private terraces and hammocks. In the grounds is a pool with a little waterfall, very restful and great views, superb spot.

$$$-$$ Los Mangos
A short walk south of the village, T2642-0076, www.hotellosmangos.com.
Large site comprising 9 bungalows, each accommodating 3 people. Also 10 rooms, some with shared bath, some for 4 people. Yoga classes run from an open-sided pagoda on the grounds. Different and fun and lots of free mangos (when in season).

$$ Cabinas Mar y Cielo
On the beach, T2642-0261.
Has 6 rooms, sleeping 2-5 people, all with bath, fan and sea view. Recommended.

$$ Horizontes
On road to Cóbano, T2642-0534, www.horizontes-montezuma.com.
Language school, restaurant, pool, hot water. Highly recommended.

$$ Montezuma Paradise
10 mins' walk out of town, on the road to Cabuya, past the waterfall entrance, T2642-0271.
Very friendly owners have rooms with shared bath and 1 with private bath, overlooking the ocean and minutes from a secluded beach cove.

$$-$ La Cascada
5 mins' walk out of town, on the road to Cabo Blanco, close to the entrance to the waterfalls, T2642-0057.
Lovely hotel with pretty, well-kept rooms and a wide hammock terrace overlooking the ocean for relaxing. Restaurant serves local food for breakfast, lunch and dinner.

$ El Tucán
At the top of the road down to the beach, T2642-0284.
Wooden hotel on stilts, clean, small wood-panelled rooms, shared shower and toilet, fan, mosquito net on window. Recommended.

$ Hotel El Capitán
On the main street, T2642-0069.
Old wooden house with an endless variety of rooms, most with shared cold-water bath, but some with private bath. Very friendly owners and good location, can get a little noisy, good for backpackers.

$ Lucy
Follow road south past Los Mangos, T2642-0273.
One of the oldest hotels in town and one of the most popular budget options, due to its location on the sea. 10 rooms with fans, some with sea view. Shared bath, pleasant balcony. Ultra-friendly Tica owner. Restaurant next door opens during high season. Recommended.

$ Pensión Arenas
On the beach, T2642-0308.
Run by Doña Meca, rustic small rooms, with fan, shared bath, no frills but pleasant balcony and sea view. Free camping. Laundry service. Cheap.

Around Montezuma

$$$$ Milarepa
Playa Santa Teresa, on beach, T2640-0023, www.milarepahotel.com.
Nice bamboo bungalows, open-air bathroom.

$$$ Celaje
Cabuya, on beach, T2642-0374, www.celaje.com.
Very good Italian restaurant. Pool, rooms with bath, hot water, good.

$$$-$$ Los Caballos
3 km north on road to Cóbano from Montezuma, T2642-0124.
Has 8 rooms with bath, pool, outdoor restaurant, ocean views, gardens. 5 mins from beach. Great horse-riding trips.

$$$-$ Funky Monkey Lodge
Santa Teresa, T2640-0317, www.funky-monkey-lodge.com.
The very friendly and hospitable owners have extended their relaxed and very attractive resort. They now have 1 bungalow sleeping 8 people, 3 private bungalows and 2 apartments, sleeping 2-4 and a suite with a large balcony overlooking the ocean. They also have a rather upmarket dormitory with beds rather than bunks. Recommended.

$$$-$ Mal País Surf Camp
Mal País, T2640-0031, www.malpaissurfcamp.com.
Restaurant, pool, also has camping.

$$-$ Cabañas Bosque Mar
Mal País, T2640-0074.
Clean, large rooms, hot-water shower, attractive grounds, good restaurant on beach nearby, 3 km to Cabo Blanco Reserve.

$$-$ Cabinas Las Rocas
20 mins south of Montezuma, T2642-0393, www.caboblancopark.com.
Good but quite expensive meals, small, seashore setting, isolated.

$$-$ Frank's Place
Mal País, the road junction, T2640-0096.
Set in tropical gardens. Wide variety of rooms with private or shared bath and self-catering options available. Good range of services and local advice.

$ Cabañas Playa El Carmen
Playa Santa Teresa, T2683-0281.

Basic, very cheap cabins and camping, shared bath and kitchen. **Jungle Juice**, vegetarian restaurant, serves smoothies and meals from US$4.

$ Cabinas y Restaurante El Ancla de Oro
Cabuya, T2642-0369.
Some cabins with bath, others shared bathroom, seafood restaurant, lobster dinners US$10, filling breakfasts, owned by Alex Villalobos, horses US$20 per day with local guide, mountain bike rental, transport from Paquera launch available.

$ Casa Zen
Santa Teresa.
Smart, budget accommodation with shared bath and 1 fully furnished apartment. Camping area also available. Close to the beach, restaurant on site.

$ Mochila Inn
300 m outside Montezuma, T2642-0030.
Cabinas from US$30, also houses and apartments for around US$350 per month.

Restaurants

Montezuma

$$$ Playa de Los Artistas/Cocina Mediterránea
About 5 mins south of town on the road to Cabuya.
Best restaurant in town.

$$ Bakery Café
North end of town.
Great for breakfast, with bread, cakes and excellent vegetarian food.

$$ Brisas del Mar
Just south of the soccer ground in Santa Teresa.
Offers great local seafood – tuna or *mahi mahi* straight from the boats at Mal País. Great service and atmosphere. Highly recommended.

$$ Chico's Playa Bar
On the beach.
Popular hangout, great sushi. They stop serving food in the low season.

$$ Cocolores
On the beach behind El Pargo Feliz, T2642-0096. Closed Mon.
Good for seafood and veggie options.

$ El Pulpo Pizzeria
Santa Teresa
Good-value pizzeria that also delivers.

$$ El Sano Banano
On the road to the beach.
Healthfood restaurant, good vegetarian food, large helpings, daily change of menu, milkshakes, fresh fruit and yoghurt, owned by Dutch/Americans, free movies with dinner.

$$ Pizza Romana
Opposite El Capitán.
Good Italian food cooked by Italians, pizzas, pesto, fresh pastas, etc.

$$-$ Tayrona
Behind Taganga.
Great pizza, Italian-owned, attractive restaurant off the main street.

$ Soda El Caracol
Located by the football field.
One of several *sodas* around town serving good Tico food, very cheap.

$ Soda Monte Sol
On the road to Cabo Blanco.
Recommended for good Mexican burritos, good value, big helpings.

$ Taganga
Located at the top of the high street, opposite El Tucán hostel.
Argentine grills, chicken and meat.

Entertainment

Montezuma
Bar Moctezuma, usually open the latest, but not as loud as the others.
Chico's Bar and **Chico's Playa Bar**, cocktail by the beach, or late-night salsa dancing and very loud reggaeton parties.
Congo Azul Bar, reggae nights Thu and Sat.

Around Montezuma

New bars are opening up every year along the beachfront at Mal País. For a treat, try a *mojito* on the terrace at the exclusive resort of **Flor Blanca** at the northern edge of Santa Teresa. **Bar Tabu**, *Santa Teresa*. Probably the most popular bar in the area, great location on the beach; good music, always lively, open late. **La Llora Amarilla**, *Santa Teresa*. Now very popular, large venue that hosts regular disco and party nights.

Mal País Surf Camp, *Mal País*. Bar open every night, live jam night on Wed.

Shopping

Sámara

Free Radical supermarket/*soda* on main road, 1 km east of town centre. Fresh ceviche, delightful pastries, beer, wine, natural juices, local honey and unusual hand-blown glass products.

Supermarket, *near Casa del Mar*. Well stocked and you can get fresh bread and croissants from **Chez Joel**.

Montezuma

There are rather pricey boutique-style souvenir and clothes shops in Montezuma, most selling a very similar range.

Librería Topsy, *T2642-0576. Mon-Fri 0800-1400, Sat 0800-1200*. Sells books and maps and will take postcards and small letters to the post office for you.

What to do

Montezuma

Aventuras en Montezuma, *T2642-0050*. Offers a similar range, snorkelling to Tortuga Island, canopy, sunset and wildlife tours for similar prices, also taxi boat to Jacó, US$35, minimum 5 people. Ivan and his staff are also very helpful as a tourist office and can advise on hotels and other matters locally and nationally. They also book and confirm flights.

Cocozuma Traveller, *T2642-0911, www. cocozumacr.com*. Tico-owned company, now one of the best in Montezuma. Runs all the usual tours including horse rides and Isla Tortuga. Their boat taxi now runs to Jacó (US$40), Sámara (US$40) and Tamarindo (US$40). They will also arrange hotels, transfers, car rental and have quadbikes for hire. Very helpful staff are happy to give information about the area.

Montezuma Eco Tours, *on the corner opposite Soda Monte Sol, T2642-1000, www. montezumaecotours.com*. Offer a wide range of tours, including shuttle to Cabo Blanco (US$3), kayaking/snorkelling at Isla Cabuya (US$25 per person), day trip to Isla Tortuga (US$40 per person), horse rental (US$25) and bike rental (US$5 per day). Also boat/road transfers to Jacó/Tamarindo for around US$150 for up to 6 people.

Montezuma Expeditions, *top of the high street, T2642-0919, www.montezuma expeditions.com*. Very efficient set up organizing private and group transport around the country. Trips cost US$35-US$48 per person, and include San José, La Fortuna (Arenal), Monteverde and Jacó.

Zuma Tours, *Cóbano, T8849-8569, www. zumatours.net*. Lots of information available on their website.

Transport

Montezuma

Bus To **Paquera** daily at 0530, 0815, 1000, 1215, 1400 and 1600, connecting with the car and passenger ferry to **Puntarenas** central docks. Tickets available in advance from tourist information centre; be at bus stop outside **Hotel Moctezuma** in good time as the bus fills up quickly, US$2.60, 1 hr (paved road). To **Cabuya** US$1, buses run 4 times a day. Change at Cóbano for **Mal País** – 2 buses run daily from Cóbano, 1100 and 1400 (check as times can change).

Taxi To **Cóbano** US$5. To **Paquera** US$20.

Central
Pacific coast

West of the central highlands lies a narrow lowland strip of African palm with just the occasional cattle ranch. But, for the visitor, it is the miles of beaches stretching from Jacó almost continuously south to Uvita that are the real attraction. Parque Nacional Manuel Antonio is a major destination with developed services. Further south, the beaches are quieter and the Parque Nacional Marino Ballena, which is harder to get to, is barely developed; but it's of interest to divers and whalewatchers.

Puntarenas and around

a decaying port and pleasure resort

West of San José and the Meseta Central, the Pan-American Highway descends 800 m to Esparza, an attractive town that was repeatedly sacked by pirates in the 17th century, belying its peaceful nature today. A further 15 km west, Barranca marks the turning for Puntarenas, no more than six avenues wide, which fills a 5-km spit thrusting east–west into the Gulf of Nicoya. Once the country's main Pacific port with rail links to the Central Highlands, it has since been superseded by Caldera a few kilometres to the south.

The northern side of the peninsula, around Calle Central, has a market, banks, a few grimy hotels and the fishing docks. It is run down and neglected, typical of small tropical ports. In an effort to reinvent itself as a tourist destination, the southern side is made up of the **Paseo de las Turistas**, a seafront esplanade that draws crowds to the hot, sometimes dirty beach, especially at weekends.

Most people come to Puntarenas to party, but the town boasts a handful of modest attractions. In the cultural centre by the main church and tourist office, you'll find the mildly diverting **Museo de la Historia Marina** ① *T2661-5036, Tue-Sun 0945-1200, 1300-1715, US$1.80.* **Puntarenas Marine Park** ① *T2661-5272, www.parquemarino.org, daily 0900-1700, US$10 children US$5,* offers 28 large aquariums showing Costa Rica's marine life. In the gulf are several islands including the **Islas Negritas**, a biological reserve reached by passenger launches.

Puntarenas is popular with Tico tourists, but largely overlooked by foreign travellers, who use it as nothing more than a transport hub; from Puntarenas, you can take the ferry to the southern Nicoya Peninsula, or a bus north or south to other parts of the country without returning to San José. If heading for Nicoya, see page 101. If heading to Santa Elena/Monteverde, see page 75.

Esparza to the Pacific coast

From Esparza on the Pan-American Highway a road runs 21 km southeast to **San Mateo** (from where a road runs northeast to Atenas and the Central Highlands; see page 50). Just before San Mateo, at Higuito de San Mateo, is **Las Candelillas** ① *T2428-9157*, a 26-ha farm and reforestation project with fruit trees and sugar cane. There is a day use recreational area with showers, pool and riding, trails and bar/restaurant.

From San Mateo a road runs south to **Orotina**, which used to be an important road/rail junction on the San José–Puntarenas route. Today the area is home to **Original Canopy Tour** at **Mahogany Park** ① *T2257-5149, www.canopytour.com*, which charges US$45 to fly through the trees; transportation is available.

West of Orotina the road forks northwest to the port of **Caldera**, via Cascajal, and southwest to the Pacific coast at Tárcoles.

Listings Puntarenas and around

Where to stay

Puntarenas
Accommodation is difficult to find from Dec-Apr, especially at weekends.

$$$$-$$$ Tioga
On the beachfront with Calle 17, T2661-0271, www.hoteltioga.com.
54 rooms; those with balconies are much better, with views. Private bath, a/c, TV and telephone. Restaurant, pool, very good.

$$ La Punta
Av 1, Calle 35, T2661-0696.
Good spot 1 block from car ferry, with bath, hot water, secure parking, good pool. American-owned, big rooms, friendly, clean.

$$-$ Gran Hotel Chorotega
On the corner of Calle 1, Av 3 near the banks and market, T2661-0998, www.hotelchorotega.com.
Clean rooms with private bath, cheaper with shared. Efficient and friendly service. Popular with visiting business people. A good deal.

Restaurants

Puntarenas

$$ Casa de Mariscos
Calle 7-9, T2661-1666. Closed Wed.
On the beachfront, good seafood, reasonable prices.

$$ La Yunta
On the beachfront at Calle 19, T2661-3216.
A popular steakhouse, open all night.

$ Soda Macarena
Opposite the Muelle de Cruceros (dock).
Handy while waiting for buses.

Transport

Puntarenas
Bus Terminal for San José is at Calle 2, Av 2-4. Buses every 40 mins, 0415-1900 to **San José**, 2 hrs, US$4.30. Daily bus to **Santa Elena** for Monteverde, 0750, 1350, 1415, 5 hrs, US$2.50. Buses south to **Quepos** from main bus station, 6 daily via **Jacó**, US$$2.00, 4 hrs, return 0430, 1030, 1630. To **Liberia** with **Empresa Pulmitan**, first at 0600, last 1500, 4 hrs, US$1.50. To **Tilarán** via **Cañas** at 1130 and 1630, US$2. Good café at bus terminal.

Ferry The ferry dock is about 1 km from Puntarenas bus station, local buses run between the 2, otherwise walk or get a taxi (US$2-3).

Check which dock your ferry leaves from. For the **Nicoya Peninsula** see page 101. To **Playa Naranjo** at 0630, 1000, 1420, 1930, returning at 0800, 1230, 1730, 2100, 1½ hrs. T2661-1069, www.coonatramar.com, for exact times. Pedestrians US$1.70, motorbikes US$6, cars US$24.

Buses meet the ferry for **Nicoya** (through Carmona, 40 km unpaved, 30 km paved road, crowded, noisy, frequently break down, US$1.25, 2¼ hrs), **Sámara** (US$1.30), **Coyote**, **Bejuco** and **Jicaral**.

From the same dock a car ferry goes to **Paquera** at 0500, 0900, 1100, 1400, 1700, 2030, returning at 0530, 0900, 1100, 1400, 1700, 2000, 1½ hrs, US$1.70, T2661-2084, www.navieratambor.com, to check the times. On arrival, get on the bus (which waits for the ferry) as quickly as possible (to **Cóbano**, 2-3 hrs, US$1.25, bad road, to **Montezuma** US$2.60, 1½ hrs at least); pay on the bus, or get a taxi. Note: last bus meets the 1700 ferry only.

The Costanera to Quepos

wildlife reserves and attractive surf beaches

The Costanera or coastal road passes through Jacó, Manuel Antonio and Quepos and on to Dominical before heading inland to San Isidro de El General, or continuing south to Palmar Norte. If you want a popular beach, pick somewhere before Manuel Antonio. Beyond Manuel Antonio, although not deserted, you'll find things a lot quieter. If driving, leave nothing of value in your vehicle; thefts, robberies and scams are regularly reported. The Costanera is plied by all long-distance buses heading to the southern zone.

Reserva Biológica Carara
Daily 0700-1600, US$15.

Between Orotina and Jacó the Carara Biological Reserve (5242 ha) is rich in wildlife. Three trails lead through the park: one, lasting a couple of hours, leaves from close to Tarcoles bridge; the others, lasting a little over one hour, leave from the ranger station to the south. The reserve protects a transitional zone from the dry north coast of the country to the very humid region of the southeast. Spider monkeys, scarlet macaws and coatis can all be seen in the reserve.

One of the most popular free experiences in Costa Rica is to peer over the side of the Río Tárcoles bridge to see the opaque sediment-filled waters broken by the bony backs of the somnolent crocodiles below. It's easy to find the spot to stop, as cars cram the roadside, especially at dawn and dusk when scarlet macaws can be seen returning to their roosts from Carara Biological Reserve on the southern banks of the river.

You can get a closer look by taking a boat tour with **Jungle Crocodile Safari** ① *T2241-1853, www.junglecrocodilesafari.com*, or José's **Crocodile River Tour** ① *T2637-0795, www.crocodile rivertour.com, US$25 per person from the dock in Tárcoles, US$35 round trip from Jacó.*

Next to Carara is **La Catarata** ① *T2236-4140, 0800-1500, 15 Dec-15 Apr, US$7.50*, a private reserve with an impressive waterfall with natural pools for bathing. Take the gravel road up the hill beside **Hotel Villa Lapas**: it's 5 km to the entrance and a 2.5-km hike to falls and pools, but it's worth the effort. There are signs on the main road.

Jacó

A short distance from Carara is Jacó, a large stretch of sandy beach, with a lively and youthful energy. It is popular with surfers and weekenders from San José and comes with a rough'n'ready, earthy commercial appeal. If you want to learn to surf, this is as good a place as any, with several surf shops offering courses and boards for rent. If you want to party with crowds on their annual holiday, it's a great spot. If you're looking for peace and quiet, go elsewhere.

Jacó to Quepos

From Jacó the potholed road runs down the coastline with lovely views of the ocean. The beaches are far quieter and, if you have a car, you can take your pick. A few kilometres south is **Playa Hermosa**, which is right on the main road and has a popular surfing beach. If travelling by car, 20 km further and a few kilometres off the road is **Playa Bejuco**, **Esterillos Centro** and **Playa Palma**, near Parrita; definitely worth exploring. Beyond **Parrita** (Banco Nacional, Banco de Costa Rica, a gas station and a few stores) the road travels through a flat landscape of endless African palm plantations. Many of the plantation villages are of passing interest for their two-storey, balconied houses laid out around a central football pitch, a church of some denomination and the obligatory branch of AA. The carriageway narrows to single track on bridges along this road so take care if you're driving, especially at night.

Quepos

Developed as a banana exporting port by United Brands, Quepos was forced to reinvent itself following the devastation of banana plantations in the region overwhelmed by Panama disease, in the early 1950s. Endless rows of oil-producing African palm have replaced the bananas and Quepos has long since shrugged off the portside image, to the extent that few even bother to explore the dock at the southern end of town.

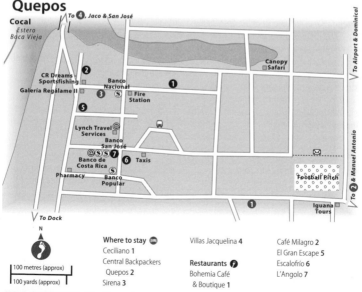

Quepos

To Jaco & San José · Cocal · Estero Boca Vieja · Canopy Safari · CR Dreams Sportsfishing · Banco Nacional · Galería Regálame II · Fire Station · Lynch Travel Services · Banco San José · Banco de Costa Rica · Taxis · Pharmacy · Banco Popular · Football Pitch · Iguana Tours · To Airport & Dominical · To Manuel Antonio · To 2 & Manuel Antonio · To Dock

N

100 metres (approx)
100 yards (approx)

Where to stay 🛏
Ceciliano **1**
Central Backpackers
  Quepos **2**
Sirena **3**
Villas Jacquelina **4**

Restaurants 🍴
Bohemia Café
  & Boutique **1**
Café Milagro **2**
El Gran Escape **5**
Escalofrío **6**
L'Angolo **7**

Southeast of Quepos, a winding road, lined with hotels, bars, restaurants and stores rises and falls for 7 km before reaching the stunning coastline of Parque Nacional Manuel Antonio (see below) and nearby beautiful beaches. Quepos plays an important role as a service town for local and foreign tourists. It is cheaper than the Manuel Antonio road, there is no shortage of restaurants, bars and shops, and regular buses make the journey to the national park. Tell the bus driver where you are going and you'll be dropped at your chosen hotel.

Listings The Costanera to Quepos map p114

Where to stay

Reserva Biológica Carara

$$$$ Villa Caletas
Punta Leona, to the south of the reserve,
T2637-0505, www.hotelvillacaletas.com.
One of Costa Rica's most distinctive hotels. French-owned, divine rooms and 14 villas atop a mountain with amazing views, spectacular sunsets, lush gardens, pool, restaurant, boat and nature tours.

Jacó

Accommodation in Jacó is overpriced; look for discounts May-Nov.

$$$$ Doce Lunas Hotel
Quebrada Seca, 400 m east of the Costanera,
T2643-2211, www.docelunas.com.
Located on the edge of the jungle, 2 km from the beach, Doce Luna is a tranquil and verdant retreat. Rooms are spacious and tastefully attired with hardwood furniture and all modern conveniences including cable TV, minibar, coffee-maker, a/c. Wedding and yoga packages available.

$$$ Hotel Mar de Luz
Av Pastor Díaz, next to the Subway,
T2643-3000, www.mardeluz.com.
A family-orientated hotel with a sustainable ethos, solar panels, pool and comfortable rooms with all the usual amenities, some with kitchenettes. Cool, clean, quiet and secluded from the downtown mayhem.

$$$ Hotel Paraíso Escondido
150 m east of the Catholic church on Calle Los Cholos, T2643-2883, www.hoteljaco.com.
Romantic villa-style lodging. All rooms with a private bath, patio and a/c, rooms cheaper with fan. Pool and laundry service. The owner often meets arriving buses. Good spot and worth the price.

$$$ Posada Jacó
Calle Bohío, T2643-1951, www.posadajaco.com.
Hidden on a quiet side street next to a river, Posada Jacó is a low-key option with limited ocean views and a small pool. They have 6 comfortable suites equipped with a/c, cable TV, safe, kitchenette, fridge, microwave, phone and coffee-maker. Intimate and easy-going.

$$$-$ Room2board hostel and surf school
10 m south of Bahía Azul, in front of the beach, T2643-4949, www.room2board.com.
Upscale 'boutique' hostel with stylish private rooms ($$$), shared rooms ($$) and dorms ($). Lots of amenities including Wi-Fi, TVs, pool, yoga room, lockers, laundry. Surf camp crowd and atmosphere.

$$-$ Buddha House Boutique Hostel
Av Pastor Díaz, T2643-3615,
www.hostelbuddhahouse.com.
A cheery 'boutique' party hostel with a mixture of rooms, with or without private bath ($$), and spacious 5-bed dorms ($). Services include surfboard rental, surf lessons, yoga, massage, tours, pool and hammocks. Laid-back and friendly.

$$-$ Hotel Kangaroo
At the southern end of town, T2643-3351,
www.hotelkangaroo.info.
Mix of dorms and private rooms, but it's the atmosphere that keeps people happy and recommending this place.

Jacó to Quepos

$$$ Beso del Viento
Playa Palo Seco, 5 km, T2779-9674,
www.besodelviento.com.
Surrounded by palm trees a block from the
beach, French-owned Beso del Viento is an
intimate little B&B with 12 stylish rooms, a
restaurant and an oval-shaped pool.

$$$ Hotel Pelícano
Esterillos Este, T2778-8105, www.
pelicanbeachfronthotel.com.
50 m from the Pacific Ocean, with
13 boutique rooms, café-restaurant, pool,
private airstrip at the back, beach at the
front. French/Canadian owners, great spot.
Recommended.

$$$ Hotel Sandpiper Inn
T2643-7042, www.sandpipercostarica.com.
A 2-storey hotel with 2 spacious oceanfront
rooms with custom-made furniture and
rustic tile work, all well equipped, a/c,
coolers, Wi-Fi and cable TV. Also pool,
restaurant, sportfishing.

Quepos

It's difficult to find accommodation on Sat
Dec-Apr and when schools are on holiday.
There are many cheap *cabinas* (**$**), some
clean, some grungy, most of them clustered
on the east side of town.

$$$ Hotel Sirena
Near bus station, T2777-0572,
www.lasirenahotel.com.
The best option in town for its price
bracket. La Sirena has 14 quite good rooms
overlooking a small pool, restaurant/tiki bar
and garden, all with mini-fridge, digital safe,
a/c, cable TV. Breakfast included.

$$ Villas Jacquelina
550 m north of Puente Lolo, T8345-1516,
www.villasjacquelina.com.
A villa-style B&B with an eco-friendly ethos,
pool, patios, balconies and mountain views.

Comfortable no-frills rooms feature crisp
sheets and bright artwork, cheaper with
shared bath. Friendly, clean, US/Tico-owned.

$$-$ Central Backpackers Quepos
Playa Manuel Antonio road,
in front of the INVU, T2777-2321,
www.centralbackpackers.hostel.com.
Friendly, quiet, low-key hostel, simple and
economical. Dorms and private rooms
available. Friendly, basic, family-run.

$ Ceciliano
Towards the eastern side of town, on the road
leading to Manuel Antonio, T2777-0192.
Family-run, quiet, small rooms, with bath,
hot. One of many cheapies, not great, but OK
for budget wanderers. Good central location.

Restaurants

Jacó
There are lots of *sodas* in Jacó.

$$$ Sunrise Grill Breakfast Place
Centre of town. Closed Wed.
Breakfast from 0700.

$$$ Wishbone
On the main street.
Big plates of Mexican food, from US$6.

$$ Chatty Cathy's
On the main drag.
A popular dining spot.

$$ La Ostra
Centre of town.
Good fish in this pleasant open-air restaurant
open all day.

$$ Wahoo
Just within the centre to the north.
Good Tico food, mainly fish.

Jacó to Quepos

$ Doña María's Soda
Parrita, T8842-3047.
Small central market, tasty *casados*.

Quepos
There are many good restaurants along the road towards Manuel Antonio.

$$$-$$ Bohemia Café & Boutique
Av 3, Calle Central-2. Tue-Sun.
Friendly healthfood restaurant with a bohemian ambiance and indie clothing for sale. The coconut Mahi Mahi is a good choice, followed by the chocolate volcano. Flavourful.

$$$-$$ El Gran Escape
Central, T2777-0395.
Lively collection of restaurants and bars offering Tex Mex, pizza and sushi. Good food and service, recommended.

$$ Escalofrío
Next to Dos Locos.
Pizza, pasta and ice cream to die for from US$4.

Cafés, snacks and bakeries
The municipal market (for fruit and bread) is at the bus station.

Café Milagro
On the waterfront, T2777-0794, www.cafemilagro.com.
Best espresso, cakes, pies, Cuban cigars, souvenirs, freshly roasted coffee for sale; another branch on the road to Manuel Antonio.

L'Angolo
Opposite Dos Locos.
Serves a mix of breads, olives, hams and everything you'd need for self-catering or picnicking in style.

What to do

Quepos
Language schools
Costa Rica Spanish Institute, *T2234-1001, www.cosi.co.cr.*

Escuela D'Amore, *halfway between Quepos and the national park, T2777-1143, www. escueladamore.com.* Immersion school, living with local families, in a great setting overlooking the ocean.

Tour operators
Amigos del Río, *opposite the football pitch, T2777-0082, www.amigosdelrio.net.* River rafting, kayaking, canopy and horse-riding tours, good guides.
Iguana Tours, *close to the church on the football pitch, T2777-2052, www.iguanatours. com.* Excellent local knowledge with many tours available. Friendly and helpful.
Lynch Travel Services, *right in the centre of town, T2777-0161, www.lynchtravel.com.*

Transport

Jacó
Bus From **San José** Coca Cola bus station, Calle 16, Av 1-3, 7 daily, 2½ hrs, US$4.30, arrive at Plaza Jacó-Complex terminal at north end of town, next to **Pizza Hut**. Also several buses to/from Puntarenas and **Quepos**.

Quepos
Air There are several daily flights from **San José**, with **Sansa** (US$63-79) and **Nature Air**, from around US$50 one-way. The **Sansa** office is under Hotel Quepos, T2777-0683.

Bus There are 6 buses to Quepos daily from the Terminal Tracopa, Calle 5, Av 18-20, 4 hrs, US$6.30. From Quepos, there are buses northwest along the coast to **Puntarenas**, 7 daily, 3½ hrs, 2 daily buses via **Dominical** to **San Isidro de El General**, T2771-4744, 0500 and 1330, 3½ hrs, US$4, connections can be made there to get to the Panamanian border, return 0700, 1330.

Taxi Taxis congregate opposite the bus terminal, just up from **Dos Locos** restaurant. Minibuses meet flights.

From the southeastern corner of Quepos, a road winds up, over and round the peninsula of Punta Quepos, passing the flourishing hotels, restaurants, bars and stores along the length of this rocky outcrop.

Travelling the road for the first time, you can't fail to be impressed by the beauty of the views. And at night, you can't help being blinded by the neon lights that speckle the hillside – evidence of the vibrant tourist trade. At times it is difficult to believe a national park flourishes on the other side of the watershed. The impact on what was once an attractive stretch of jungle-clad coastline is indisputable. For some it is an environmental catastrophe, for others it is a demonstration of the importance of planning to protect.

With 683 ha of mangrove swamps and beaches, home to a rich variety of fauna and flora, Manuel Antonio National Park can rightly claim to be the country's second best wildlife reserve, after Volcán Poás. Just 7 km south of Quepos on a paved road, three beautiful, forest-fringed beaches stretch along the coastline and around the headland of Punta Catedral: **Espadilla Sur**, **Manuel Antonio** and **Puerto Escondido**. Iguanas and white-faced monkeys often come down to the sand.

In addition to enjoying the beaches, hiking is also good in the park. A 45-minute trail, steep in places, runs round the Punta Catedral between Espadilla Sur and Manuel Antonio beaches. If you're early and quiet, it is possible to see a surprising amount of wildlife. A second walk to Puerto Escondido, where there is a blowhole, takes about 50 minutes. The map sold at the entrance shows a walk up to a mirador, with good views of the coastline.

Essential Parque Nacional Manuel Antonio

Opening hours and entry fee

Tuesday-Sunday 0700-1600. US$15.

Services and facilities

Guides are available, but not essential, at the entrance. You can buy breakfast and other meals from the stalls just before the river, where cars can be parked and minded for US$1 by the stallholders. Basic toilets, picnic tables and drinks are available by the beaches. Cold water showers can be found at Manuel Antonio and Espadilla Sur beaches.

When to go

It's best to go early or late in the day to see the wildlife.

Manuel Antonio has been a victim of its own success, with some of the animals becoming almost tame. But for all the criticism of recent years, it is still beautiful and highly enjoyable. Overdevelopment outside the park and overuse within has led to problems of how to manage the park with inadequate funds. You are not allowed to feed the monkeys but people do, which means that they can be a nuisance, congregating around picnic tables expecting to be fed and rummaging through bags given the chance. Leave no litter and take nothing out of the park, not even seashells.

The range of activities in the area outside the park is slightly bewildering. Sea kayaking is possible, as is mountain biking, hiking, canopy tours, canyoning, deep-sea fishing and even quad biking. Most hotels will assist with booking trips and there are agencies in Quepos that can also advise. **Note** The beaches in the park are safer than those outside, but rip tides are dangerous all along the coast. Beaches slope steeply and the force of the waves can be too strong for children.

Listings Parque Nacional Manuel Antonio

Where to stay

There are hotels all along the road from Quepos to Manuel Antonio, many of them expensive. Many shut in the low season; in high season, it's best to book ahead. The area is full to bursting at weekends with locals camping on the beach.

$$$$ Makanda by the Sea
Down a dirt road leading to Punta Quepos from opposite Café Milagro, T2777-0442, www.makanda.com.
11 villas and studios with superb open design. An idyllic and romantic paradise spot.

$$$$ Sí Como No
T2777-0777, www.sicomono.com.
A superb hotel with beautiful touches of design using stunning stained glass, all the comforts you would expect, and service par excellence plus a cinema.

$$$$-$$$ Costa Verde
At the train carriage restaurant and reception, T2777-0584, www.costaverde.com.
Apartments for 2-4 people, with kitchenette and bath, 2-bedroom villas available, well appointed, pool and a couple of restaurants. Several nature trails out the back. Recommended.

$$$ Coyaba Tropical
Manuel Antonio road, 1 km south of Quepos, T2777-6279, www.coyabatropical.com.
This excellent, homely B&B is housed in a tastefully restored Spanish colonial building, complete with pool, jacuzzi and lush gardens. Tasteful rooms and friendly hospitable hosts.

$$ B&B Casa Buena Vista
T2777-1002, www.casabuenavista.net.
A private house offering a breathtaking view and wonderful breakfast terrace, friendly owner. Shared kitchen, breakfast included.

$$ Hotel Manuel Antonio
T2777-1237, www.hotelmanuelantonio.com.
Good breakfast, camping possible nearby, ask in the restaurant. Handy, just minutes from the national park and the beach.

Transport

Bus There are several buses to the park daily from the Terminal Tracopa in **San José**. At weekends buy your ticket the day before; buses fill to standing room only very quickly. Roads back to San José on Sun evening are packed. A regular bus service runs roughly ½-hourly from beside **Quepos** market, starting at 0545, to Manuel Antonio, last bus back at 1700, US$0.35.

Car If driving, there is ample guarded parking in the area, US$6.

Taxi From **Quepos**, approximately US$10. Minibuses meet flights from San José to the airport at Quepos (see above), US$2.25.

★ Playa Matapalo

Some 30 km southeast from the congestion of Quepos towards Dominical the unpaved coastal road drifts almost unnoticed through Playa Matapalo, where you'll find an expansive, beautiful sandy beach recommended for surfing, relaxing and playing with your ideas of paradise. Other activities, in an overwhelmingly Swiss community, include fishing, horse riding and hiking to mountain waterfalls.

Dominical

Some 12 km further on, at the mouth of the Río Barú, is Dominical, a small town with a population of a few hundred. No more than 500 m from one end to the other it's popular with surfers and often busy. Hotel prices soar in high season and most hotels are close to noisy bars. Treks and horse-riding trips to waterfalls are possible if the beach is too much to bear. Just north of the town **Hacienda Barú** has a **national wildlife preserve**, with activities like abseiling, canopy tours and nature walks (see below). If you want to brush up your Spanish try the **Adventure Education Center** ① *T2787-0023, www.adventurespanishschool. com*, with an immersion Spanish school. They have schools in Arenal and Turrialba as well. But most people come here for the surfing; if you want to learn, visit the **Green Iguana Surf Camp** ① *T8825-1381, www.greeniguanasurfcamp.com*, who provide board hire, group lessons, individual lessons and package deals.

Punta Dominical is 4 km south of town (no transport). A poor dirt road follows a steep path inland up the Escaleras (stairs) to some secluded accommodation blending beach and rainforest.

Uvita

If you get the impression the southern Pacific coast is about beaches, you'd be right. The village of Uvita, 18 km south of Dominical, has beautiful beaches all along the coastline. You can walk in the nearby forests, swim in nearby waterfalls or at the beach, take a boat trip and watch birds. Ballena Marine National Park (see below) protects over 5000 ha of Pacific coral reef and humpback whales can be sighted at nearby Isla Ballena between December and April.

The road south from Uvita is paved all the way to Palmar Norte and access to the beaches of Playa Ballena and Playa Bahía has become easier in recent years with development of the area.

Parque Nacional Marino Ballena

There is a nominal entrance fee of US$6 which is rarely collected.

The vast majority of Ballena (Whale) Marine National Park is coastal waters – 5161 ha against 116 ha of protected land – which may go some way to explaining why there isn't a lot to see at this least-developed national park. The underwater world is home to coral reefs and abundant marine life that includes common and bottle-nosed dolphins as well as occasional visits from humpback whales at times seen with their calves.

Although there is a rarely staffed **rangers station** ① *T2786-7161*, in Bahía, and signposts line the Costanera, the infrastructure in the park is non-existent. Along the beach at Bahía is a turtle-nesting project administered by the local community. As with the park itself, the organization is very ad hoc – visitors and volunteers are welcome. Beachcombing is good, as is snorkelling when the tides are favourable. Boat trips to the island can be arranged from Bahía and diving is starting up with the most recommended local being Máximo Vásquez, or Chumi as he is known. The coastal road continues south beside **Playa Tortuga**, passing small communities of foreigners hiding and enjoying one of the quietest spots near a beach in Costa Rica, to join the Pan-American Highway at Palmar Norte (see page 126).

Listings Quepos to Palmar Norte

Where to stay

Dominical

$$$$ Cascadas Farallas
About 5 km from Dominical, T2787-4137,
www.waterfallvillas.com.
Wonderfully romantic Balinese-style villas overlooking the falls. Set up for spiritual work, including yoga retreats, spa treatments, weddings and honeymoons.

$$$ Bella Vista Lodge
Punta Dominical, T305-975 0003,
www.bellavistalodge.com.
Great view, good large meals, owned by local American, organizes trips in the area. There are also houses to rent.

$$$ Hacienda Barú
About 2 km north of Dominical, T2787-0003,
www.haciendabaru.com.
A 332-ha reserve that began life as a private reserve in 1972. Cabins sleeping 3 or more with private bath, hiking and riding. So much to see and do in such a small area. There is a canopy observation platform, tree climbing, night walks in the jungle, several self-guided trails and a butterfly garden.

$$$ Pacific Edge
Costanera Km 48, Punta Dominical,
T2200-5428, www.pacificedge.info.
4 large cabins with great views of ocean and rainforest.

$$$ Villas Río Mar Jungle and Beach Resort
Out of town, 500 m from beach, T2787-0052,
www.villasriomar.com.

40 bungalows with bath, fridge and fan, pool, jacuzzi, tennis court, trails, riding, all-inclusive.

$$-$ Tortilla Flats
Formerly Cabinas Nayarit, right on the seafront, T2787-0033.
Rooms sleeping up to 3 people, with private bath and hot water. A bit overpriced if just for 2.

$ Cool Vibes Beach Front Hostel
Main street, 100 m south of Restaurante El Coco, T8353-6428, www.hosteldominical.com.
Funky backpackers' place with a rustic open dorm, ocean views and friendly crowds. No private rooms. Kitchen, Wi-Fi, coffee, lockers, surfboard rental and lessons. Cheap and cheerful.

Uvita

$$$$ La Cusinga Eco-Lodge
Km 166 Costanera Sur, T2770-2549,
www.lacusingalodge.com.
Situated on a 240-ha private nature reserve, La Cusinga Eco-Lodge has several luxury rooms surrounded by forest, some with expansive views of the Pacific ocean. 3 meals included.

$$$-$$ Canto de Ballenas
6 km south of Uvita, close to Parque Nacional Marino Ballena, T2248-2538,
www.hotelcantoballenas.com.
Rustic but fine wooden cabins in a simple landscaped garden. Great spot in a quiet location.

$$$-$ Flutterby House
In Bahía near Uvita, T2743-8221,
www.flutterbyhouse.com.
A funky, quirky hostel with a chilled-out
scene. A range of accommodation is
available from simple wooden shacks and
dorms to tree houses or private rooms.
Home-grown veg and an emphasis on
sustainability. Rustic and low-key.

$$ La Ballena Roja Beach Bungalows
200 m from Marino Ballena National Park,
Playa Chaman–Playa La Colonia, T8361-
4829, www.laballenarojauvita.com.
Charming and simple rooms, rustic chic, with
modern amenities and access to a shared
balcony where you can catch sea breezes.

$$-$ Cabinas Los Laureles
Uvita village, 400 m northeast of
Banco de Costa Rica, T2743-8008.
Nice location, *cabinas* and rooms with
private bathroom, simple and quite good.

$$-$ Cascada Verde
Uvita village, up the hill,
www.cascadaverde.org.
Hostal, educational retreat and organic farm,
German-run, vegetarian food, yoga and
meditation workshops available. Pay for a
bed, hammock or camp, or work for your
lodgings. Long-term lodgings preferred,
great spot if you take to the place.

$$-$ The Tucan Hotel
Uvita village, just off the main road,
T2743-8140, www.tucanhotel.com.
Low-key and pleasant spot in Uvita. Dorm
and private rooms, kitchen available, Wi-Fi
and advice on local travel.

Restaurants

Dominical

$$ Jazzy's River House
Down the main street.
More an open-house-cum-cultural-centre,
occasionally have meals followed by an
open-mic set up on Wed.

$$ Restaurant El Coco
In town.
Serves good food and rents budget rooms.

$$ San Clemente
In town.
A good mix of Tex Mex with big servings.

$$ Thrusters
In town.
A hip spot for the surf crowd, front restaurant
offers sushi.

$ Soda Nanyoa
In town.
Offers Costa Rican specialities.

Transport

Dominical
Bus To **Quepos** 0545, 0815, 1350 (Sat and
Sun) and 1450, US$3.20. To **San Isidro**, 0645,
0705, 1450, 1530, 1 hr, US$2.50. To **Uvita** at
0950, 1010, 1130 (weekends) 1710 and 2000,
US$1.10. To **Ciudad Cortés** and **Ciudad Neily**
0420 and 1000. To **San José**, 0545, 1340 (Sat
and Sun), 7 hrs.

Uvita
Bus From **San José** Terminal Coca Cola,
Mon-Fri 1500, Sat and Sun 0500, 1500, return
Mon-Fri 0530, Sat and Sun 0530, 1300, 7 hrs,
US$8.90. From **San Isidro** daily 0800, 1600,
return 0600, 1400. From **Dominical**, last bus
1700 or 1800, US$1,10.

Southern
zone

Heading through the Talamanca mountains, the Pan-American Highway reaches its highest point at Cerro de la Muerte (Peak of Death) and passes El Chirripó, Costa Rica's highest peak at 3820 m, as the scenic road drops down through the valley of the Río de El General to the tropical lowlands of the Pacific coast and the border with Panama. Private reserves along the route are ideal for birdwatching – here the resplendent quetzal enjoys a quieter life than its Monteverde relations – and mountain streams are stocked with trout providing both sport and food. Lodges and hotels are usually isolated, dotted along the highway. Towards Costa Rica's most southerly point, the Península de Osa is a nature haven of beautiful pathways, palm-fringed beaches and protected rainforest, well worth the effort if you have the time.

The Pan-American Highway runs for 352 km from San José to the Southern Zone and on to the Panama border. It's a spectacular journey along a generally good road but challenging if you're driving, with potholes, occasional rockslides during the rainy season, roadworks and generally difficult conditions.

From Cartago, the route heads south over the mountains, beginning with the ascent of **Cerro Buena Vista** (3490 m), a climb of almost 2050 m to the continental divide. A little lower than the peak, the highest point of the road is 3335 m at Km 89, which travels through barren *páramo* scenery. Those unaccustomed to high altitude should beware of mountain sickness brought on by a too-rapid ascent. For 16 km the road follows the crest of the Talamanca ridge, with views of the Pacific 50 km away and, on clear days, of the Atlantic, 80 km to the east.

Some 4.5 km east of Km 58 (Cañón church) is **Genesis II**, a privately owned 40-ha cloudforest National Wildlife Refuge, at 2360 m, bordering the **Tapantí-Macizo de la Muerte National Park**. Accommodation is available here and at several other places along the way. At Km 78 is **Casa Refugio de Ojo de Agua**, a historic pioneer home overlooked but for a couple of picnic tables in front of the house. At Km 80 a steep, dramatic road leads down the spectacular valley of the Río Savegre to **San Gerardo de Dota**, a birdwatchers' paradise. The highest point is at Km 89.5, where temperatures are below zero at night.

San Isidro de El General

The drop in altitude from the highlands to the growing town of San Isidro passes through fertile valleys growing coffee and raising cattle. The huge **cathedral** on the main plaza is a bold architectural statement, with refreshing approaches to religious iconography inside. The **Museo Regional del Sur** ⓘ *Calle 2, Av 1-0, T2771-5273, Mon-Fri 0800-1630, 1330-1630, free*, is in the old marketplace, now the **Complejo Cultural**. The 750-ha **Centro Biológico Las Quebradas** ⓘ *7 km north of San Isidro, T2771-4131, Tue-Fri 0800-1400, Sat and Sun 0800-1500, closed Oct*, has trails and dormitory lodging for researchers. San Isidro de El General is also the place to stock up for a trip into Parque Nacional Chirripó and to climb Cerro Chirripó Grande (3820 m), see below.

★ Parque Nacional Chirripó

US$15 plus US$10 per night, crowded in season, make reservations through the Oficina de los Parques Nacionales (OPN) in San Gerardo, T2742-5083, open 0630-1200, 1300-1630. Get the latest information from www.sangerardocostarica.com. If you want to walk or climb in the park, get food in San Isidro and book accommodation at the OPN. The bus to San Gerardo leave from the bus station in the market south of the cathedral plaza. The blue and white bus marked San Gerardo leaves at 0930, 1400 and 1845, taking 1½ hrs, US$1.60. Return buses at 0515, 1130 and 1600.

San Isidro de El General is west of Costa Rica's highest mountain **Cerro Chirripó Grande** (3820 m) in the middle of Parque Nacional Chirripó (50,150 ha). Treks starts from San Gerardo de Rivas (see below). The views from the hilltops are splendid and the high plateau near the summit is an interesting alpine environment with lakes of glacial origin and diverse flora and fauna. The park includes a considerable portion of cloudforest and the walk is rewarding.

Climbing the Chirripó peaks

The early-morning climb to the summit of Cerro Chirripó, Costa Rica's highest mountain (3820 m), is a refreshing slog after the relative comforts often encountered in Costa Rica. The hike takes you through magnificent cloudforest draped in mosses and ephiphytes before entering a scorched area of *páramo* grasslands with incredible views to the Pacific and Atlantic coastlines on clear days. The widlife – birdlife in particularly – is incredible and, even if you don't see it, you will certainly hear it. The trek itself is not difficult but it is tiring, being almost consistently uphill on the way and a knee-crunching, blister-bursting journey down.

From the *refugio* inside the park, you can also explore the nearby Crestones, a volcanic outcrop that has been etched on to the minds of every Costa Rican, and the creatively named Sabana de los Leones and Valle de los Conejos. There are useful orientation maps on www.sangerardocostarica.com.

If you wish to climb Cerro Chirripó you must make advance reservations by calling the **MINAE** park service office in San Gerardo (T2771-5116), the access town to Chirripó, around 12 km northeast of San Isidro de El General. After phoning for reservations you are given a couple of days to pay by bank deposit to guarantee your space. Visitors are not allowed into the park without reservations at the *refugio*. During the dry season it's often full, so it's a good idea to make arrangements as soon as possible. Start in the early morning for the eight- to 10-hour hike to the *refugio*. The cost is US$15 entry for each day spent in the park, plus US$10 shelter fee per night. Guides are available. The *refugio* has simple but adequate accommodation, with space for about 80 people and a large kitchen area.

The cold (it's often frosty in the morning) comes as a bit of a shock after other regions of Costa Rica, but you can rent blankets and sleeping bags from the *refugio*; gas cookers are also available for hire (US$2). There are sufficient water supplies en route although you will need to carry your food supplies. Electrical power at the *refugio* is only for a couple of hours each night, so be sure to bring a torch/flashlight. The top of Chirripó is located a further 5 km beyond the Crestones base camp.

In addition to the high camp there is a shelter about halfway up, Refugio Llano Bonito (2500 m), which is simple and occasionally clean, with a wooden floor, two levels to sleep on, no door but wind protection, drinking water and toilet. It's about four hours' walk from San Gerardo and three hours' walk on to Refugios Base Crestones. Plan for at least two nights on the mountain, although you can do it with only one night if you're tight for time, rising very early to summit on the second day in time to go all the day down in one hit. While nights can be cold, daytime temperatures tend to be warm to hot, so go prepared with sunscreen and hat. In the rainy season, trails up the plateau are slippery and muddy, and fog obscures the views. Time your descent to catch the afternoon bus back to San Isidro.

For a general update on San Gerardo and climbing Chirripó, visit www.sangerardo costarica.com.

Parque Nacional Chirripó neighbours **Parque Internacional La Amistad** (193,929 ha), established in 1982, and together they extend along the Cordillera de Talamanca to the Panamanian border, comprising the largest area of virgin forest in the country with the greatest biological diversity.

San Gerardo de Rivas

There's full information about the town, including accommodation, at www.san gerardocostarica.com.

In a cool, pleasant spot, San Gerardo de Rivas is at the confluence of the Río Blanco and the Río Pacífico Chirripó. Close to Parque Nacional Chirripó entrance, it is the starting point for the climb up **Cerro Chirripó Grande** (3820 m). If you haven't booked accommodation at the *refugio* in San Isidro you can try booking at the MINAE office (see box, page 125).

As interest in this quiet area grows, new tours are appearing, including trips to local waterfalls (US$40) and nature tours.

Handy for weary legs after the climb, there are **hot springs** ① *daily 0700-1800, entrance US$5*, in the area. Before crossing the concrete bridge turn left to 'Herradura' for 10 minutes then look for the sign after Parque Las Rosas; go down to the suspension bridge, cross the river and continue for 10 minutes to the house where you pay.

Buenos Aires to Paso Real

Continuing southeast, a good road sinks slowly through the Río General valley where the Talamanca Mountains dominate the skyline. At Km 197 (from San José), the change from coffee to fruit is complete; at the junction for **Buenos Aires** is the huge **Del Monte** cannery. The town, a few kilometres off the Pan-American Highway, has some simple accommodation.

Heading 17 km east towards the mountains is the **Reserva Biológica Durika**, a privately owned reserve of roughly 800 ha, aiming to create a self-sustained community in the Talamanca mountains. Accommodation is available in some rustic cabins.

South along the highway, the small towns of Térraba and Boruca are the most prominent remains of the nation's indigenous population. The community of **Boruca**, with a small *hostal* ($), has a small, poorly maintained museum, but every year the **Fiesta de los Diablitos** on the last day of December and first two days of January, and the last day of January and the first two days of February in **Rey Curre**, see the culture come alive in a festival of music, dance and costume. There is a daily bus to Boruca from Buenos Aires at 1130 (1½ hours).

At **Paso Real** the highway heads west to Palmar Norte, with a turning towards San Vito (see below) and the Panamanian border.

Palmar Norte and Palmar Sur

Taking a sharp turn at Paso Real (straight on for San Vito, see below), the Pan-American Highway heads west to Palmar Norte (Km 257, with gas station) from where the Costanera leads to Ciudad Cortés and the beach towns of the Central Pacific coast (see page 111).

Crossing the Río Grande de Terraba leads to Palmar Sur, which is 90 km from the Panamanian border. There are several very large pre-Columbian stone spheres in the area. Some, measuring 1.5 m in diameter and accurate to within 5 mm, are in a banana plantation close to town. Their purpose is a matter of conjecture although recent theories claim that they represented the planets of the solar system, or that they were border markers.

South of Palmar Sur

Through a matrix of cooperative banana and African plantations, a road leads south from Palmar Sur to **Sierpe**, on the Río Sierpe, where there are several small hotels and the departure point for boats to Bahía Drake, see page 134.

The Pan-American Highway heads southeast from Palmar Sur first to **Chacarita** (33 km), where a road turns off to the Osa Peninsula; it continues to **Río Claro** (another 26 km) where a road leads to Golfito; and then, another 15 km further on, the highway reaches **Ciudad Neily**, which is 16 km from the border at **Paso Canoas** (see Costa Rica–Panama box, page 174).

Listings Travelling the Pan-American Highway

Where to stay

$$$$ Hotel de Montaña Savegre
San Gerardo de Dota, T2740-1028,
www.savegre.com.
Set in a private nature reserve 9 km from Los Quetzales National Park, complete with waterfalls and trout fishing. Prices include meals.

$$$ Trogón Lodge
San Gerardo de Dota, T2740-1051,
www.grupomawamba.com.
23 fine wooden cabins with private bathroom, set in beautiful gardens connected by paths and used by dive-bombing hummingbirds.

$$ Hotel and Restaurant Georgina
Km 95, T2770-8043.
At almost 3300 m, Costa Rica's highest hotel, basic, clean, friendly, good food (used by southbound **Tracopa** buses), good birdwatching; ask owners for directions for a nice walk to see quetzals.

San Isidro de El General

$$$-$$ Talari Mountain Lodge
10 mins from San Isidro on the road to San Gerardo, T2771-0341, www.talari.co.cr.
8-ha farm, with bath, riverside cabins, known for birdwatching, rustic.

$$ Rancho La Botija
Out of town on the road to San Gerardo, T2770-2147, www.rancholabotija.com.
Restaurant, pool, hiking to nearby petroglyphs, open 0900 at weekends, great restaurant littered with fragments of *botijas*. Recommended.

$$-$ Hotel Los Crestones
In town, T2770-1200,
www.hotelloscrestones.com.
Big rooms have a TV, plus there's a pool. Wheelchair accessible.

$ Hotel Chirripó
South side of Parque Central, T2771-0529.
Private or shared bath, clean, very good restaurant, free covered parking, recommended.

San Gerardo de Rivas
Accommodation is on road to the park.

$$$-$$ Pelícano
T2742-5050, www.hotelpelicano.net.
11 rooms sleeping between 2 and 5 people, with great views, a bar and restaurant. Beautiful setting with countless birds. Also has a pool.

$$-$ Casa Mariposa Hostel and Guesthouse
50 m noth of entrance to Parque Nacional Chirripó, T2742-5037,
www.hotelcasamariposa.net.
A rustic family-run guesthouse with staggering views and affordable dorm beds (**$**), private rooms (**$$**), kitchen, internet, free tea and coffee and hot bath tub. Good reports. Recommended.

$$-$ El Urán
At the very top, closest to the park entrance, T2742-5003, www.hoteluran.com.
Simple, clean rooms, lots of blankets and a restaurant that will feed you early before setting out.

Buenos Aires to Paso Real

$$-$ Cabañas
Durika Biological Reserve, T2730-0657, www.durika.org.
Rustic cabins. Includes 3 vegetarian meals a day, with a wide range of activities including walks, hikes to the summit of Cerro Durika and cultural tours (around US$10 per person on top of the daily rate).

South of Palmar Sur

$$ Río Sierpe Lodge
Sierpe, T2384-5595, www.riosierpelodge.com.
All-inclusive plan with an emphasis on fishing.

Restaurants

San Isidro de El General

$$ La Cascada
Av 2 and Calle 2, T2771-6479.
Balcony bar where the bright young things hang out.

$$ Restaurant Crestones
South of the main plaza, T2771-1218.
Serves a good mix of snacks, drinks and lively company.

$$ Restaurant El Tenedor
Calle Central, Av Central-1, T2771-0881.
Good food, big pizzas, friendly. Recommended.

$$ Soda Chirripó
South side of the main plaza.
Gets the vote from the current gringo crowd in town.

$ La Marisquería
Corner of Av 0 and Calle 4.
Simple setting but great ceviche.

$ Soda J&P
Indoor market south of the main plaza.
The best of many.

What to do

San Isidro de El General
Ciprotur, *Calle 4, Av 1-3, T2771-6096, www. ecotourism.co.cr.* Good information on services throughout the southern region.
Selvamar, *Calle 1, Av 2-4, T2771-4582, www. exploringcostarica.com.* General tours and the main contact for out-of-the-way destinations in the southern region.

Transport

San Isidro de El General
Bus Terminal at Av 6, Calle Central-2 at the back of the market and adjacent streets but most arrive and depart from bus depots along the Pan-American Highway. To **Quepos** via **Dominical** at 0500 and 1330, 3 hrs, US$4. However, **Tracopa** buses coming from **San José**, going south go from Calle 3/Pan-American Highway, behind church, to **Palmar Norte**, US$5.20; **Paso Canoas**, 0830-1545, 1930 (direct), 2100; **David** (Panama) direct, 1000 and 1500; **Golfito** direct at 1800; **Puerto Jiménez**, 0630, 0900 and 1500. Waiting room but no reservations or tickets sold. **Musoc** buses leave from the intersection of Calle 2-4 with the Pan-American Highway.

Most local buses leave from bus terminal to the south of the main plaza. Buses to **San Gerardo de Rivas** and **Cerro Chirripó** leave 0500 and 1400, return 0700 and 1600.
Taxi A 4WD taxi to San Gerardo costs about US$20 for up to 4 people.

Palmar Norte and Palmar Sur
Air Daily flights with **Sansa** (from US$65) and **Nature Air**, San José–Palmar Sur (from US$101, 1 way).

Bus Express bus to **Palmar Norte** from Terminal Alfaro, with **Tracopa** from **San José**, 7 daily 0600-1800, 5 hrs, US$9.70, via

San Isidro de El General, 5 buses return to the capital 0445-1300. 5 buses daily to **Sierpe** for the boat to **Bahía Drake** (page 134) 45 mins, US$0.30. Also buses north to **Dominical** and south to the **Golfito** and the Panamanian border.

(page 134)

Sierpe
Bus and boat 5 buses daily to **Palmar Norte**, 0530-1530, 45 mins, US$0.30. Boats down Río Sierpe to **Bahía Drake**, 1½ hrs, US$70 per boat. Many hotels in Drake have boats; may be able to get a lift, US$15 per person.

Paso Real to San Vito

some of the country's best coastal views

The road from Paso Real to San Vito is paved, in good condition and offers some great views as the road rapidly falls through the hills. La Amistad International Park has few facilities for visitors at present, but one secluded lodge is found way up in the hills beyond Potrero Grande, just south of the Paso Real junction on the way to San Vito. Near the border is San Vito. Originally built by Italian immigrants among denuded hills, it is a prosperous but undistinguished town.

On the road from San Vito to Ciudad Neily at Las Cruces are the world-renowned **Wilson Botanical Gardens** ① *T2773-4004, www.ots.ac.cr*, owned by the **Organization for Tropical Studies**, 6 km from San Vito. In 360 ha of forest reserve are over 5000 species of tropical plants, orchids, other epiphytes and trees with 331 resident bird species. It is possible to spend the night here if you arrange it first with the **OTS** ① *San José, T2240-6696 ($$$$ per person all-inclusive), US$32 per person for day visits with lunch*. On the same road is **Finca Cántaros** ① *T2773-3760*, specializing in local arts and crafts, owned by Gail Hewson Gómez. It's one of the best craft shops in Costa Rica – worth a look even if you don't buy anything.

Border with Panama–Sabalito
Heading east from San Vito, a good gravel road, paved in places, runs via Sabalito (Banco Nacional) to the Panama border at Río Sereno (see border crossing box for Costa Rica–Panama, page 174). There are buses from Sabalito to San José.

(see border crossing box for Costa Rica–Panama, page 174)

Listings Paso Real to San Vito

Restaurants

Paso Real to San Vito

$$ Lilianas
San Vito.
Still showing homage to the town's Italian heritage with good pasta dishes and pizza.

$ Restaurant Nelly
San Vito, near Cabinas Las Huacas.
Good wholesome truck-drivers' fare.

Transport

Paso Real to San Vito
Bus Direct buses **San José** to San Vito, 4 daily, 0545, 0815, 1130 and 1445, from Terminal Alfaro, Calle 14, Av 5; direct bus San Vito–San José 0500, 0730, 1000, 1500, 6 hrs, *corriente* buses take 8 hrs, US$11. Alternative route, not all paved, via Ciudad Neily (see below); from San Vito to **Las Cruces** at 0530 and 0700; sit on the left coming up, right going down, to admire the wonderful scenery; return buses pass Las Cruces at 1510.

Some 31 km north of the border a road branches south at Río Claro (several *pensiones* and a fuel station) to the former banana port of Golfito, a 6-km-long linear settlement bordering the Golfo Dulce and steep forested hills. While elements of hard sweat and dock labour remain, Golfito's prominence today comes from being a free port, set up in 1990, selling goods tax free at about 60% of normal prices. Check out www.golfito.info for information on lodging and activities in the area.

Golfito also provides boat and ferry access to Puerto Jiménez and the Osa Peninsula, and popular fishing and surfing beaches to the south of the town.

Entering the town from the south heading north there are a few hotels where the road meets the coast. In 2 km is the small town centre of painted buildings with saloon bars, open-fronted restaurants and cheap accommodation – probably the best stop for budget travellers. Nearby is the dilapidated *muellecito* used by the ferries to Puerto Jiménez and water taxis. One kilometre north are the container port facilities and the **Standard Fruit Company**'s local HQ, though many of the banana plantations have been turned over to oil palm and other crops. Beyond the dock is the free port, airstrip and another set of hotels.

The **Refugio Nacional de Fauna Silvestre Golfito**, in the steep forested hills overlooking Golfito, was created to protect Golfito's watershed. Rich in rare and medicinal plants with abundant fauna, there are some excellent hikes in the refuge. Supervised by the University of Costa Rica, they have a field office in Golfito.

Thirty minutes by water taxi from Golfito, you can visit **Casa Orquídeas** ① *T2775-1614, tours last about 2½ hrs, US$5 per person, US$20 minimum, closed Fri*, a family-owned botanical garden with a large collection of herbs, orchids and local flowers and trees, that you can see, smell, touch and taste.

To the north of Golfito is the **Parque Nacional Piedras Blancas** tropical wet forest. The area was being exploited for wood products, but has been steadily purchased since 1991 with help from the Austrian government and private interests, notably the classical Austrian violinist Michael Schnitzler. All logging has now ceased and efforts are devoted to a research centre and ecotourism, concentrated in an area designated **Parque Nacional Esquinas**. Near the village of **La Gamba** a tourist lodge has been built (see Where to stay, below). La Gamba is 6 km along a dirt road from Golfito, or 4 km from Briceño on the Pan-American Highway between Piedras Blancas and Río Claro.

Beaches around Golfito

Playa de Cacao is about 6 km (1½-hour walk) north of Golfito round the bay, or a short trip by water taxi. Further north is the secluded beach of **Playa San Josecito** with a couple of adventure-based lodges.

About 15 km by sea south of Golfito, and reached by water taxi or a long bus journey (US$2 by colectivo ferry from the small dock; 0600 and 1200, return 0500, 1300), **Playa Zancudo** is a long stretch of clean golden sound, dotted with a few rustic hotels ideal for relaxing and lazing away the days. Still further south is **Pavones**, where a world record left-hand wave has elevated the rocky beach to the realm of surfing legend. South of Pavones, towards the end of the peninsula and at the mouth of the Golfo Dulce is **Punta Banco**.

Ciudad Neily, Paso Canoas and the Panama border

Ciudad Neily is an uninspiring town providing useful transport links between San Vito in the highlands and the coastal plain, and is roughly 16 km from Paso Canoas on the border with Panama (see Costa Rica–Panama box, page 174). Paso Canoas is a little piece of chaos with traders buying and selling to take advantage of the difference in prices between Costa Rica and Panama. With little to hold you, there's not much reason to visit unless you're heading to Panama. If misfortune should find you having to stay the night, there are some reasonable options.

Listings Golfito and around

Where to stay

Golfito
It can be difficult to get a hotel room at weekends.

$$$ Esquinas Rainforest Lodge
Near La Gamba, 6 km from Golfito, T2741-8001, www.esquinaslodge.com.
Full board, private baths, verandas overlooking the forest, tours, all profits to the local community.

$$ Sierra
Northernmost part of town, near the airport and free zone, T2775-0666.
With 72 double rooms, a/c, a couple of pools and a restaurant. Rooms are better than you'd think from the outside.

$ Del Cerro
Close to the docks, T2775-0006.
Offering 20 simple rooms sleeping 1-6, private bathroom, laundry services, fishing boat rentals.

$ Golfo Azul
T2775-0871.
Has 20 large, comfortable rooms, with bath and a/c, good restaurant.

$ La Purruja Lodge
4 km south of Golfito, T2775-5054, www.purruja.com.
5 duplex cabins with bath, plus camping US$2 per tent.

$ Mar y Luna
T2775-0192.
Has 8 rooms sleeping 2-4, with bath, fan, restaurant on stilts above the sea, quiet spot, good deal.

$ Melissa
Behind Delfina, T2775-0443.
Has 4 simple rooms, with private bath, clean and quiet, great spot overlooking bay. Parking available. Recommended.

Beaches around Golfito

$$$ Tiskita Jungle Lodge
Punta Banco, T2296-8125, www.tiskita.com.
A 162-ha property including a fruit farm, with excellent birdwatching, 14 cabins overlooking the ocean. Cool breezes, waterfall, jungle pools, trails through virgin forest – great spot.

$$$-$$ Cabinas La Ponderosa
Pavones, T2776-2076, www.cabinaslaponderosa.com.
Owned by 2 surfers, large cabins, fan or a/c, with bath (hot water), walking, horse riding, fishing, diving and surfing; also house for rent (sleeps 6), restaurant.

$$ Los Cocos
Playa Zancudo, Golfito, T2776-0012, www.loscocos.com.
Beachfront cabins with private bathroom, hot water, mosquito net, fan, kitchenette, refrigerator, veranda. Also provide boat tours and taxi service. Discounts for longer stays. Heavenly.

$$-$ Mira Olas
Pavones, T2776-2006, www.miraolas.com.
Comfortable cabins with kitchen and fan, low
monthly rates, jungle trail, peaceful garden
filled with colourful birdlife, 5 mins from the
beach. Highly recommended.

$$-$ Sol y Mar
Playa Zancudo, T2776-0014,
www.zancudo.com.
4 screened cabins, hot water, fan, 3-storey
rental house (US$700 per month), 50 m from
ocean, bar/restaurant, meals 0700-2000,
home-baked bread, great fruit shakes,
volleyball with lights for evening play,
badminton, paddleball, boogie boards,
library. Highly recommended.

$ The Yoga Farm
Punta Banco, www.yogafarmcostarica.org.
A laid-back retreat, set on a mountainside
surrounded by primary rainforest and
near the beach. A great place to get back
to nature. Price (per person) includes
accommodation, food and yoga.

Restaurants

Golfito
Many seafood places along the seafront.

$$ Cubana
Near post office.
Good, try *batidos*.

$$ El Uno
Near Cubana.
Good, reasonably priced seafood.

$$ La Dama del Delfín Restaurant
Downtown. Closed for dinner and Sun.
Breakfast from 0700. Snacks, home-
baked goods.

$ La Eurekita
Centre.
Serves a mean breakfast of *huevos rancheros*.

Beaches around Golfito

$$ Bar y Restaurant Tranquilo
Playa Zancudo.
A lively spot between **Zancudo Beach Club**
and **Coloso del Mar**.

$$ Macondo
Playa Zancudo.
Italian restaurant which also has a couple
of rooms.

$ Soda Katherine
Playa Zancudo, T2776-0124.
From US$4, great Tico fare; also simple cabins.

What to do

Beaches around Golfito
The Yoga Farm, *Punta Banco, www.yoga
farmcostarica.org.* Yoga, horse riding and
hikes through the rainforest. Also organize
homestay with an indigenous family.

Transport

Golfito
Air Several daily flights to **San José**, with
Sansa (US$71 one-way). Runway is all-
weather, tight landing between trees;
2 km from town, taxi US$0.50.

Boat There is a boat service between
Golfito and **Puerto Jiménez**, leaving the
dock in Golfito at 1130, US$2.50, 1½ hrs,
returning at 0600, or chartering a water taxi
for US$60, up to 8 passengers, is possible.
   Water taxis in and around Golfito, **Froylan
Lopex**, T8824-6571, to **Cacao Beach**, **Punta
Zancudo**, **Punta Encanto** or to order, US$20
per hr up to 5 persons.
   Docks Banana Bay Marina (T2775-0838,
www.bananabaymarina.com) accommodate
boats up to 150 ft and might be an option if
heading south on a boat, but you'll need to
ask nicely and be a bit lucky.

Bus From **San José** 0700 (8½ hrs) and 1500 (6 hrs express) daily from Terminal Alfaro, return 0500 (express), 1300, US$12.40; from **San Isidro de El General**, take 0730 bus to Río Claro and wait for bus coming from Ciudad Neily. To **Paso Canoas**, US$1.30, hourly from outside Soda Pavo, 1½ hrs. To **Pavones** at 1000 and 1500, return at 0430 and 1230, 3 hrs, US$1.80. A spit of land continues south to Punta Burica with no roads and only a couple of villages.

Ciudad Neily, Paso Canoas and the Panama border

Bus The terminal in Ciudad Neily is at the northern end of town, beside the Mercado Central. Daily bus to **San José**, with **Tracopa**, from main square (6 daily, US$12.40, 7 hrs, on Sun buses from the border are full by the time they reach Ciudad Neily). Buses arrive at Av 5 and Calle 14 in San José. Services to **San Vito** inland and to **Palmar**, **Cortés** and **Dominical** (0600 and 1430, 3 hrs). Also to **Puerto Jiménez** at 0700 and 1400, 4 hrs. Bus for **Golfito** leaves from town centre every 30 mins. The Pan-American Highway goes south (plenty of buses, 20 mins, US$0.65) to Paso Canoas on the Panamanian border; see also Costa Rica–Panama box, page 174. Colectivo US$1.80, very quick.

To **San José**, 0400, 0730, 0900, 1500 (T2223-7685), or go to Ciudad Neily and change. International buses that reach the border after closing time wait there till the following day. Hourly buses to **Ciudad Neily**, ½ hourly to **Golfito**.

★ Península de Osa

home to a park world famous for its diversity of wildlife

Across the Golfo Dulce is the hook-shaped appendage of the Osa Peninsula. Some distance from most other places of interest in the country, the journey is worthwhile for the peninsula's Parque Nacional Corcovado, with some of the best rainforest trekking and trails in the country.

Getting to the peninsula is becoming easier. There is a daily ferry service from Golfito arriving at the small dock in Puerto Jiménez; bus services run from San José, passing through San Isidro de El General, Palmar North and from the south at Ciudad Neily; and boats ply the coastal route from Sierpe to Bahía Drake. You can also fly from San José.

Puerto Jiménez *See map, page 135.*

Once a gold-mining centre, Puerto Jiménez still has the feel of a frontier town although most miners were cleared from the Parque Nacional Corcovado area over 20 years ago.

Today, Puerto Jiménez is a popular destination with its laid-back, occasionally lively atmosphere, reasonable beaches nearby and, of course, the beautiful national park on the Pacific side of the peninsula. Look out for *El Sol de Osa* (www.soldeosa.com), an up-to-date community-information service. A particular charm of Puerto Jiménez, barely five blocks square, is its relative freedom from road traffic; scarlet macaws can be seen roosting in the trees around the football pitch. There are good local walks to the jungle, where you will see monkeys and many other birds, and to beaches and mangroves as well. There is a seasonal migration of humpbacks between October and March.

Around Puerto Jiménez

Geological treasures can be seen at the gold mine at **Dos Brazos**, about 15 km west of town; ask for the road that goes uphill beyond the town, to see the local gold mines. Several colectivo taxis a day go to Dos Brazos, last bus back at 1530 (often late); taxi US$7.25. You can also take a long walk to **Carate** (see below), which has a gold

Essential Península de Osa

Avoid the rainy season. Bring umbrellas (not raincoats, which are too hot), because it will rain, unless you are hiking, in which case you may prefer to get wet. There are a few shelters, so only mosquito netting is indispensable. Bring all your food if you haven't arranged otherwise; in the whole peninsula you'll only find food and accommodation in Puerto Jiménez and Agujitas. The cleared areas (mostly outside the park, or along the beach) can be devastatingly hot. Chiggers (*coloradillas*) and horseflies infest the horse pastures and can be a nuisance, similarly sandflies on the beaches; bring spray-on insect repellent. Another suggestion is vitamin B1 pills (called thiamine, or *tiamina*). Mosquitoes are supposed to detest the smell and leave you alone. Get the Instituto Geográfico maps, scale 1:50,000. Remember finally that, as in any tropical forest, you may find some unfriendly wildlife, like snakes (fer-de-lance and bushmaster snakes may attack without provocation), and herds of peccaries. You should find the most suitable method for keeping your feet dry and protecting your ankles; for some, rubber boots are the thing, for others light footwear that dries quickly.

mine. Branch to the right and in 4 km there are good views of the peninsula. A topographical map is a big help, obtainable from Instituto Geográfico in San José. At **Cabo Matapalo** on the tip of the peninsula, 18 km south of Puerto Jiménez, are several expensive sleeping options.

To reach Puerto Jiménez from the Pan-American Highway (70 km), turn right about 30 km south of Palmar Sur; the road is paved to Rincón, thereafter it is driveable with many bridge crossings. There is a police checkpoint 47 km from the Pan-American Highway.

Bahía Drake

Arriving by boat from Sierpe, Bahía Drake provides a northern entrance point to the Osa Peninsula and Parque Nacional Corcovado. In March 1579, Sir Francis Drake careened his ship on Playa Colorada in Bahía Drake. There is a plaque commemorating the 400th anniversary of the famous pirate's nautical aberration in **Agujitas**. Life in the bay is not cheap and, combined with transport, costs can quickly mount up. Bahía Drake, which continues south merging seamlessly with Agujitas, is a popular destination for divers with Isla del Caño nearby. Open Water PADI courses (US$340) are available at **Cabinas Jinetes de Osa** or through **Caño Divers** at Pirate Cove.

Listings Península de Osa *map p135*

Where to stay

Puerto Jiménez
For more Jiménez hotels, see www.jimenezhotels.com.

$$$$ Iguana Lodge
5 km southeast of Puerto Jiménez behind the airstrip, T8829-5865, www.iguanalodge.com.
4 cabins, good swimming and surfing.

$$$-$$ Cabinas Puerto Jiménez
On the gulf shore with good views, T2735-5090, www.cabinasjimenez.com.
Remodelled big rooms, many with private decks looking out to the gulf, spotless. Wi-Fi.

$$-$ Cabinas Marcelina
Main street, T2735-5007.
With bath, big, clean, friendly and totally renovated, nice front yard, small discount for youth hostelling members.

$ Hotel Oro Verde
Main street, T2735-5241.
Run by Silvia Duirós Rodríguez, 10 clean, comfortable rooms, with bath and fan, some overlooking the street.

$ Pensión Quintero
Just off main street, T2735-5087.
Very simple wooden building, but clean, cheap and good value (price per person); will store luggage. Ask for Fernando Quintero, who rents horses and has a boat for up to 6 passengers, good value; he is also a guide, recommended.

Around Puerto Jiménez
Cabo Matapalo

$$$$ El Remanso Rainforest Beach Lodge
T2735-5569, www.elremanso.com.
Houses and cabins for rent, all fully equipped and with ocean views, an oasis of peace.

$$$$ Lapa Ríos Wilderness Resort
T2735-5130, www.laparios.com.
The cream of the crop. Includes meals. 14 luxury palm-thatched bungalows on private 2400-ha reserve (80% virgin forest, US owners Karen and John Lewis), camping trips, boats can be arranged from Golfito. Idyllic, fantastic views. Recommended.

Puerto Jiménez

Where to stay 🛏
Cabinas Marcelina **3**
Cabinas Puerto
  Jiménez **4**
Iguana Lodge **1**
Oro Verde **9**

Pensión Quintero **11**

Restaurants 🍴
Agua Luna **1**
Carolina &
  Escondido Trex **2**

Il Giardino **3**
Juanita's Mexican
  Bar & Grille **4**
Marisquería Corcovado **5**
Pizzamail.it **6**

Bahía Drake

$$$$ Aguila de Osa Inn
The normal landing point, T2296-2190,
www.aguiladeosa.com.
Includes meals; fishing, hiking, canoeing
and horse riding available, comfortable
cabins made with exotic hardwoods.
Recommended.

$$$$ La Paloma Jungle Lodge
T2239-0954, www.lapalomalodge.com.
Price per person includes meals. 9 cabins
with bath, guided tours with resident
biologist. Packages.

$$$ Cabinas Jinete de Osa
T2236-5637, www.costaricadiving.com.
Good hotel, run by 2 brothers from Colorado.
Diving a speciality, PADI courses offered.
Spacious and airy rooms, all with bath, hot
water, fan. Recommended.

$$$ Rancho Corcovado Lodge
In the middle of the beach, T2786-7059.
www.ranchocorcovado.com. Price per
person. Simple, rustic rooms, many with
view, all with bath. Friendly Tico owners, nice
open-air restaurant on beach serves *comida
típica*. Camping permitted.

$$$-$$ Pirate Cove
Northern end of the beach, T2786-7845,
www.piratecove.com.
Very nice tent-like cabins emulate an
outdoor experience minus the mud. US$55
per person shared bath, US$70 with bath,
3 meals included.

$ Bella Vista Lodge
On the beach at the southern end of town,
T2770-8051.
The only budget option in town and
disappointing. Basic rooms, 2 with bath,
3 shared (even more basic), meals (US$3-5)
not included.

Restaurants

Puerto Jiménez

$$$ Agua Luna
On the seashore near the dock, T2735-5033.
Stylish setting, beautifully presented
but pricey.

$$$ Il Giardino
Just off the main street.
Quiet little Italian, intimate setting and
good food.

$$$-$$ Carolina
Main street, T2735-5185.
Highly recommended for fish (everything
actually), good prices. **Escondido Trex** office
at back of restaurant.

$$$-$$ Pizzamail.it
Parque Central.
Authentic, Italian-style stone-baked pizzas,
thin crusts and tasty.

$$ Juanita's Mexican Bar and Grille
Central, T2735-5056.
Happy hour, crab races, good Mexican fare,
seafood from US$4.

$$-$ Marisquería Corcovado
Seafront, east of the dock.
An unpretentious local eatery where you
can pick up some of the best seafood in
town, including great ceviche and fish fillets.
Good value.

What to do

Puerto Jiménez
Aventuras Tropicales, *opposite the football
pitch, T2735-5195, www.aventurastropicales.
com.* Can book accommodation and has a
couple of computers with internet.
MINAE office, *facing the airstrip, T2735-5036,
for booking dormitory lodging and camping
facilities in Corcovado National Park.*
Surcos Tours, *T8603-2387, www.surcostours.
com.* Single and multi-day hiking tours of
Corcovado National Park, birdwatching

tours and trips to Matapalo rainforest. Recommended.

Tonsa Tours, *see map*. Run by the quiet Jaime, provides many of the normal tours and also jungle treks across to Carate. Not for the faint-hearted, but certain to be fascinating.

Transport

Puerto Jiménez

Air There are daily flights to Puerto Jiménez and **Golfito** with Sansa (US$71) and **Nature Air** (from US$114 one-way) from **San José**.

Bus 1 block west of the main street. A café by the bus terminal is open Sat 0430 for a cheap and reasonable breakfast. From **San José**, just outside Terminal Atlántico Norte (C 12, Av 9-11), there are 2 buses daily to Puerto Jiménez at 0600 and 1200 via San Isidro, US$12.60, 8 hrs, return 0500, T2735-5189. There are also buses from **San Isidro**, leaving from the Pan-American Highway at 0930 and 1500, US$8, returns at 0400 and 1300, 5 hrs. To **Ciudad Neily** at 0500 and 1400, 3 hrs, US$3.80. A few colectivos to **Carate** depart from outside **Restaurant Carolina** daily 0530 and 0600, cost US$7. Service may be restricted in the wet season. Local bus is US$1.80.

Sea There is a boat service between **Golfito** and Puerto Jiménez, leaving the dock in Golfito at 1130, US$2.50, 1½ hrs, returning at 0600, or chartering a water taxi for US$60, up to 8 passengers, is possible.

Parque Nacional Corcovado

an ideal spot for just walking along endless beaches

Corcovado National Park, including Reserva Biológica Isla del Caño (84 ha), comprises over 42,469 ha – just under half the Osa Peninsula. Consisting largely of tropical rainforest, swamps, miles of empty beaches and some cleared areas now growing back, it is located on the Pacific Ocean at the western end of the peninsula. The park is also filled with birds, mammals and six species of cat.

At **Carate** there is a dirt airstrip and a store, run by Gilberto Morales and his wife Roxana (they rent rooms, but they are often full of gold miners; they also have a tent for hire, but take a sleeping bag). There are several luxury options here and a couple more lodges 30 minutes' walk west along the beach.

Five minutes' walk further down the beach is **La Leona** park wardens' station and entrance to the park. To go beyond here costs US$7 per day, whether you are walking along the beach to La Sirena (18 km, six hours, take sun protection), or just visiting for the day. Beyond here to the end of **Playa Madrigal** is another 2½ hours' walk, partly sandy, partly rocky, with some rock pools and rusty shipwrecks looking like modern sculptures. The shore rises steeply into the jungle, which grows thickly with mangroves, almonds and coconut palms. Check with wardens about high tide so you don't get stuck. There are a couple of rivers along the beach, the first, Río Madrigal, is only about 15 minutes beyond La Leona (lovely and clear, deep enough for swimming about 200 m upstream, a good place for spotting wildlife). The best place for seeing wildlife, though, is La Sirena, where there are paths inland and the terrain is flatter and more isolated.

You can head inland from Sirena on a trail past three conveniently spaced shelters to **Los Patos**, after passing several rivers full of reptiles (20 km, six to nine hours depending on conditions). The wooden house is the ranger station with electricity, TV and four beds available at US$1.75 per night; meals are possible if you don't bring your own food.

Essential Parque Nacional Corcovado

Park information

If short of time and/or money, the simplest way to the park is to take the pickup truck from outside **Tonsa Tours** in Puerto Jiménez to Playa Carate (most days at 0600 and 1400, 2½ hours, US$7 one way, returning at 0800 and 1600, ask in advance about departure). Or call **Cirilo Espinosa** (T2735-5075), or **Ricardo González** (T2735-5068) for a 4WD jeep taxi. It is possible to book a flight from Puerto Jiménez to Carate or La Sirena in the park for US$99 per person, minimum five people. Ask at the airstrip or call T2735-5178.

The **MINAE office** (Puerto Jiménez, near the airport, T2735-5036, daily 0830-1200, 1300-1700), will give permits for entering the park (US$7) and will book accommodation at La Sirena, see Where to stay, below. Hiking boots and sandals are useful if you are walking in the park.

Its balcony is a great observation point for birds, especially the redheaded woodpecker. From Los Patos you can carry on to the park border then, crisscrossing the Río Rincón to **La Palma** (small *hostal*), a settlement on the opposite side of the peninsula (13 km, six more hours), from where there are several 'taxis' making the one-hour trip to Puerto Jiménez (see above). An offshoot of this trail will lead you to a raffia swamp that rings the **Corcovado Lagoon**. The lagoon is only accessible by boat, but there are no regular trips. Cayman and alligator survive here, sheltered from the hunters.

From Sirena you can walk north along the coast to the shelter at **Llorona** (plenty of waterfalls), from which there is a trail to the interior with a shelter at the end. From Llorona you can proceed north through a forest trail and along the beach to the station at **San Pedrillo** on the edge of the park. You can stay here, camping or under roof, and eat with the rangers, who love company. From San Pedrillo you can take the park boat (not cheap) to **Isla del Caño**, a lovely (staffed) park outpost.

Listings Parque Nacional Corcovado

Where to stay

See also details of the MINAE office, under Park information above.

$$$$ Casa Corcovado Jungle Lodge
Along the coast from San Pedrillo, T2256-3181, www.casacorcovado.com.
Outside the park in the forest, but with 500 m of beach more or less opposite Isla del Caño, 14 bungalows, many facilities, packages from 2 nights full board with boat transport (2 hrs) from Sierpe.

$$$ Corcovado Lodge
30 mins' walk west of Carate along the beach, T2257-0766, www.costaricaexpeditions.com.
20 walk-in tents with 2 campbeds in each, in a beautiful coconut grove with hammocks

overlooking the beach; to be sure of space book through **Costa Rica Expeditions** in San José, see page 42.

$$$ La Leona Eco-Lodge
30 mins' walk west of Carate along the beach, T2735-5705, www.laleonaecolodge.com.
Rustic tent cabins, crocodile spotting, rappelling, yoga and night hikes. Price per person.

$ La Sirena
Book through MINAE, Puerto Jiménez, near the airport, T2735-5036.
In dorms, maximum 20 people (reservation essential), take sheets/sleeping bag. Also camping, no reservation needed, 3 meals available. Bring mosquito netting.

This steep-sided and thickly wooded island and national park of 24 sq km lies 320 km off the Osa Peninsula, on the Cocos Ridge, which extends some 1400 km southwest to the Galápagos Islands. There is virtually nothing on the island, apart from a few endemic species, but you can visit for some of the world's best diving.

The BBC Discovery Channel shot some dramatic silhouetted images of tiger sharks here for their *Blue Planet* series. Historically, though, it was a refuge for pirates who are supposed to have buried great treasure here, though none has been found by the 500 or so expeditions looking for the 'x' that marked the spot. Travel by chartered boat can be made in Puntarenas, after a government permit has been obtained, or you can take a scuba-diving cruise on the **Okeanos Agressor** ① *T2232-0572 ext 60 (in US: PO Drawer K, Morgan City, LA 70381, T504-385-2416).* The twice-monthly 10-day trips are understandably expensive (about US$4235 for 10 days).

Caribbean
coast

Heading east from San José, the central highlands quickly fall away to the sparsely populated flat Caribbean lowlands. The tropical rainforest national parks of Tortuguero and Barra del Colorado, leading through coastal canals and waterways, are a nature lover's paradise with easily arranged trips, normally from San José, into the rainforest. South of the distinctly Caribbean city of Puerto Limón, coastal communities have developed to provide comfortable hangouts and laid-back beachlife for all budgets.

San José to the coast

the third largest of Costa Rica's national parks, with abundant wildlife

Parque Nacional Braulio Carrillo

The Parque Nacional Braulio Carrillo was created to protect the high rainforest north of San José from the impact of the San José–Guápiles–Puerto Limón highway. It extends for 47,583 ha and encompasses five different types of forest with hundreds of species of bird, jaguar, ocelot and Baird's tapir. Various travel agencies offer naturalist tours, approximately US$75 from San José. San José to Guápiles and Puerto Limón buses go through the park.

The entrance to the **Quebrada González centre** ① *daily 0800-1530, US$15*, is on the highway, 23 km beyond the Zurquí tunnel, just over the Río Sucio at the Guápiles end and has an administration building. To get there, take any bus to the Atlantic and ask to be dropped off. There are three trails: **Las Palmas**, 1.6 km (you need rubber boots); across the road are **El Ceibo**, 1 km, circular; and **Botarrama**, entry 2 km from Quebrada González. The trail has good birdwatching and the views down the Río Patria canyon are impressive. The Zurquí centre near the tunnel has been closed but may open again soon, so ask at headquarters. It has services and the 250-m **Los Jilqueros** trail to the river.

Beyond Quebrada González (1.5 km) is **Los Heliconios** ① *entry US$7*, a butterfly garden with an insect museum and amphibians. Adjoining it, **Reserva Turística El Tapir** ① *entry US$7*, has a 20-minute trail and others of one to two hours.

An ingenious **Rainforest Aerial Tram** ① *Tue-Sun 0630-1600, Mon 0900-1530, 90 mins' ride costs US$60, students with ID and children half price, children under 5 are not allowed; office in San José, Av 7, Calle 7, behind Aurola Holiday Inn, T2257-5961, www.rainforestadventure. com*, lifts visitors high into the rainforest, providing a fascinating up-close and personal view of the canopy life. The price includes a guided nature walk. It's best to go as early as possible for birds. Tourist buses arrive from 0800. There's also a zip-wire, trekking tour, birding tour and serpentarium. US$114 covers everything. There's a guarded car park for private vehicles and restaurant for meals in the park. It can be difficult to get reservations during the high season. The San José office organizes an all-inclusive package leaving around 0800 daily, with pickups at most major hotels.

Further on, at the Soda Gallo Pinto is the **Bosque Lluvioso** ① *T2224-0819, daily 0700-1700, entry US$15*, a 170-ha private reserve. It is at Km 56 on the Guápiles highway (**Rancho Redondo**), with a restaurant and trails in primary and secondary forest.

The turn-off at Santa Clara to Puerto Viejo de Sarapiquí is 13 km before Guápiles. At the junction is **Rancho Robertos** (T2711-0050), a good, popular and reasonable roadside restaurant. For Guápiles, see below. Nearby is a **Tropical Frog Garden**, an interesting short stop if you have the time.

There is a private reserve bordering the Parque Nacional Braulio Carrillo called **Río Danta**, with 60 ha of primary rainforest and short limited treks (US$4) arranged with meals (US$6-9). For information contact **Mawamba Group** ① *T2223-2421, must be pre-arranged, no drop-ins.*

Puerto Viejo de Sarapiquí

Puerto Viejo de Sarapiquí is 40 km north of the San José–Limón highway and 20 km from La Virgen to the southwest. Once an important port on the Río Sarapiquí, only occasionally do launches ply the Río Colorado to the Canales de Tortuguero. There is reported to be a cargo boat once a week to Barra del Colorado (no facilities, bring your own food, hammock, sleeping bag) and on to Moín, about 10 km by road from Puerto Limón. There is little traffic, so you will need luck and a fair amount of cash. There is good fishing on the Río Sarapiquí.

La Selva Biological Station ① *T2766-6565, www.ots.ac.cr, 3½-hr guided natural history walk with bilingual naturalists daily at 0800 and 1330-1600, US$30 per person*, on the Río Puerto Viejo, is run by the **Organization for Tropical Studies**. The floral and faunal diversity is unbelievable. Several guided and self-led walks, including a **Sarapiquí River Boat Tour**, are available, but to visit it is essential to book in advance. Accommodation is also available.

The Río Sarapiquí flows into the San Juan, forming the northern border of Costa Rica. The Río San Juan is wholly in Nicaragua, so you technically have to cross the border and then return to Costa Rica. This will cost US$5 and you will need a passport and visa. Trips on the **Río Sarapiquí** and on the **Río Sucio** are beautiful (US$15 for two hours); contact William Rojas in Puerto Viejo (T2766-6108) for trips on the Río Sarapiquí or to Barra del Colorado and Tortuguero. There is a regular boat service to Tortuguero on Monday and Thursday, returning on Tuesday and Friday, costing US$55 per person.

Las Horquetas de Sarapiquí

Some 17 km south of Puerto Viejo, near Las Horquetas de Sarapiquí, is **Rara Avis** ① *T2764-1111, www.rara-avis.com*, rustic lodges in a 600-ha forest reserve owned by ecologist Amos Bien. This admirable experiment in educating visitors about rainforest conservation takes small groups on guided tours (rubber boots provided), led by biologists. You must be prepared for rough and muddy trails, lots of insects but great birdwatching and a memorable experience.

Guápiles, Guácimo and Siquirres

One hour from San José, Guápiles is the centre of the Río Frío banana region. It is another 25 km from Guácimo to Siquirres, a clean, friendly town and junction for roads from Turrialba with the main highway and former railways.

Matina

Some 28 km beyond Siquirres, heading north at the 'techo rojo' junction is Matina, a small, once-busy town on the railway but off the highway. Today, it is an access point to Tortuguero and the less well-known private **Reserva Natural Pacuare**, 30 km north of Puerto Limón, which is accessible by canal from Matina. Run by Englishman John Denham, the reserve has a 6-km stretch of **leatherback turtle-nesting beach** protected and guarded by the reserve. Volunteers patrol the beach in May and June, measuring and tagging these magnificent marine turtles. For volunteer work, contact Carlos Fernández, **Corporación de Abogados** ① *Av 8-10, Calle 19, No 837, San José, T2234-5890, c.fernandez@turtleprotection. org, organization information at www.turtleprotection.org.*

Listings San José to the coast

Where to stay

Puerto Viejo de Sarapiquí

$$$$-$$$ Selva Verde Lodge
Out of town, heading west a few kilometres towards La Virgen, T2761-1800, www. selvaverde.com.
On over 200 ha of virgin rainforest reserve, 40 double rooms, 5 bungalows for 4, includes meals, caters mainly for tour groups. Sensitively set in the rainforest with extensive trail system, rafting, canoeing and riding through property; tours with biologists organized.

$$$ El Bambú
In centre north of park, T2766-6359, www.elbambu.com.
Mini-resort-style lodgings with 40 comfortable rooms, fan, cable TV, pool, gym, including breakfast, very pleasant.

$$$ El Gavilán Lodge
On the southern bank of the Río Sarapiquí, reached by taxi, T2234-9507, www.gavilanlodge.com.
Includes breakfast, set in 100-ha private reserve by the river pier, good restaurant, good jungle paths, riding and river tours, 12 rooms private bath, garden jacuzzi, special group and student/researcher rates, day trips and overnight trips from San José.

$$ Posada Andrea Cristina
Just out of town near the main road junction, T2766-6265, www.andreacristina.com.
Comfortable small cabins, set amongst tropical gardens, and a fantastic treehouse for those who want to get close to the canopy. Good local knowledge.

$ Mi Lindo Sarapiquí
Overlooking park, T2766-6074.
Has 6 spotless rooms with bath, fan, hot water and restaurant downstairs. Recommended.

Las Horquetas de Sarapiquí

$$$ River-Edge Cabin and Waterfall Lodge
T2764-1111, www.rara-avis.com.
Accommodation at **Rara Avis**, the lodge is a beautiful 8-room jungle lodge in an idyllic setting, the cabin is deeper in the rainforest for even more seclusion. There is also treetop

accommodation and rates for backpackers at Las Casitas.

Guápiles, Guácimo and Siquirres

$$$ Casa Río Blanco
About 6 km west of Guápiles look out for the big yellow road sign, take 1st right before the Río Blanco bridge and follow signpost for 1 km, T2710-4124, www.casarioblanco.com.
Accommodates 12 guests in comfortable cabins, with breakfast, run by Herbie and Annette from Amsterdam. Beautiful gardens and a great spot for people interested in the environment. Recommended.

$$ Centro Turístico Pacuare
Siquirres, T2768-8111, www.centroturistico pacuare.com.
Motel-style lodging with 60 reasonable, functional rooms, with or without a/c. Amenities include restaurant, bar, pool table, café, soccer field and large pool.

Transport

Puerto Viejo de Sarapiquí
Bus Buses stop on north side of park. From **San José** 7 daily from Gran Terminal del Caribe, 1½ hrs, US$3.45, through PN Braulio Carrillo, or through Heredia, 4 daily, 3½ hrs, US$4.20. From **Ciudad Quesada**, 5 daily, 2½ hrs.

Car To get there by car from **San José**, after passing through the Parque Nacional Braulio Carrillo take Route 4, a paved road which turns off near Santa Clara to Puerto Viejo; it bypasses Río Frío and goes via Las Horquetas. A more scenic but longer route leaves from **Heredia** via San Miguel and La Virgen, and on to Puerto Viejo.

Guápiles, Guácimo and Siquirres
Bus In Guápiles, buses leave from a central terminal a block to the north of the church. Regular buses to **San José** and **Puerto Limón**. Buses to **Puerto Viejo de Sarapiquí** every 2½ hrs, and to **Río Frío** every 1½ hrs.
    For Siquirres, at least 1 bus per hr leaves Gran Terminal del Caribe in **San José**, 2½-hr journey, US$2.90.

Puerto Limón and the Caribbean coast
the country's most important port and biggest carnival

Puerto Limón is on a rocky outcrop on an almost featureless coastline. Between Puerto Limón and the Río San Juan on the Nicaraguan border, the long stretch of Atlantic coastline and its handful of small settlements is linked by a canal system that follows the coastline.

The region encompasses Parque Nacional Tortuguero (page 145), famed for its wildlife and turtle-nesting beaches, and Refugio Nacional de Fauna Silvestre Barra del Colorado (page 149). The Río San Juan forms the border between Costa Rica and Nicaragua; however, the border is not mid-river, but on the Costa Rican bank. English is widely spoken along the coast.

Puerto Limón *See map, page 144.*
Built on the site of the ancient indigenous village of Cariari, Columbus dropped anchor at Punta Uvita, the island off the coastline, on his fourth and final voyage. The climate is very humid and it rains almost every day. With a mainly black population and a large Chinese contingent, the town has a distinctly Caribbean feel, expressed particularly during carnival but in most bars every weekend. Puerto Limón is not a popular stopover, but experienced

travellers may have an interest in exploring Limón. Beware of theft at night and remember it is a port; there are a lot of drunks roaming the streets.

Parque Vargas and the seafront promenade at the rocky headland are popular places for social gatherings and killing time, making for ideal people-watching territory, especially in the evening. Parque Vargas, sadly rather run down, has an impressive botanical display with a colourful mural depicting the history of Limón and a bandstand.

On the upside, the nightlife is good, particularly for Caribbean music and dancing, culminating in carnival every October, Costa Rica's largest festival (see Festivals, below). There is a small **Museo Etnohistórico de Limón** ① *Calle 2, Av 2, Mon-Fri 0900-1200, 1300-1600*, featuring material relating to Columbus' arrival in Limón. The cargo docks are still active with international crews making regular journeys, as well as being the landing point for pristine floating palaces cruising the Caribbean.

Around Puerto Limón

Playa Bonita and **Portete** have pleasant beaches about 5 km along the coastal road from Puerto Limón. **Moín**, a further 1.5 km east along the road, is the sight of the international docks, which exports some 2.8 million bunches of bananas annually. The docks are also the departure point for barges to Tortuguero and Barra del Colorado (eight hours). Boats also run from Moín to Tortuguero (see below) and may be hired at the dockside. Buses run to Moín every 40 minutes from 0600-1740, 30 minutes, US$0.10. If shipping a vehicle, check which dock. Some simple accommodation options are available if you end up waiting here.

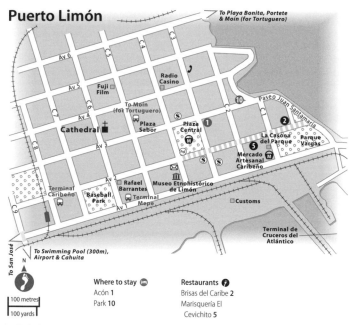

Puerto Limón

To Playa Bonita, Portete & Moín (for Tortuguero)

Av 6
Av 5
Radio Casino
Fuji Film
Av 4
To Moín (for Tortuguero)
Plaza Sabor
Plaza Central
Cathedral
Paseo Juan Santamaría
La Casona del Parque
Parque Vargas
Av 3
Mercado Artesanal Caribeño
Av 2
Rafael Barrantes
Museo Etnohistórico de Limón
Terminal Caribeño
Baseball Park
Terminal Mepe
Customs
To San José
To Swimming Pool (300m), Airport & Cahuita
N
Terminal de Cruceros del Atlántico

100 metres
100 yards

Where to stay 🛏
Acón 1
Park 10

Restaurants 🍴
Brisas del Caribe 2
Marisquería El Cevichito 5

Where to stay

Puerto Limón

$$ Park
Av 3, Calle 1-2, T2798-0555.
Neat little hotel with 34 rooms, sea-facing,
quiet and cool, restaurant good.

$$-$ Acón
*On corner of main square, Calle 3, Av 3,
T2758-1010.*
Big rooms with private bath, a/c, clean, safe,
good restaurant, a bit run down, popular
daily disco **Aquarius** except Mon.

Restaurants

Puerto Limón

$$ Brisas del Caribe
Facing Parque Vargas, Av 2, Calle 1, T2758-0138.
Cheap noodles, meat and seafood, and
good service.

$$ Marisquería El Cevichito
Av 2, Calle 1-2, T2758-1380.
Good fish, steaks and ceviche and good
spot for people-watching.

Festivals

Puerto Limón
Just before 12 Oct Carnival is Costa Rica's
biggest; it's crowded and prices rise, but it's
definitely worth seeing.

Transport

Puerto Limón
Bus Town bus service is irregular and
crowded. Service from **San José** with
CoopeLimón, T2233-3646 and **Caribeño**,
T2222-0610, at least every hour, 0500-2000,
daily. Arrive and depart from Calle 2, Av 1-2,
2½ hrs, US$5.30. Also services to **Guápiles**
and **Siquirres**, US$1.30. From same stop buses
to Siquirres/Guápiles, 13 daily, 8 direct. Near
Radio Casino on Av 4, Calle 3-4, buses leave
for **Sixaola** on the Panamanian border, 1st
0500, last 1800, US$5.30, stopping at **Cahuita**.
Puerto Viejo and **Bribri** en route; for more on
crossing the border at Sixaola to Panama, see
border crossing box for Costa Rica–Panama,
page 174). To **Manzanillo**, at 0600, 1430,
returning 1130, 1900, 1½ hrs, US$4.20. To
Moín from Calle 5, Av 3-4, every 30 mins
from 0600-2200, US$0.40.

★ Parque Nacional Tortuguero
extensive park protecting turtle-nesting sites and rainforest

Tortuguero (Tortuguero Information Centre, T8833-0827, safari@racsa.co.cr) is a
29,068-ha national park, with a marine extension of over 50,000 ha, conserving
the Atlantic nesting sites of the green and leatherback turtle and the Caribbean
lowland rainforest inland. As with much of Costa Rica, getting the timing right to
see this natural phenomenon is essential. The green turtles lay their eggs at night
on the scrappy, rather untidy beach from June to October, with the hatchlings
emerging from the depths of their sandy nests until November at the latest.
Leatherbacks can be seen from March to June. Hawksbill and loggerheads also
nest at Tortuguero but numbers are minimal. Trips to look for nesting turtles are
carefully monitored and you must be accompanied by a licensed guide at all times.
For details, see Tour operators and Transport, in Listings section, below.

While your visit may not coincide with those of the turtles, the canals of jungle-fringed waterways behind the beach, full of abundant bird and insect life, are always a pleasure.

A **visitor centre**, close to the village of Tortuguero, has information on the park and the turtles. Round the back of the headquarters there is a well-marked and recommended 1.4-km nature trail. In the centre is a small gift shop. To the northern end of the village is the **Caribbean Conservation Corporation**, which has played a fundamental role in the creation and continued research of the turtle nesting grounds. There's an interesting and very informative **Natural History Museum** ① *T2224-9215 (San José), www.conserve turtles.org, daily 1000-1200, 1400-1730, donation US$1*. Information about all this and more can be found on the village website, www.tortuguerovillage.com.

A guide is required for trips along the beach at night and is recommended for trips through the waterways. If travelling with a lodge, tours will be arranged for you. If organizing independently, contact the information kiosk in the village for instructions and to link up with a registered guide. To visit the turtles at night you must pay US$15 park entrance fee and US$5 each for a guide. A guide and tour in no way guarantees you will see a turtle or hatchlings. **Note** Do not swim at Tortuguero as there are sharks.

Tours through the water channels are the best way to see the rainforest, ideally in a boat without a motor. The canal, bordered with primary rainforest, gives way to smaller channels and, drifting slowly through forest-darkened streams, the rainforest slowly comes alive with wildlife including birds – over half of those found in Costa Rica – monkeys, sloths and, for the lucky, alligators, tapirs, jaguars, ocelots, peccaries, anteaters and even manatees. You can hire a canoe and guide for about US$8 per hour per person in a boat without motor, or US$15 with a motor, minimum of four people. Night tours cost US$20 per person per hour. Fishing tours, with all equipment included, cost US$35 per person, with a minimum of two people. Take insect repellent. See Tour operators, below.

Listings Parque Nacional Tortuguero

Where to stay

Top-end hotels normally target package deals; walk-in rates given where available. There are many cheap *cabañas* in town; the boatmen or villagers will help you find them. Staying in town is better for the local economy.

Tortuguero village

$$ Casa Marbella
In front of the Catholic church, T2709-8011, http://casamarbella.tripod.com.
B&B with 4 small rooms, with private bath. Run by local guide Daryl Loth. Good source of information and in the centre of the village.

$$ Miss Junie's
T2709-8102.
Has 12 good cabins at the north end of town.

$ Cabinas Tortuguero
T2709-8114, tinamon@racsa.co.cr.
5 little cabins, each sleeping 3 with private bath, pleasant garden with hammocks. Nice spot.

Beyond Tortuguero village
Places out of the village, best visited as part of a package, include:

$$$$ Mawamba Lodge
T2293-8181, www.grupomawamba.com.
Comfortable cabins with fans, pool, walking distance to town. Turtle beaches are behind the property.

$$$$-$$$ Pachira Lodge
Across the canal from town, T2257-2242, www.pachiralodge.com.

3-day/2-night package includes transport, food, tours with bilingual guide, US$309 per person.

$$$ Laguna Lodge
T2272-4943, www.lagunatortuguero.com.
50-odd cabins, with bath and fan, restaurant, bar, beautiful gardens, pool and conference room.

$$$ Tortuga Lodge
T2521-6099 (San José), www. costaricaexpeditions.com.
Price per person includes meals. Very comfortable accommodation, in big rooms, each with veranda or balcony.

$$$ Turtle Beach Lodge
T2248-0707, www.turtlebeachlodge.com.
2- to 7-day packages from US$210 in 48 ha of beautifully landscaped tropical grounds.

$$ Caribbean Paradise
1 channel back from Tortuguero, T2232-2174, www.caribbeanparadisetortuguero.com (difficult to reach, try going direct when you arrive).
Run by Tico Carlos and his wife Ana, includes 3 meals. 20 simple rooms, no set itinerary, personal service, activities as you want them. A refreshing change from the general offering and very enjoyable.

$ Caño Palma Biological Station
6 km north of Tortuguero, administered by the Canadian Organization for Tropical Education and Rainforest Conservation (in Canada T905-683 2116).
Basic rooms for volunteer staff. Price per person, includes meals. A good place for serious naturalists or just for unwinding, accommodation for up to 16 in wooden cabin, freshwater well for drinking and washing. Minimum stay 2 weeks.

Restaurants

Tortuguero village

$$ Café Caoba
Cheap and has excellent pizza, sandwiches and shrimp.

$$ Miss Junie's
North end of the village.
Very popular, has good local dishes, reservation necessary.

$$ The Vine
Pizzas and sandwiches.

$ El Dolar
Simple restaurant, small menu, good *casado*.

$ Restaurant El Muellecito
T2710 6716.
Also has 3 simple cabins.

What to do

Tour operators
From San José Most people visit Tortuguero as part of a tour from San José flying into the airport, or catching an agency bus and boat from Matina. It is possible to travel to Tortuguero independently (see Transport, below). Tours from San José include transport, meals, 2 nights' lodging, guide and boat trips for US$215-330 per person (double occupancy).
Caño Blanco Marina, *2 Av, 1-3 C, San José, T2256-9444 (San José), T2710-0523 (Tortuguero).* Runs a daily bus-boat service San José–Tortuguero at 0700, US$50 return. Book in advance – if you miss the boat, there is nothing else in Caño Blanco Marina.
Mawamba, *T2223-2421, www.grupo mawamba.com.* Minimum 2 people, 3 days/2 nights, daily, private launch so you can stop en route, with launch tour of national park included. Accommodation at the very comfortable **Mawamba Lodge**, 3-day/2-night package, Tue, Fri, Sun US$330. Other accommodations have very similar packages, with the difference being the level of comfort in the hotel. **Ilan Ilan Lodge**

(T2255-3031, www.ilan-ilanlodge.com), is one of the more affordable at US$215 for 2 nights, US$160 for 1 night (but not really long enough to be worth it).

Tours from Puerto Viejo de Sarapiquí, including boat trip to Tortuguero, meals, 2 nights' lodging, guide and transport to San José cost US$275-400 per person (double occupancy). *Riverboat Francesca* (T2226-0986, www.tortuguerocanals.com), costs US$200-220 per person 2-day, 1-night trips exploring the canals for exquisite wildlife, sportfishing. Longer packages are also available.

From Puerto Limón Organizing a package trip from **Puerto Limón** is more difficult. **Viajes Tropicales Laura** (T2795-2410, www.viajestropicales laura.net), have been highly recommended, daily service, open return US$60 if phoned direct, more through travel agencies, pickup from hotel, will store luggage, lunch provided, excellent for pointing out wildlife on the way. An inclusive 2-day, 1-night package a from Puerto Limón with basic accommodation, turtle-watching trip and transport (no food) costs from US$99 per person.

Guides Several local guides have been recommended, including **Johnny Velázquez**; **Alberto**, who lives next to Hotel Mary Scar; **Rubén Bananero**, who lives in the last house before you get to the National Park office, sign on pathway, recommended for 4-hr tour at dusk and in the dark; **Chico**, who lives behind Sabina's Cabinas, US$2 per hr, and will take you anywhere in his motor boat; **Ernesto**, who was born in Tortuguero, and has 15 years' experience as a guide, contact him at Tropical Lodge or through his mother, who owns Sabina's Cabinas; **Rafael**, a biologist who speaks Spanish and English (his wife speaks French), and lives 500 m behind Park Rangers' office (ask rangers for directions); he also rents canoes. **Ross Ballard**, a Canadian biologist who can be contacted through Casa Marbella.

Daryl Loth lives locally and runs **Tortuguero Safaris** (T8833-0827,

safari@racsa.co.cr). **Barbara Hartung** of **Tinamon Tours** (T2709-8004, www. tinamontours.de), a biologist who speaks English, German, French and Spanish, is recommended for boat, hiking and turtle tours in Tortuguero (US$5 per person per hr; all-inclusive trips from Limón 3-days, 2-nights, US$140 per person). Both Daryl and Barbara are strong supporters of using paddle power, or at most electric motors. There are several boats for rent from Tortuguero, ask at the *pulpería*. The use of polluting 2-stroke motors is outlawed in Tortuguero, and the use of 4-stroke engines is limited to 3 of the 4 main water channels.

Transport

Air Daily flights from **San José** with **Nature Air** (US$$91).

Boat It is quite possible to travel to Tortuguero independently, but more challenging than the all-inclusive packages. There are a couple of options. From **Limón**, regular vessels leaves from the Tortuguero dock in **Moín**, north of Limón, US$50 return. It is a loosely run cooperative, with boats leaving at 1000. There is also a 1500 service that runs less frequently. If possible, book in advance through the Tortuguero Information Centre (check the times; they change frequently). If you are in a group you may be able to charter a boat for approximately US$200.

An alternative route is between **Puerto Veijo de Sarapiquí** and Tortuguero. Boats leave Puerto Viejo on Mon and Thu, returning on Tue and Fri. US$55 per person.

Bus and boat From **San José**, the bus/ boat combination is the cheapest option and a mini-adventure in itself. Take the 0900 bus to Cariari from the Terminal Gran Caribe, arriving around 1045. Walk 500 m north to the ticket booth behind the police station where you can buy you bus/boat ticket to Tortuguero. Take the 1200 bus to **La Pavona**, arriving around 1330. Take 1 of the boats to Tortuguero, which will arrive about 1500. The journey is about US$10 1-way. Don't be talked into a package if you're not interested – there are plenty of services to choose from in Tortuguero. The return service leaves at 0830 and 1330 giving you 1 or 2 nights in Tortuguero.

Alternative routes include the 1030 bus from San José to Cariari, changing to get the 1400 bus to La Geest and the 1530 boat to Tortuguero. Or 1300 bus San José–Cariari, 1500 bus Cariari to La Pavona, 1630 boat La Pavone to Tortuguero.

It is also possible to take a bus from Siquirres to **Freeman** (unpaved road, US$1.70), a Del Monte banana plantation, from where unscheduled boats go to Tortuguero; ask around at the bank of the Río Pacuare, or call the public phone office in Tortuguero (T2710-6716, open 0730-2000) and ask for **Johnny Velázquez** to come and pick you up, US$57, maximum 4 passengers, 4 hrs. Sometimes heavy rains block the canals, preventing passage there or back. Contact **Willis Rankin** (T2798-1556) an excellent captain who will negotiate rampaging rivers. All riverboats for the major lodges leave from Hamburgo or Freeman. If the excursion boats have a spare seat you may be allowed on.

Barra del Colorado

secluded national wildlife refuge

The canals here are part artificial, part natural; originally they were narrow lagoons running parallel to the sea separated by a small strip of land. Now the lagoons are linked and it is possible to sail as far as Barra del Colorado, in the extreme northeast of Costa Rica, 25 km beyond Tortuguero. They pass many settlements. The town is divided by the river, the main part being on the northern bank.

The **Refugio Nacional de Fauna Silvestre Barra del Colorado** (81,213 ha) is difficult to access. The reserve and the Parque Nacional Tortuguero share some boundaries, making for a far more effective protected zone. The fame of the region's fauna extends to the waters, which are world renowned for fishing.

Once across the Río Colorado (which in fact is the south arm of the Río San Juan delta), you can walk to Nicaragua along the coast, but it is a long 30-km beach walk; take food and lots of water. Most hikers overnight en route. Seek advice before setting out.

Listings Barra del Colorado

Where to stay

$$$$-$$$ Silver King Lodge
T2711-0708, www.silver kinglodge.com.
Price per person. Deluxe sport-fishing hotel, 5-night packages includes flights, meals, rooms with bath and a/c. Pool.

$ Tarponland Lodge
T2710-2141.
Cabins, run by Guillermo Cunningham, very helpful and knowledgeable. If you have a tent you may be able to camp at **Soda La Fiesta**, lots of mosquitoes.

sleepy beach towns offering surfing, diving and trekking

Penshurst

South of Limón, a paved road shadows the coastline normally separated by little more than a thin line of palms. Beyond Penshurst is the **Hitoy Cerere Biological Reserve**. If you have time, camping is easy in the hills and there are plenty of rivers for swimming. Further south the road leads to Cahuita, Puerto Viejo and on towards Manzanillo – low-key beach resorts, with lively centres, comfortable hideaways and coastal and nature opportunities to explore. If heading for the Panamanian border, going inland just north of Puerto Viejo takes you through Bribri and on to Sixaola; see also the border crossing box for Costa Rica–Panama, page 174). From Penshurst it is 11.5 km to Cahuita.

Cahuita and Parque Nacional Cahuita

Entry to the park US$15. The official entrance to the park is at Puerto Vargas, about 5 km south of Cahuita, where the park headquarters, a nature trail, camping facilities and toilets are situated. Take the bus to Km 5, then turn left at the sign. You can enter the park for free from the southern side of Cahuita, which is ideal for relaxing on the beach, but leave a donation. If you have the option,

Cahuita

Playa Negra

Caribbean Sea

Plaza

Laundrette

Cahuita Tours

Highway 36

To Highway 36

To Highway 36

N

100 metres
100 yards

Where to stay
Bungalows Aché **4** *C6*
Cabinas Iguana **3** *B1*
Cabinas Nirvana **25** *B1*
El Encanto B&B Inn **7** *B3*
Jenny's Cabinas **12** *B6*
Kelly Creek **13** *C6*

La Casa de las Flores **1** *B5*
La Diosa **2** *A1*
Magellan Inn **15** *A1*
Restaurant & Bungalows
  Bluspirit **8** *B4*
Sol y Mar **22** *C6*

Restaurants
Chao's Paradise **3** *A1*
Coral Reef **1** *B5*
La Casa Creole **5** *A1*
La Fe **8** *B5*
Mango Tango Pizzeria **17** *B5*
Miss Edith's **6** *A5*

visit during the week when it is quieter. There is a tourist complex in the area and the marisquería (seafood restaurant), at Puerto Vargas park entrance has a jovial host who also has rooms.

The small town of **Cahuita** hides 1 km back from the main road and has a sleepy feel. A laid-back community, it's a good place to hide away in one of the secluded spots or to party in the centre of town. There are no banks; money exchange is difficult except occasionally for cash dollars (**Cahuita Tours** changes dollars and traveller's cheques). Take plenty of colones from Limón. The nearest banks are in **Puerto Viejo** and **Bribri** (20 km away) but several places accept credit cards.

North of the town is **Playa Negra**, a beautiful black-sand beach ideal for swimming or just lazing about in a hammock, while to the south is the national park. Most people stay in Cahuita to explore the park.

Cahuita National Park (1068 ha) is a narrow strip of beach protecting a coral reef offshore and a marine area of 22,400 ha. The length of the beach can be walked in about three hours; you'll pass endless coconut palms and interesting tropical forest, through which there is also a path. It is hot and humid, so take drinking water, but a wide range of fauna can be seen, as well as howler monkeys, white-faced monkeys, coatis, snakes, butterflies and hermit crabs. Over 500 species of fish inhabit the surrounding waters and reef tours are available. An old Spanish shipwreck can be seen and reached without a boat. Snorkellers should take care to stay away from the coral, which is already badly damaged by agricultural chemicals and other pollutants. The park extends from the southern limit of Cahuita town southeast to Puerto Vargas.

Note Cahuita and Puerto Viejo have suffered from what locals believe is a lack of support and investment from central government. An undercurrent of problems, partially based on the perception that everyone on the Caribbean coast takes drugs, does mean that you may be offered drugs. If you are not interested, just say no.

★ Puerto Viejo de Talamanca

Puerto Viejo is a good base and a quietly happening party town, with a number of good beaches stretching out to the south. Activities in the area are numerous and you could spend many days exploring the options. There is reef diving nearby, or you can head south to Mandoca for lagoon diving from canoes. Surfers seek out the glorious **Salsa Brava** wave, which peaks from December to February. Away from the beach, nature trips range from tough treks

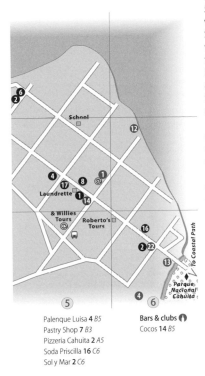

Palenque Luisa **4** *B5*
Pastry Shop **7** *B3*
Pizzeria Cahuita **2** *A5*
Soda Priscilla **16** *C6*
Sol y Mar **2** *C6*

Bars & clubs 🎵
Cocos **14** *B5*

in Gandoca–Manzanillo Wildlife Refuge (see below) through to gentle strolls around the self-guided botanical gardens to the north of town. There are also several cultural trips to KeKöLdi and Bribri indigenous reserves and options to take dug-outs to the inland town of Yorkin. The **Asociación Talamanqueña de Ecoturismo y Conservación** ⓘ *ATEC, main street, T2750-0398, www.ateccr.org*, provides tourist information, sells locally made crafts and T-shirts, and also offers guide services, rainforest hikes, snorkelling and fishing trips. The **South Caribbean Music Festival** takes place in the lead up to Easter.

Around Puerto Viejo
There are a number of popular beaches southeast along the road from Puerto Viejo. Traffic is limited, buses occasional, but it is walkable. About 4 km away is **Playa Cocles**, which has some

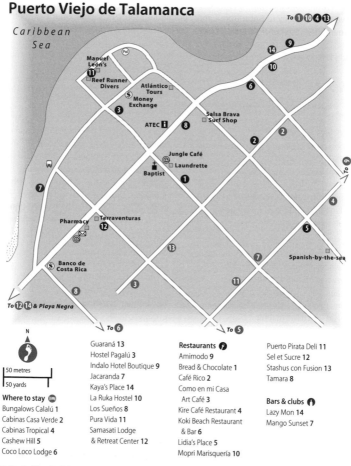

Puerto Viejo de Talamanca

Caribbean Sea

of the best surfing on this coast, and 2 km further on is **Playa Chiquita**, with many places to stay. Next is **Punta Uva**, beyond which, after another 5 km, you arrive in **Manzanillo**, followed by white-sand beaches and rocky headlands to **Punta Mona** and the **Gandoca-Manzanillo Wildlife Refuge** ① *ANAI, T2224-6090*, a celebration of Costa Rican diversity largely left alone by prospectors and tourists alike. Among other projects, marine scientists are interested in the protection of the giant leatherback turtle. Volunteer work is possible.

Bribri

At **Hotel Creek**, north of Puerto Viejo, the paved road heads through the hills to the village of Bribri, at the foot of the Talamanca Range Indigenous Reserve. Halfway between is **Violeta's Pulpería**. From Limón, **Aerovías Talamaqueñas Indígenas** fly cheaply to **Amubri** in the reserve (there is a *casa de huéspedes* run by nuns in Amubri). Villages such as Bribri, Chase, Bratsi, Shiroles and San José Cabécar can be reached by bus from Cahuita. There are several buses daily to Bribri from Limón. Continuing south is Sixaola, on the border with Panama; see also border crossing box for Costa Rica–Panama, page 174.

Listings South from Puerto Limón *maps p150 and p152*

Where to stay

Penshurst

$$$ Los Aviarios del Caribe
30 km south of Limón just north of Penshurst, T2750-0775, www.slothsanctuary.com.
A sloth rescue sanctuary with a small nature reserve. The friendly owners offer canoe trips in the Estrella river delta and there's a volunteer programme if you have time to spare. Recommended.

$$$ Selva Bananita Lodge
20 km from Puerto Limón at Cerro Mochila heading inland at Bananito, T2253-8118, www.selvabananito.com.
7 cabins on secluded farm, solar heating, primary rainforest tours, tree climbing, horses and bikes to rent.

Cahuita and Parque Nacional Cahuita
Beware of theft on the beach and drug pushers who may be undercover police.

$$$ El Encanto Bed and Breakfast Inn
Playa Negra, T2755-0113, www.elencantocahuita.com.
Attractive place built by very stylish French owners, among shady gardens with pool. 3 bungalows with private bath, hot water,

fan, mosquito net, terrace and hammocks and 1 3-bedroom apartment. Yoga and massage are available.

$$$ La Casa de las Flores
Cahuita, T2755-0326, www. lacasadelasfloreshotel.com.
Centrally located, 200 m north of park entrance, this Italian-run hotel is modern and very clean. The black and white minimalism is quite harsh in the bedrooms.

$$$-$$ La Diosa
Playa Grande, past Playa Negra, T2755-0055, www.hotelladiosa.net.
Colourful bungalows with luxury jacuzzi, a/c, private hot-water bath, hammocks, pool, gym, massage, games room, internet, surf/kayak equipment – all this and on the beach. Cheaper out of season.

$$$-$$ Magellan Inn
2 km north of Cahuita, T2755-0035, www.magellaninn.com.
Includes breakfast, 6 beautifully decorated rooms with bath and fan, and 10,000-year-old pool (honestly) set in peaceful gardens and with renowned French Creole restaurant.

$$ Bungalows Aché
By the entrance to the national park, T2755-0119, www.bungalowsache.com.

A little off the beaten track in a very tranquil and attractive location. Well-kept bungalows with private hot-water bath, mosquito nets, coffee-maker, fridge and hammocks, friendly owners.

$$ Kelly Creek
Within a couple of blocks of the centre of town, by entrance to national park, T2755-0007, www.hotelkellycreek.com.
Large rooms with veranda, ceiling fan to assist fresh sea breezes, good service and great spot.

$$ Restaurant and Bungalows Bluspirit
Just out of town on the road to Playa Negra, T2755-0122, www.bungalowsbluspirit.com.
Gorgeous split-level bungalows with private bath, hot water and hammocks, by the beach. Run by a very friendly couple who also serve fresh fish and Italian home-cooked meals in their bar and restaurant.

$$-$ Cabinas Iguana
800 m north of Cahuita, T2755-0005, www.cabinas-iguana.com.
Swiss-owned, very friendly, cabins or houses to rent, kitchen, fan, mosquito netting, balcony, clean, waterfall-fed pool, nice location. Big 2-for-1 book swap. Very good value.

$$-$ Cabinas Nirvana
Towards Playa Negra, T2755-0110, www.cabinasnirvana.com.
Wooden rooms in a very tranquil spot, hot water private bath, pool in gardens.

$$-$ Jenny's Cabinas
Heading to the beach, T2755-0256, www.cabinasjenny.com.
Balconies with view, Canadian-owned, bath, fan, breakfast available, running water, close to the sea but surrounding area a bit scruffy.

$ Sol y Mar
On the road to national park, T2755-0237.
Friendly owners have rooms that sleep 2-6 people, with private hot-water bath. Rooms are a little tatty, but fine and some very spacious. Their local restaurant is good for breakfast.

Puerto Viejo de Talamanca
Discounts are often available May-Nov.

$$$$ Samasati Lodge & Retreat Center
Near Hone Creek on junction between Cahuita and Puerto Viejo, T2224-1870, www.samasati.com.
Beautiful mountain location with 100-ha reserve, vegetarian restaurant, meditation courses, reservation recommended. Rates per person.

$$$ Cabinas Casa Verde
Central, T2750-0015, www.cabinascasaverde.com.
Comfortable rooms with hammocks, private bath, cracked tile showers in beautiful gardens. A pool and open-air jacuzzi add to the relaxation. The owner collects Central American poison dart frogs and keeps them in tanks dotted around the grounds; ask to take a look, even if you are not a guest. Very nice owners and staff. Recommended.

$$$ Cashew Hill
South of town, T2750-0256, www.cashewhilllodge.co.cr.
Redeveloped in the last few years, although retaining rustic charm. 6 family-orientated rooms, with both private and shared bath, fans and mosquito nets. Set in 1 ha of beautiful gardens on the rolling hills above the town; a mirador looks out over the jungle tops to the sea. Yoga massage retreats and classes available. Quiet, very chilled atmosphere.

$$$ Coco Loco Lodge
South of town, T2750-0281, www.cocolocolodge.com.
Quiet spot in expansive garden south of town, nice thatched wooden and stone cabins, some fully equipped with kitchen and cable TV. Popular. English, German and Spanish spoken.

$$$-$$ Bungalows Calalú
On the road to Cocles, T2750-0042, www.bungalowscalalu.com.
A range of bungalows with and without kitchen, also pool and beautiful butterfly garden in the grounds.

$$$-$$ Kaya's Place
Playa Negra, T2750-0690,
www.kayasplace.com.
Beautifully hand built with reclaimed wood, each room is a little different and accommodation ranges from simple to more luxurious *cabinas*. Opposite the beach, a nice chilled spot.

$$ Cabinas Tropical
Close to the coast, T2750-2064,
www.cabinastropical.com.
8 spotless rooms, some with fridges, with good mattresses, private bath and hot water. Pleasant gardens with shaded garden house for relaxing. The German owner, Rolf Blancke, a tropical biologist, runs tours.

$$ Guaraná
Opposite Lulu Berlu Gallery, T2750-0244,
www.hotelguarana.com.
Very attractive hotel if a little pricey, well kept. All rooms with private, hot water bath, fans, mosquito nets, private balconies and hammocks. They also have a communal kitchen and parking space.

$$ Indalo Hotel Boutique
Corner of Calle 219A and Av 67, T2750-0826,
www.hotelboutiqueindalo.com.
Simple but tasteful rooms with youthful, minimalist contemporary decor, outdoor decking and gravel veranda. Spanish-owned, quiet, friendly, hospitable and good value.

$$ Jacaranda
A few blocks back (see map), T2750-0069,
www.cabinasjacaranda.net.
A very relaxed spot away from the beach set in beautiful gardens, with mosaic pathways and private areas to relax. Rooms are fixed with colourful throws and side lights, showers are spacious. Very attractive place, hot water throughout, fans, mosquito nets. Communal kitchen. Massages can be booked to take place in a pagoda in their flower garden.

$$-$ Pura Vida
A few blocks back from the main street (see map), T2750-0002, www.hotel-puravida.com.
German/Chilean-run, friendly, very clean, hammocks. Sadly lacking in character but recommended.

$ Hostel Pagalú
2 blocks from the bus stop towards the MegaSuper, T2750-1930, www.pagalu.com.
Clean, decent, professional, chilled-out hostel. Accommodation is in tidy 4- to 6-bed dorms with clean sheets and hot-water showers, or simple but comfortable private rooms, with ($$) or without private bath. Also common areas, free coffee and tea, parking, lockers, Wi-Fi.

$ La Ruka Hostel
500 m south of Salsa Brava, just out of town, T2750-0617, www.larukahostel.com.
Laid-back and friendly backpacker place, fun and sociable, but not crazy wild. Lodging includes 3 dorms sleeping 6-8 persons and 2 private double rooms, all with private bath. There are also hammocks, snorkel and fin rentals, surf board rentals, dogs, cats.

$ Los Sueños
Main street (on map), T2750-0369,
www.hotellossuenos.com.
Laid-back and very relaxing, just 4 colourful and bright rooms.

Around Puerto Viejo

$$$$ Tree House Lodge
Punta Uva, T2750-0706,
www.costaricatreehouse.com.
Dutch owner Edsart has 4 apartments – 2 of which are the most unusual in Costa Rica: the treehouse and the beach suite (there is also a beach house). All are fully equipped with kitchen facilities and hot water, and all are equally luxurious.

$$$$-$$$ Aguas Claras
4.5 km from Puerto Viejo on road to Manzanillo, T2750-0131, www.aguasclaras-cr.com.
5 beautiful cottages each painted a different colour with pretty white wooden gables and balconies. All fully equipped and very close to the beach. **Restaurant Miss**

Holly serves gourmet breakfast and lunch. Recommended.

$$$ La Finca Chica
Playa Cocles, T2750-1919, www.fincachica.com.
A good choice for couples or families, very attractive wooden *casitas* and bungalows dotted around a verdant 1-ha jungle property. Rustic but comfortable, with all modern amenities. Recommended.

$$$ La Kukula
Playa Chiquita, T2750-0653, www.lakukulalodge.com.
Located 300 m from the beach, a 'tropical-contemporary' jungle-shrouded lodge with a range of rooms, suites and bungalows, all with hot water, mosquito nets and private terraces. Amenities include a rancho-bar and pool.

$$$ Pachamama Jungle River Lodge
Punta Uva, T8486-7086, www.pachamamacaribe.com.
Managed by a happy couple from southern France, Pachamama is located 200 m from the beach at the mouth of a jungle river. Great *casas* and *casitas* equipped with modern appliances and, most importantly, hammocks.

$$$ Physis Caribbean
Playa Cocles, T2750-0941, www.physiscaribbean.net.
A hospitable B&B with a tropical garden and a range of comfortable wood-panelled rooms equipped with a/c, TV, Wi-Fi, dehumidifier and stereo system. Cosy place, helpful owners.

$$$ Shawandha
Playa Chiquita, T2750-0018, www.shawandhalodge.com.
Beautiful bungalows in the jungle with a calm and private feel and fantastic mosaic showers. Massages available. Very stylish restaurant serving French-Caribbean fusion, pricey.

$$$-$$ La Costa de Papito
Playa Cocles, T2750-0080, www.lacostadepapito.com.
11 beautifully designed bungalows with all the style you'd expect from Eddie Ryan

(**Carlton Arms Hotel**, New York). Rooms with fan and bath. Great owners who love to make their guests happy. Recommended. They now host **Pure Jungle Spa** (T2750-0536, www.purejunglespa.com, Tue-Sat), or by appointment. Treatments are organic, handmade and sound good enough to eat, from chocolate facials to banana body wraps.

$$ Selvin Cabins and restaurant
Playa Uva, T2750-0664.
With room and dormitory accommodation. Cheap.

$$-$ Walaba Hostel
Punta Uva, T2750-0147, www.walabahostel.com.
Close to nature, this bohemian hostel has 2 dorms with bunks, a large living room with TV and DVD, shared kitchen and 1 private attic with views of the garden.

Restaurants

Cahuita and Parque Nacional Cahuita
If the catch is good restaurants have lobster.

$$$ La Casa Creole
*Playa Negra, by the **Magellan Inn**, 2 km north of Cahuita, T2755-0104 (for reservations). Mon-Sat 0600-0900.*
A culinary feast of French and Creole creations, from US$8. Recommended.

$$$-$$ Pizzeria Cahuita
Beach road, next to the police station.
Thin-crust Italian-style pizzas and pastas. Great desserts too, try the tiramisu.

$$ Chao's Paradise
T2755-0421, Playa Negra.
Typical Caribbean food and seafood specials, good little reggae bar, with oropendula nests overlooking the beach.

$$ Coral Reef
Next to Coco's Bar, Cahuita.
Very accommodating local management can cook to your tastes, great local food with seafood specialities.

$$ Mango Tango Pizzeria
Cahuita.
Great home-made pasta with a wide variety if Italian sauces, quite a rarity in these parts, good pizza, good restaurant.

$$ Miss Edith's
Cahuita, T2755-0248. Daily until 2130.
Almost legendary. Delicious Caribbean and vegetarian food, nice people, good value, no alcohol licence, take your own, many recommendations for breakfast and dinner, but don't expect quick service.

$$ Restaurant Palenque Luisa
Cahuita.
Has the distinctly tropical feel with split-bamboo walls, sand floors and a good *menú típico*.

$$ Sol y Mar
Cahuita. Open 0730-1200, 1630-2000, need to arrive early and wait at least 45 mins for food.
Red snapper and volcano potato are especially wicked, US$5; also good breakfasts, try cheese, egg and tomato sandwich, US$2. Good value.

$$-$ La Fe
Opposite Coco's Bar, Cahuita.
Large variety of dishes all centred round rice and beans, good typical food.

$ Soda Priscilla
Opposite Sol y Mar, Cahuita.
Good budget breakfast *pinto*, eggs and fresh juices.

Puerto Viejo de Talamanca

$$$ Amimodo
North end of town, overlooking the beach, beyond Standord's.
Fine Italian restaurant with prices to match. Reputedly fantastic. Weekend Latin nights. Doesn't always come with a smile.

$$$ Koki Beach Restaurant and Bar
Downtown waterfront, www.kokibeach. blogspot.com.
If you want to splash out, a very popular bar-restaurant, style and interior a cut above most places in Puerto Viejo. They serve mainly seafood and meat dishes, including mussels, filet mignon, sea bass in jalapeño sauce and sautéed octopus.

$$$-$$ Mopri Marisquería
Waterfront, opposite Lazy Mon.
This unpretentious open-air restaurant serves really excellent, fresh seafood – try the fish fillet in coconut sauce. If you were wondering, Mopri is Caribbean slang for cousin, the Spanish word *primo* reassembled. Highly recommended.

$$$-$$ Stashus con Fusion
200 m south of town towards the beaches, T2750-0530.
Flavourful international offerings include tandoori coconut fish, Mexican smoked chipotle chicken and guava green vegetable curry. Convivial outdoor seating with candles and occasional live music. Romantic and intimate.

$$ Café Rico
Corner of Calle 217 and Av 69, opposite Cabinas Casa Verde.
Great coffee and breakfasts at this funky café owned by a friendly Englishman. Also book exchange, laundry and tourist information. Recommended.

$$ Como en mi Casa Art Café
Behind Cabinas Los Almendros, near the Sat organic market, www.comoenmi casacostarica.wordpress.com.
Small, friendly, bohemian café serving fresh food prepared with love. Offerings include salads, smoothies, hummus dips, breakfasts, coffee and home-made chocolate. An emphasis on local organic ingredients.

$$ Kire Café Restaurant
Av 71.
Affordable and friendly open-air eatery. They serve smoothies, salads, pizzas, burgers, *casados* and *comida típica*, all prepared and served Argentine-style.

$$ Puerto Pirata Deli
On the beach, 50 m east from the bus station.

Funky, friendly place on the beach. They serve raw food and Ayruvedic-inspired Mediterranean dishes, organic, vegetarian, wheat-free. Chilled-out, great place. Try the smoothies.

$$ Sel et Sucre
100 m south of the bus stop, www.seletsucrecr.com.
Delicious sweet and savory crêpes, salads, waffles, chocolate fruit fondues, coffee, cocktails and smoothies. Authentically French, recommended.

$$ Tamara
Main street, T2750-0148. Open 0600-2100.
Local good fish dishes, popular throughout the day and packed at weekends.

$$-$ Bread and Chocolate
Centre of town (see map).
A breakfast café well-known for its home baking and the morning menu is filled with good, home-made choices, ranging from eggs, bacon and fresh bread to oatmeal with apple and cinnamon. Cakes, mint and nut brownies and divine chocolate truffles are also home-made and the café is well recommended.

$ Lidia's Place
South of centre.
Good typical food and to-die-for chocolate cake that does not hang round.

Cafés and bakeries

Pan Pay
Beachfront.
Good bakery. Also serve great breakfasts: eggs with avocado, fresh bread and tomato salsa, omelettes, pastries, etc. A good place to read the paper and nod at the locals – a very popular spot in the morning.

Around Puerto Viejo

$$ El Living
Playa Cocles.
Pizza, drinks and music, very laid-back and good prices.

$$ La Isla Inn
Playa Cocles.
Serves Japanese Caribbean fusion, including sushi, soups, salads and stir-fry.

$$ Magic Ginger
Hotel Kasha, Playa Chiquita.
Restaurant and bar serving gourmet French cooking, seafood specials and exotic salads.

$$ Rest Maxi
Manzanillo.
Reggae-style restaurant serving typical Caribbean food and seafood specials.

$ Aguas Dulce
Playa Cocles.
Ice creams, pastries and sandwiches.

Bars and clubs

Cahuita and Parque Nacional Cahuita
Rikki's Bar and **Cocos Bar** in the centre of Cahuita; the latter is the livelier of the two and hosts reggae nights on Fri and live music.

Coffee Bar
On the shore near Cabinas Jenny.
A good reggae spot.

Puerto Viejo de Talamanca
Puerto probably has the most lively nightlife on Costa Rica's entire Caribbean coast and has always run on an unspoken rota – each bar having a particular night, and this is still (loosely) the case. 2 solid fail-safes are **Lazy Mon,** on the downtown beach front, and **Mango Sunset**, 20 m from the bus stop.

What to do

Cahuita and Parque Nacional Cahuita
Snorkelling equipment and **surfboards** available for rent. **Horses** can be hired, but try to ensure they are in good shape. **Bicycles** can be hired for about US$7 per day and you cycle to Puerto Viejo and the Panamanian border through some beautiful scenery.

Tour operators

Wide range of activities available including water sports and nature tours.

Cahuita Tours, *T2755-0232, exotica@racsa. co.cr.* Excursions by jeep and glass-bottomed boat tours over the reefs, bike, diving and snorkelling equipment rental, international telephone service (ICE) and Western Union money transfer. **GrayLine** bus travel can be arranged here.

Roberto's Tours, *office located at his restaurant (Roberto's) on the main street.* Very nice people run all the usual tours of the area including snorkelling and diving.

Willies Tours, *T2755-0267, www.willies-costarica-tours.com.* Willie is most helpful and knows everything about Cahuita and surrounding areas. He runs tours to Tortuguero, Panama, Bribri indigenous reserve and whitewater rafting in the Pacuare river. The office is located opposite Restaurant Palenque on the main street, where he also runs an internet café.

Puerto Viejo de Talamanca

Tours in Puerto Viejo include canopy, snorkelling, boat trips and diving in Cahuita and Manzanillo, trips to an indigenous reserve, rafting in Pacuare, kayaking, birdwatching, etc.

ATEC is the easiest source of information (www.ateccr.org) and the original provider of information and tours combining eco-tourism and conservation but you can also try **Terraventuras** (T2750-0750, www. terraventuras.com); **Exploradores Outdoors** (T2750-6262, www.exploradoresoutdoors. com); **Atlántico Tours** (T2750-0004); **Reef Runner Divers** (T2750-0480, www. reefrunner divers.com); **Yuppi and Tino** (T2750-0621) in Puerto Viejo; and **Aguamar Adventures**, in Manzanillo, who have been operating since 1993, and offer diving courses and local trips. Snorkel tours from US$35, tank dives from US$50.

Penshurst

Bus Small buses leave **Limón** (Calle 4, Av 6) for **Valle de Estrella/Pandora,** 7 a day from 0500, at 2-hourly intervals, last at 1800, 1½ hrs (returning from Pandora at similar times).

Cahuita and Parque Nacional Cahuita

Bus Service direct from **San José's** Terminal del Caribe, to **Cahuita** at 0600, 1000, 1200, 1400 and 1600, return 0700, 0800, 0930, 1130 and 1630, 3½ hrs, US$7.90, T2257-8129, **Trans Mepá,** 4 hrs, US$4.50, and from **Puerto Limón,** in front of Radio Casino, 0500-1800, return 0630-2000, 1 hr, US$2, T2758-1572, both continuing to Bribri, and Sixaola (dirt road) on the Panamanian border (US$1, 2 hrs); see also border crossing box for Costa Rica–Panama, page 174. The bus drops you at the crossing of the 2 main roads in Cahuita.

Puerto Viejo de Talamanca

Bus Daily services from **San José** from Gran Terminal del Caribe at 0600, 1000, 1200, 1400 and 1600, return at 0730, 0900, 1100 and 1600, 4 hrs, US$9; from **Limón** daily from Radio Casino, 0500-1800, return 0600-2000, 1½ hrs; 30 mins from **Cahuita,** US$0.80. To **Manzanillo** at 0700, 1530, 1900, returning 0500, 0830, 1700, ½ hr, US$0.80. To **Sixaola (on the Panamanian border)** 5 daily, 0545 until 1845, 2 hrs, US$2; see also border crossing box for Costa Rica–Panama, page 174.

Around Puerto Viejo

Bus Express bus to **Manzanillo** from Terminal Sixaola, **San José,** daily, 1600, return 0630. From **Limón** daily 0600, 1430, return 1130, 1900, 1½ hrs.

Background

History

Spanish settlement

During his last voyage in September 1502, Columbus landed on the shores of what is now Costa Rica. Rumours of vast gold treasures (which never materialized) led to the name of Costa Rica (Rich Coast). The Spaniards settled in the Meseta Central, where the numbers of several thousand sedentary indigenous farmers were soon greatly diminished by the diseases brought by the settlers. Cártago was founded in 1563 by **Juan Vásquez de Coronado**, but there was almost no expansion for 145 years, when a small number left Cártago for the valleys of Aserrí and Escazú. They founded Heredia in 1717, and San José in 1737. Alajuela, not far from San José, was founded in 1782. The settlers were growing in numbers but were still poor and raising only subsistence crops.

Independence and coffee

Independence from Spain was declared in 1821 whereupon Costa Rica, with the rest of Central America, immediately became part of Mexico. This led to a civil war during which, two years later, the capital was moved from Cártago to San José. After Independence, the government sought anxiously for some product which could be exported and taxed for revenue.

Coffee was successfully introduced from Cuba in 1808, making Costa Rica the first of the Central American countries to grow what was to become known as the golden bean. The Government offered free land to coffee growers, thus building up a peasant landowning class. In 1825 there was a trickle of exports, carried by mule to the ports. By 1846 there were ox-cart roads to Puntarenas. By 1850 there was a large flow of coffee to overseas markets which was greatly increased by the opening of a railway in 1890 from San José and Cártago to Puerto Limón along the valley of the River Reventazón. From 1850, coffee prosperity began to affect the country profoundly: the birth rate grew, land for coffee was free, and the peasant settlements started spreading, first down the Reventazón as far as Turrialba, then up the slopes of the volcanoes, then down the new railway from San José to the old Pacific port of Puntarenas.

Banana industry

Bananas were first introduced in 1878 making Costa Rica the first Central American republic to grow them. It is now the second largest exporter in the world. Labour was brought in from Jamaica to clear the forest and work the plantations. The industry grew and in 1913, the peak year, the Caribbean coastlands provided 11 million bunches for export. Since then the spread of disease has lowered exports and encouraged crop diversification. The United Fruit Company turned its attentions to the Pacific littoral, especially in the south around the port of Golfito. Although some of the Caribbean plantations were turned over to cacao, *abacá* (Manila hemp) and African palm, the region has regained its ascendancy over the Pacific littoral as a banana producer. By the end of the century over 50,000 ha were planted to bananas, mostly in the Atlantic lowlands.

In the 1990s Chiquita, Dole and Del Monte, the multinational fruit producers, came under international pressure over labour rights on their plantations. Two European campaign groups targeted working conditions in Costa Rica where, despite constitutional guarantees of union freedom, there was a poor record of labour rights abuse. Only 10% of Costa Rica's 50,000 banana workers were represented by unions. The rest preferred to join the less political *solidarista* associations, which provide cheap loans and promote savings, and thus avoid being blacklisted or harassed. Del Monte agreed in 1998 to talk to the unions after a decade of silence, while Chiquita declared its workers were free to choose trade union representation.

Democratic government

Costa Rica's long tradition of democracy began in 1889 and has continued to the present day, with only a few lapses. In 1917 the elected president **Alfredo González** was ousted by **Federico Tinoco**, who held power until 1919, when a counter-revolution and subsequent elections brought Julio Acosta to the presidency. Democratic and orderly government followed until the campaign of 1948 when violent protests and a general strike surrounded disputed results. A month of fighting broke out after the Legislative Assembly annulled the elections, leading to the abolition of the constitution and a junta being installed, led by **José Figueres Ferrer**. In 1949 a constituent assembly drew up a new constitution and abolished the army. The junta stepped down and **Otilio Ulate Blanco**, one of the candidates of the previous year, was inaugurated. In 1952, Figueres, a socialist, founded the Partido de Liberación Nacional, and was elected president in 1953. He dominated politics for the next two decades, serving as president in 1953-1958 and 1970-1974. The PLN introduced social welfare programmes and nationalization policies, while intervening conservative governments encouraged private enterprise. The PLN was again in power 1974-1978 (**Daniel Oduber Quirós**), 1982-1986 (**Luis Alberto Monge**), 19861-1990 (**Oscar Arias Sánchez**) and 1994-1998 (**José María Figueres**, son of José Figueres Ferrer).

President Arias drew up proposals for a peace pact in Central America and concentrated greatly on foreign policy initiatives. Efforts were made to expel Nicaraguan contras resident in Costa Rica and the country's official proclamation of neutrality, made in 1983, was reinforced. The Central American Peace Plan, signed by the five Central American presidents in Guatemala in 1987, earned Arias the Nobel Peace Prize, although progress in implementing its recommendations was slow. In the 1990 general elections, **Rafael Angel Calderón Fournier**, a conservative lawyer and candidate for the Social Christian Unity Party (PUSC), won a narrow victory, with 51% of the vote, over the candidate of the PLN. Calderón, the son of a former president who had been one of the candidates in the 1948 disputed elections, had previously stood for election in 1982 and 1986. The president's popularity slumped as the effects of his economic policies were felt on people's living standards, while his Government was brought into disrepute by allegations of corruption and links with 'narco' traffickers.

PLN government, 1994 and 1998

In the February 1994 elections another former president's son was elected by a narrow margin. **José María Figueres** of the PLN won on economic policies. Figueres argued against neo-liberal policies, claiming he would renegotiate agreements with the IMF and the World Bank, but in his first year of office a third Structural Adjustment Programme was approved. A subsequent National Development Plan and a Plan to Fight Poverty contained a wide range of measures designed to promote economic stability and to improve the quality of life for many sectors of society.

1998, 2002 elections

In 1998 the elections were won by the PUSC candidate, **Miguel Angel Rodríguez**. Thirty percent of voters abstained. The new president took office in May 1998, promising to make women, the young and the poor a priority for his government. Typically for Costa Rica, the elections of early 2002 ran on a frenzy of neutrality. **President Pacheco** stimulated just enough support to win after the election went to a run-off.

2006 and beyond

Having successfully convinced Costa Rica's Congress to change the constitution and allow re-election, Oscar Arias was elected president in 2006, 16 years after serving his first term.

In the 2010 elections, the PLN put forward Vice-President Laura Chinchilla against the libertarian candidate Otto Guevara, becoming Costa Rica's first female president. She proved to be a socially conservative president, opposing gay marriage and supporting the ban on a morning after pill, but she did declare a moratorium on oil exploration. She ended her term with historically low approval ratings, thanks mainly to her fiscal reforms.

The 2014 elections saw a second round run-off between PLN candidate and former San José mayor, Johnny Araya Monge, and centre-left Citizens' Action Party candidate Luis Guillermo Solís Rivera. But Araya dropped out of the race, leaving Solís to claim the presidency with 78% of the vote.

Culture

People

In all provinces over 98% of the population is white and mestizo except in Limón where 33.2% is black and 3.1% indigenous, of whom only 5000 survive in the whole country. There are three groups: the Bribri (3500), Boruca (1000) and Guatuso. Although officially protected, the living conditions of the indigenous population are very poor. In 1992 Costa Rica became the first Central American country to ratify the International Labour Organization treaty on indigenous populations and tribes. However, even in Limón, the percentage of blacks is falling: it was 57.1% in 1927. Many of them speak Jamaican English as their native tongue. Much of the Caribbean coastland, especially in the north, remains unoccupied. On the Pacific coastlands a white minority owns the land on the hacienda system which has been rejected in the uplands. About 46% of the people are mestizos. The population has risen sharply in the mountainous Peninsula of Nicoya, which is an important source of maize, rice and beans.

Music and dance

This is the southernmost in our string of 'marimba culture' countries. The guitar is also a popular instrument for accompanying folk dances, while the *chirimía* and *quijongo*, already encountered further north, have not yet totally died out in the Chorotega region of Guanacaste Province. This province is indeed the heartland of Costa Rican folklore and the Punto Guanacasteco, a heel-and-toe dance for couples, has been officially decreed to be the 'typical national dance', although it is not in fact traditional, but was composed at the turn of the last century by Leandro Cabalceta Brau during a brief sojourn in jail. There are other dances too, such as the *botijuela*, *tamborito* and *cambute*, but they are not traditional, being are performed on stage when outsiders need to be shown some native culture.

Among the country's most popular native performers are the duet Los Talolingas, authors of *La Guaria Morada*, regarded as the 'second national anthem' and Lorenzo 'Lencho' Salazar, whose humorous songs in the vernacular style are considered quintessentially Tico.

Some of the Republic's rapidly deculturizing indigenous groups have dances of their own, like the *Danza de los Diablitos* of the Borucas, the *Danza del Sol* and *Danza de la Luna* of the Chorotegas and the *Danza de los Huesos* of the Talamancas. A curious ocarina made of beeswax, the *dru mugata* is still played by the Guaymí people and is said to be the only truly pre-Columbian instrument still to be found. The drum and flute are traditional among various groups, but the guitar and accordion are moving in to replace them. As in the case of Nicaragua, the Caribbean coast of Costa Rica, centred on Puerto Limón, is inhabited by black people who came originally from the English-speaking islands and whose music reflects this origin. The sinkit seems to be a strictly local rhythm, but the calypso is popular and the cuadrille, square dance and maypole dance are also found. There is also a kind of popular hymn called the *saki*. Brass, percussion and string instruments are played, as well as the accordion.

Land & environment

Costa Rica lies between Nicaragua and Panama, with coastlines on the Caribbean (212 km) and the Pacific (1016 km). The distance between sea and sea ranges from 119-282 km. A low, thin line of hills between Lake Nicaragua and the Pacific is prolonged into northern Costa Rica with several volcanoes (including the active Volcán Arenal), broadening and rising into high and rugged mountains and volcanoes in the centre and south. The highest peak, Chirripó Grande, southeast of the capital, reaches 3820 m. Within these highlands are certain structural depressions; one of them, the Meseta Central, is of paramount importance. To the southwest this basin is rimmed by the comb of the Cordillera; at the foot of its slopes, inside the basin, are the present capital San José, and the old capital, Cártago. Northeast of these cities, about 30 km away, four volcano cones rise from a massive common pedestal. From northwest to southeast these are Poás (2704 m), Barva (2906 m), Irazú (3432 m) and Turrialba (3339 m). Irazú and Poás are intermittently active. Between the Cordillera and the volcanoes is the Meseta Central: an area of 5200 sq km at an altitude of between 900 and 1800 m, where two-thirds of the population live. The northeastern part of the basin is drained by the Reventazón through turbulent gorges into the Caribbean; the Río Grande de Tárcoles drains the western part of it into the Pacific.

There are lowlands on both coasts. On the Caribbean coast, the Nicaraguan lowland along the Río San Juan continues into Costa Rica, wide and sparsely inhabited as far as Puerto Limón. A great deal of this land, particularly near the coast, is swampy; southeast of Puerto Limón the swamps continue as far as Panama in a narrow belt of lowland between sea and mountain.

The Gulf of Nicoya, on the Pacific side, thrusts some 65 km inland; its waters separate the mountains of the mainland from the 900-m-high mountains of the narrow Nicoya Peninsula. From a little to the south of the mouth of the Río Grande de Tercels, a lowland savannah stretches northwest past the port of Puntarenas and along the whole northeastern shore of the Gulf towards Nicaragua. Below the Río Grande de Tercels the savannah is pinched out by mountains, but there are other banana-growing lowlands to the south. Small quantities of African palm and cacao are now being grown in these lowlands. In the far south there are swampy lowlands again at the base of the Península de Osa and between the Golfo Dulce and the borders of Panama. Here there are 12,000 ha planted to bananas. The Río General, which flows into the Río Grande de Térraba, runs through a southern structural depression almost as large as the Meseta Central.

Wildlife

Costa Rica's diversity is due to the fact that Central America is the meeting place of two of the world's major biological regions – the Nearctic to the north and the Neotropical to the south. It has a remarkable geological and climatic complexity and consequently an enormous range of habitats, from rainforests, dry forests, cloudforests and mangroves to wetlands.

When to go

In terms of wildlife, the best time to visit depends, obviously, on where you are and what you want to see, whether it's the sight of hundreds of thousands of migrating raptors passing over Central America between August and December, or that of nesting turtles along the coast. The exact dates of the turtle season vary with the species, but June to October are peak times for many. In practise, planning will be required to get the timing right.

Spotting wildlife

Use local, **experienced guides** as these people will know what species are around and where to look for them and will often recognize bird calls and use these as an aid to spotting them. You should take **binoculars**; get a pair with a reasonable magnification and good light-gathering configurations (ie 10x40 or 8x40) for use in the dim light of the rainforests. They will also need to be reasonably waterproof. Another enormous aid to wildlife watching is a strong torch or, better still, a powerful **headlamp**. The latter not only leaves your hands free but it also helps when trying to spot eye shine of nocturnal mammals, the light reflected back from their eyes direct to yours. Some places, such as Monteverde Cloud Forest Reserve, offer excellent night walks with guides, but with care you can equally well arrange your own. Another strategy to use is to select a likely looking spot – such as a fruiting fig or a watering hole (in dry country) – and wait for the animals to come to you.

Mammals

In Central America mammals tend to be secretive, indeed the majority are nocturnal; hence the need for night walks if you are serious about finding them, though, even then, good views are comparatively rare. That said, you will certainly see some delightful creatures, with views of primates being more or less guaranteed. The rainforests throughout the region contain **spider monkeys**, **howler monkeys** and/or **capuchin monkeys**. The howlers are probably the most noticeable because, as their name suggests, they are inclined to make a huge row at times, especially early in the mornings and in the late afternoons. You've a good chance of seeing **black howler monkeys** in the rainforests of Costa Rica. The **spider monkey** is a much more agile, slender primate, swinging around high in the canopy, using its prehensile tail as a fifth limb. The smaller, **white-throated capuchins** are also commonly seen, moving around quite noisily in groups, searching for fruit and insects in the trees and even coming down to the ground to find food. Smaller again is the **red-backed squirrel monkey**. The most likely places to see them are Corcovado and Manuel Antonio national parks.

Another mammal you are very likely to see in the southern countries of the region are sloths. Good places to look are Reserva Monteverde and the forests of Tortuguero and Manuel Antonio. As they tend to stay in one area for days at a time, local guides are excellent at pointing them out. The most easily seen of the carnivores is not, sadly, the longed-for **jaguar**, but the ubiquitous **white-nosed coati**, a member of the racoon family. The females and their offspring go around in groups and are unmistakable with their long, ringed tails, frequently held in the air, and their long snouts sniffing around for insects and fruit in trees and on the ground. At many tourist sites, they hang around waiting to be fed by the visitors, in particular in the popular lowland national parks. Members of the cat family are rarely seen; those in the area include the **jaguar, puma, ocelot** and **margay**. All are more likely to be seen at night, or, possibly, at dawn and dusk. Tortuguero national park is a possibility for the jaguar and the other small cats. The largest land mammal in Central America is **Baird's tapir**, weighing up to 300 kg. It is a forest species and very secretive, particularly so in areas where it is hunted. Corcovado and Santa Rosa national parks are all places it might be seen, at least there is a reasonable chance of seeing its hoof prints. It might be seen at waterholes or be spotted swimming in rivers. More likely to be seen are **peccaries**, especially the collared peccary, medium sized pig-like animals that are active both day and night. The **collared peccary** can be found in both dry and rainforests throughout the region, while the **white-lipped peccary** is more common in wetter, evergreen forests. Both live in herds, of up to 100 individuals in the case of the white-lipped species. Found throughout the area, in drier, woodland patches, the **white-tailed deer** can easily be spotted, especially at dawn or dusk, or their bright eyeshine can be seen at night if you are out in a car or on foot with a torch. Also found is the smaller **red brocket**; this, though, is a rainforest species and is more elusive. Rodent species you might come across include the **agouti**, which looks rather like a long-legged guinea pig and can be seen moving around on the forest floor. Considerably larger and stockier is the nocturnal **paca**, another forest species found throughout the region, often near water where they hide when chased by predators. **Bats** will usually be a quick fly past at night, impossible to identify but for the jagged flight path which is clearly not that of a bird.

Finally, marine mammals in the area include **whales, dolphins** and **manatees**. Whales and dolphins occur along both the Pacific and Atlantic coasts.

Birds

It is true, the early bird gets the worm and the earlier you get up, the more species you'll see. **Toucans** and the smaller **toucanets** are widespread throughout tropical areas. Another popular sighting is the **scarlet macaw** easily spotted near Puerto Juárez. **Hummingbirds** too are a common sighting, frequently drawn to sugar-feeders. The **harpy eagle** is extremely rare with sightings on the Osa Peninsula a possibility.

To find the **resplendent quetzal**, a brilliant emerald green bird, with males having a bright scarlet breast and belly and ostentatious long green streamers extending as much as 50 cm beyond the end of its tail, Monteverde Cloud Forest Reserve or the less atmospheric Eddie Serrano Mirador are a couple of the best places to go.

In addition to the quetzal, Costa Rica, containing around 850 bird species, is a good country to visit for birdwatchers and **Monteverde** is a hotspot. Species there include **black guans, emerald toucanets, violet sabrewings, long-tailed manakins, three wattled bellbirds** and the threatened **bare-necked umbrellabird**. Mixed flocks of small birds such as **warblers, tanagers, woodcreepers** and **wood-wrens** can also be seen in the area. La Selva Biological Station, an area of rainforest, is another area rich in rainforest species such as the **chestnut-billed toucan, mealy parrot** and **squirrel cuckoo**. A very different habitat, with, consequently, different birds, is found in the large wetland area of Parque Nacional Palo Verde. Here one can see the **jabiru, black-necked stilt, spotted rail, bare-throated tiger heron, purple gallinule** and many other waterbirds. In the dry season, ducks, including the black-bellied whistling duck, blue-billed teal, ring-necked duck and northern pintail, congregate in this area in their thousands. More rarely seen here is the white-faced whistling duck.

Of course, all along the coasts are masses of different seabirds, including pelicans, boobies and the magnificent frigate bird.

Reptiles
This covers snakes, lizards, crocodilians and turtles. Throughout the whole region, though, you are not particularly likely to see snakes in the wild; for those wishing to do so, a snake farm or zoo is the best place to go. You might, though, be lucky on one of your walks and see a boa constrictor, or, again, a guide might know where one is resting. In contrast, lizards are everywhere, from small geckos walking up walls in your hotel room, catching insects attracted to the lights, to the large iguanas sunbathing in the tree tops. The American crocodile and spectacled caiman are both found throughout the area, with the latter being seen quite frequently. Several species of both freshwater and sea turtles are present in the region. Parque Nacional Tortuguero is a good place to see freshwater turtles and four species of marine turtle, while at Ostional Beach in Santa Rosa National Park you can watch masses of olive ridley turtles coming in to lay their eggs, particularly in September and October.

Amphibians
You'll certainly hear frogs and toads, even if you do not see them. However, the brightly coloured poison-dart frogs and some of the tree frogs are well worth searching out. Look for them in damp places, under logs and moist leaf litter, in rock crevices and by ponds and streams, many will be more active at night. Monteverde and La Selva Reserves are both rich in amphibians.

Invertebrates
There are uncounted different species of invertebrates in the area. Probably, most desirable for ecotourists are the butterflies, though some of the beetles, such as the jewel scarabs, are also pretty spectacular. If you are fascinated by spiders, you can always go hunting for nocturnal tarantulas. There are butterfly farms in El Jardín de Mariposas in Monteverde that will give you a close up view of many different species. Watching leaf-cutter ants marching in long columns from a bush they are systematically destroying and taking the pieces of leaf to their nest, huge mounds on the forest floor, can be an absorbing sight, while marching columns of army ants, catching and killing all small beasts in their path, are best avoided.

Practicalities

Getting there

Air

The main international airport is at San José (see page 43). Departure tax is a flat rate of US$29 per person, regardless of nationality or immigration status, when leaving by air. Exit taxes, by air or land, and legislation regarding visa extensions, are subject to frequent change and travellers should check these details as near to the time of travelling as possible.

From Europe

From most European cities flights connect in the US at Miami, Houston, Dallas and many others with **American Airlines**, **United**, **Delta** and **Avianca**. **Iberia** have daily flights between Madrid and San José. Starting in April 2016 **British Airways** will be operating direct flights from London Gatwick to San José. There are direct charter flights in season from several European cities including Frankfurt (**Condor**).

TRAVEL TIP

Packing for Costa Rica

As far as clothes are concerned, it's simplest to think through what you'll be doing before you pack. Starting at the lower altitudes you'll need beachwear, sunglasses, a sun hat (which you'll probably need everywhere) and sun cream. When venturing on trails, shorts and a light shirt are ideal. If you're a bug magnet lightweight long trousers are perfect – even better if you can find ones that unzip above the knee. The same lightweight approach works wonders for the Central Highlands with a light sweater or jacket for the evenings when there may be a slight chill in the air. At higher altitudes you'll need something a bit thicker. Don't bother taking a raincoat unless going on very long treks. Otherwise buy an umbrella locally. Bring comfortable shoes, as well as a change if they get wet.

Invaluable personal items worth taking if you're travelling independently include: a penknife, torch (head torches are particularly useful), camera, alarm clock, strong cord, water bottle, anti-bacterial soap, wet wipes, insect repellent and the eternally useful universal sink plug. Spectacle and contact lens wearers should take a spare pair or sufficient supplies to last the trip – although it is possible to get most items in Costa Rica.

If you have personal medical requirements make sure you bring enough to last your trip.

A good pair of binoculars is useful. Birders and nature lovers will want to take field guides – they're in some of the better lodges but it's better to have your own. Divers and keen snorkellers may want to consider taking their own mask, and experienced anglers may want to travel with the lucky lure.

All this should be packed in a strong bag, the lighter the better, and ideally one that can be locked with a removable padlock that can be used on dodgy doors and lockers in cheaper hotels. Most mid- and upper-range hotels have safe boxes.

From North America

Flights from North America are many and varied. **Jet Blue** and **Spirit Airlines** are two 'no-frills' carriers connecting Fort Lauderdale to San José. Additionally, **United, American, US Airways** and **Delta** depart from a variety of points including: Atlanta, Boston, Chicago, Dallas, Houston, Los Angeles, Miami, New York, Orlando, San Francisco, Toronto and Washington DC. **Daniel Oduber International Airport**, near Liberia, is increasingly popular, conveniently located just 30 minutes from some of Guanacaste's finest beaches. Charter specials are available from time to time.

From South America

Copa and **Avianca** have the monopoly on flights from South America. Cities include Bogotá, Cali, Caracas, Cartagena, Guayaquil, Lima, Quito and Santiago.

From Mexico and Central America

Copa, Avianca and **Nature Air** connect San José with other countries in Central America; **Avianca, Interjet** and **AeroMéxico** fly direct from Mexico. Destinations include Managua, Mexico City, Panama City, San Salvador and Tegucigalpa.

Road *See also boxes, opposite and page 174.*

Road links to the north are on the Pan-American Highway at Peñas Blancas with immigration services and buses connecting to and from Pacific Nicaragua. It is also possible to cross the remote northern border close to Los Chiles, making the journey by boat to San Carlos on the Río San Juan.

The main crossing to Panama at Paso Canoas has become stringent lately, but you should have no problems entering the country provided you are able to demonstrate sufficient funds for your trip (US$500 or a bank statement or a credit card) and an onward ticket to your country of origin. The more remote crossing of Río Sereno in the highlands connects with Volcán in Panama. It is laid-back but time-consuming to navigate without your own transport. On the Caribbean coast, Sixaola links with the Panamian town of Guabito over the vertigo-inducing old banana bridge, and onwards to Changuinola and Bocas del Toro; here there is a US$7 fee to leave Costa Rica (payable by credit card only) and a US$3 *alcaldía* tax to enter Panama.

Sea

The main ports for international cargo vessels are **Puerto Limón**, with regular sailings to and from Europe, and **Caldera**, on the central Pacific coast. Contact shipping agents, of which there are many, in Puerto Limón and San José for details. Cruise vessels arrive at Caldera, Puntarenas and Puerto Limón, normally stopping for little more than 24 hours.

BORDER CROSSINGS
Costa Rica–Nicaragua

Entry requirements for Costa Rica include proof of funds (US$300) and an onward ticket.

Los Chiles–San Carlos

An intriguing crossing, usually hassle free, used by adventurers and itinerant labourers travelling to and from Nicaragua's remote Río San Juan province. Two daily river boats connect San Carlos and Los Chiles on the Río Frío, 45 minutes, check schedules locally.

Banks and money changers are in San Carlos on the Nicaraguan side, but you are strongly advised to bring dollars before setting out. Immigration on both sides is open 0800-1600. If leaving Nicaragua, before proceeding get your exit stamp in San Carlos, US$2. Entrance tax to Nicaragua, US$12. Exit tax for Costa Rica is US$7, payable by credit card only.

To travel into Costa Rica, buses run to La Quesada (San Carlos) with many onward services to La Fortuna. Onwards to Nicaragua, from San Carlos you can travel east up the Río San Juan or take a ferry across Lake Nicaragua to Isla Ometepe or Granada. There are also road connections and a few daily buses to Managua.

Peñas Blancas

This is the only Nicaragua–Costa Rica road crossing. It's hectic on the Nicaragua side with lots of helpers and hustlers who may try to sell you forms and paperwork; no purchase is necessary, however, as these are free at the immigration window. There's a branch of BCR in the customs building and no shortage of money changers, but beware being short changed.

Immigration on both sides is open Monday-Saturday 0600-2200, Sunday 0600-2000. International buses are subject to customs searches. On the Nicaraguan side, there is a municipality tax, US$1, exit tax US$2 and entrance tax, US$12. On the Costa Rican side, the exit tax is US$7, payable at a machine with passport and credit card only. If your passport in not readable, pay at the BCR.

Onwards to Costa Rica, several daily express buses depart from behind the immigration terminal, five to six hours; also to Liberia, every 30-60 minutes, 1½ hours. To Nicaragua there are buses to Rivas every 30 minutes, where you can catch connections to Granada, Managua, or Isla Ometepe. For San Juan del Sur, exit at La Virgen. Direct buses also run from Peñas Blancas to Managua, every 30 minutes, 3½ hours.

BORDER CROSSINGS
Costa Rica–Panama

Panama is an hour ahead of Costa Rica. Entry requirements include proof of funds (US$300 for Costa Rica; US$500 for Panama) and an onward ticket. International bus tickets are available at the border, but some overzealous officials may demand to see a ticket to your country of origin. On the Costa Rican side, exit tax is US$7, payable at a machine with credit card and passport prior to processing, or at the BCR. On the Panamanian side there is a municipal tax US$1-3, which is not always collected.

Paso Canoas

A busy, insalubrious, well-plied crossing on the Interamericana highway. International buses can take two to three hours to process, otherwise it's usually quick and hassle free. The town has lots of amenities, including hotels and restaurants. There are ATMs and plentiful money changers.

Immigration on both sides is open 0600-2200. Onwards to Panama, there are frequent bus connections with David, 1½ hours away, stopping at La Concepción (Bugaba) for connections to Volcán and Cerro Punta. Onwards to Costa Rica, there are connections with the central Pacific coast and direct to San José. More frequent services to the capital run from Ciudad Neilly.

Río Sereno

A minor crossing providing access to Volcán and the western Chiriquí highlands, it's quiet and cool with some reports of lengthy bureaucratic treatment. Vehicles cannot complete formalities. There's a bank with an ATM, but no exchange; bring local currency or ask who might change it.

Costa Rican immigration is open 0800-1600; Sunday till 1400. Panamanian immigration is open 0500-1700. Onward to Panama, there are dawn to dusk services from Río Sereno to Volcán, La Concepción and David. Onwards to Costa Rica, there are frequent buses to San Vito via Sabilito.

Sixaola–Guabito

A straightforward and interesting crossing divided by the Río Sixaola, which you must cross by bridge. Basic and undesirable accommodation is available. There are no banks; try money-changers or the stores, but rates are poor.

Immigration on both sides is open 0700-1700. Onwards to Panama, colectivo taxis go to Changuinola, 20 minutes away, where you can catch a bus to David, Panama City or Almirante (for the Bocas archipelago). Sometimes tourist buses go to the docks at Almirante. Onwards to Costa Rica, there is a bus station with regular services to Puerto Limón, Puerto Viejo and San José.

Getting around

Air

From San José you can fly to Arenal (La Fortuna), Dominical/Palmar Sur, Drake Bay, Golfito, Liberia, Norasa, Puerto Jiménez, Punta Islita, Quepos, Tamarindo, Tambor and Tortuguero. The two domestic airlines are **Sansa** and **Nature Air**. See Transport, page 43.

Road

Costa Rica has a total of 39,018 km of roads of which 10,133 km are paved. The Pan-American Highway runs the length of the country, from the Nicaraguan to the Panamanian borders. South of San José, the fastest route is along the scenic Costanera coast road, which rejoins the Pan-American highway at Palmar Norte. All four-lane roads into San José are toll roads. It is illegal to ride in a car or taxi without wearing seatbelts.

Bus

The good road network supports a regular bus service that covers most parts of the country. Buses are reasonably comfortable by Central American standards, most have reclining seats but no onboard toilets (highway breaks every two to three hours). Frequency declines with popularity but you can get to most places with road access eventually. San José is the main hub for buses, although you can skip down the Pacific coast by making connections at Puntarenas. Coming from Nicaragua, direct to Arenal, requires cutting in and travelling through Tilarán.

Shuttle bus companies offer transport from the capital to dozens of beach and tourism destinations in comfortable air-conditioned minibuses; they're quicker but more expensive. See Transport, page 43.

Car

Driving in Costa Rica allows for greater flexibility when travelling. Many of the nature parks are in remote areas; 4WD and high-clearance is recommended and sometimes essential; in the wet season some roads will be impassable. Always ask locals or bus drivers what the state of the road is before embarking on a journey. Do not assume that if the buses are running, a car can get through too. Wherever you travel you should expect from time to time to find roads that are badly maintained, damaged or closed during the wet season, and delays because of floods, landslides and huge potholes. Be prepared for all manner of mechanical challenges. The electronic ignition and fuel metering systems on modern emission-controlled cars are allergic to humidity, heat and dust, and cannot be repaired by mechanics outside the main centres. Standard European and Japanese cars run on fuel with a higher octane rating than is commonly available in Central America. Note that in some areas petrol stations are few and far between. Fill up when you see one as the next one may be out of fuel.

Documents Land entry procedures are simple though time-consuming, as the car has to be checked by customs, police and agriculture officials. All you need is the registration document in the name of the driver or, in the case of a car registered in someone else's name, a notarized letter of authorization. In Costa Rica, the car's entry is stamped into the passport so you may not leave the country even temporarily without it. Note that Costa

Rica does not recognize the International Driving Licence (you can drive with a regular licence for up to three months). A written undertaking that the vehicle will be re-exported after temporary importation is useful and may be requested in Costa Rica. Membership of motoring organizations can be useful for discounts such as hotel charges, car rentals, maps and towing charges.

Of course, do be very careful to keep all the papers you are given when you enter, to produce when you leave. An army of 'helpers' loiters at each border crossing, waiting to guide motorists to each official in the correct order, for a tip. They can be very useful, but don't give them your papers. Bringing a car in by sea or air is much more complicated and expensive; generally you will have to hire an agent to clear it through.

In Latin American countries it is very expensive to insure against accident and theft, especially as you should take into account the value of the car increased by duties calculated in real (that is non-devaluing) terms. If the car is stolen or written off, you will be required to pay very high duty on its value. Costa Rica insists on compulsory third-party insurance, to be bought at the border. If anyone is hurt in an accident, do not pick them up (you become liable). Seek assistance from the nearest police station or hospital if you are able to do so. You may find yourself facing a hostile crowd, even if you are not to blame. Expect frequent road checks by police, military, agricultural and forestry produce inspectors, and any other curious official who wants to know what a foreigner is doing driving around in their domain. Smiling simple-minded patience is the best tactic to avoid harassment.

Tourists who enter by car or motorcycle pay US$10 road tax, including mandatory insurance, and can keep their cars for an initial period of 90 days. This can be extended for a total period of six months, for about US$10 per extra month, at the **Instituto Costarricense de Turismo**, or at the **Customs office** ① *Av 3, Calle 14*, if you take your passport, car entry permit, and a piece of stamped paper (*papel sellado*) obtainable at any bookshop. Cars are fumigated on entry. If you have an accident while in the country do not move the vehicle and immediately contact **Policía de Tránsito** ① *San José, T2222-9330 or T2222-9245*.

Car hire Renting a car can be a surprisingly economical way to travel if you can form a group and split the costs. As with all rentals, check your vehicle carefully as the company will try to claim for the smallest of 'damages'. Most leases do not allow the use of a normal car off paved roads. Always make sure the spare tyre is in good order, as potholes are frequent. You can have tyres fixed at any garage for about US$2 in 30 minutes.

Guideline prices: smallest economy car US$38-48 per day includes unlimited mileage or US$250-310 per week; 4WD vehicle costs US$60-120 per day, US$440-770 per week, including unlimited mileage. Driver's licence from home and credit card are generally required. Loss damage waiver (LDW) insurance is mandatory and costs an extra US$11-14 per day; excess is between US$750 and US$1500. Cash deposits or credit card charges range from US$800 to US$1800, so check you have sufficient credit. Discounts for car hire are available during the 'Green Season' (May to November). If you plan to drop off a hired car somewhere other than where you picked it up, check with several firms for their charges: **Elegante**, **Ada** and **National** appear to have the lowest drop-off fees.

Insurance will not cover broken windscreens, driving on unsurfaced roads or damaged tyres. Check exactly what the hirer's insurance policy covers. In many cases it will only protect you against minor bumps and scrapes, not major accidents, or 'natural' damage (for example flooding). Ask if extra cover is available. Also find out, if using a credit card, whether the card automatically includes insurance.

Safety Spare no ingenuity in making your car secure. Avoid leaving the car unattended except in a locked garage or guarded parking space. Remove all belongings and leave the empty glove compartment open when the car is unattended. Also lock the clutch or accelerator to the steering wheel with a heavy, obvious chain or lock. Street children will generally protect your car in exchange for a tip. Note down key numbers and carry spares of the most important ones, but don't keep all spares inside the vehicle. Secure parking lots are available in most cities. There are regular reports of break-ins at national parks and other popular tourism areas. Driving at night is not recommended.

Fuel Main fuel stations have regular (unleaded) US$1.50 and diesel US$1.40 per litre; super gasoline (unleaded) is available throughout the country, US$1.62 per litre. Prices are regulated by the government.

Road tolls Costa Rica has a road toll system, with charges of between US$0.35 to US$0.55 for some of the busiest routes in the Central Highlands.

Cycling

Cycling is easier in Costa Rica than elsewhere in Central America; there is less heavy traffic and it is generally more 'cyclist friendly'. However, paving is thin and soon deteriorates; look out for cracks and potholes, which bring traffic to a crawl. The prevailing wind is from the northeast so, if making an extensive tour, travelling in the direction of Panama is slightly more favourable.

Recommended reading for all users: Baker's *The Essential Road Guide to Costa Rica*, with detailed strip maps, kilometre by kilometre road logs, motoring information plus San José map and bus guide (Bill Baker, Apdo 1185-1011, San José). The **Expedition Advisory Centre** ① *T+44-(0)20-7591-3030, www.rgs.org*, has published a booklet on planning a long-distance bike trip titled *Bicycle Expeditions*, by Paul Vickers. Published in March 1990, it is available as a PDF from the website or £5 for a photocopy. In the UK the **Cyclists' Touring Club** ① *T0844-736-8450, www.ctc.org.uk*, has information on touring, technical information and discusses the relative merits of different types of bikes.

Cycle shops have sprung up around the country offering parts and repair services.

Hitchhiking

Generally easy and safe by day, but take the usual precautions.

Sea

Ferries serve the southern section of the Nicoya Peninsula from Puntarenas. The Osa Peninsula has a regular ferry service linking Golfito and Puerto Jiménez, and Bahía Drake is reached on boats from Sierpe. Boats travel to Tortuguero from Moín, close to Puerto Limón, and from Cariari, north of Guápiles.

Maps

The **Instituto Geográfico Nacional** ① *Calle 9, Av 20-22, open 0730-1600*, at the Ministry of Public Works and Transport in San José, supplies good topographical maps for walkers. ITM has a 1:500,000 travel map of Costa Rica, available at bookstores throughout the country. Maps are also available in San José at **7th Street Books** ① *Calle 7, Av 1 and Central, T2256-8251*; **Universal** ① *Av Central and Calle 1, T2222-2222*; and **Lehmann** ① *Av Central, Calle 1-3, T2223-1212*.

Essentials A-Z

Accident and emergency

For the emergency services, dial 112 or 911.

Children

Travel with children can bring you into closer contact with Costa Rican families and generally presents no special problems; in fact, the path is often smoother for family groups. Officials tend to be more amenable where children are concerned. Always carry a copy of your child's birth certificate and passport photos. For an overview of travelling with children, visit www.babygoes2.com.

Public transport

Overland travel in Costa Rican can involve a lot of time spent waiting for public transport. It is easier to take biscuits, drinks, bread, etc with you on longer trips than to rely on meal stops where the food may not be to taste. All airlines charge a reduced price for children under 12 and less for children under 2. Double check the child's baggage allowance though; some are as low as 7 kg. On long-distance buses children generally pay half or reduced fares. For shorter trips it is cheaper, if less comfortable, to seat small children on your knee. Often there are spare seats that children can occupy after tickets have been collected. In city and local buses, small children do not generally pay a fare, but are not entitled to a seat when paying customers are standing. On sightseeing tours you should always bargain for a family rate; often children can go free. Note that a child travelling free on a long excursion is not always covered by the operator's travel insurance.

Hotels

Try to negotiate family rates. If charges are per person, always insist that 2 children will occupy 1 bed only, therefore counting as 1 tariff. If rates are per bed, the same applies. It is quite common for children under 12 to be allowed to stay for no extra charge as long as they are sharing your room.

Customs and duty free

Duty-free allowances are 500 g of manufactured tobacco, 2 kg of chocolate and 5 litres of liquor. Any amount of currency may be taken in or out, but amounts over US$10,000 must be declared. Cameras, binoculars, camping equipment, laptop computers and other portable items of personal/ professional/leisure use are free of duty.

Disabled travellers

Most airports and hotels and restaurants in major resorts have wheelchair ramps and adapted toilets. While some cities such as San José are all ramped, in general pavements are often in such a poor state of repair that walking is precarious.

Some travel companies specialize in exciting holidays, tailor-made for individuals depending on their level of disability. Disabled Travelers, www.disabledtravelers. com, provides travel information for disabled adventurers and includes a number of links, reviews and tips. You might also want to read *Nothing Ventured*, edited by Alison Walsh (Harper Collins), which gives personal accounts of worldwide journeys by disabled travellers, plus advice and listings.

Dress

Casual clothing is adequate for most occasions although men may need a jacket and tie in some restaurants. Dress conservatively in indigenous communities and small churches. Topless bathing is generally unacceptable.

Drugs

Users of drugs without medical prescription should be particularly careful, as Costa Rica imposes heavy penalties for even the simple possession of such substances. The planting of drugs on travellers, by traffickers or the police, is not unknown. If offered drugs on the street, make no response at all and keep walking. Note that people who roll their own cigarettes are often suspected of carrying drugs and are subjected to close searches.

If you are taking illegal drugs – even ones that are widely and publically used – be aware that authorities do set traps from time to time. Should you get into trouble, your embassy is unlikely to be very sympathetic.

Electricity

110 volts AC, 60 cycles, US-style plugs.

Embassies and consulates

For a list of Costa Rican embassies abroad, see www.rree.go.cr or embassy.goabroad.com.

Gay and lesbian travellers

Costa Rica is not particularly liberal in its attitudes to gays and lesbians. Having said that, times are changing (the first same-sex marriage in Central America took place in Costa Rica in 2015) and you'll find there is a gay scene with bars and clubs at least in most of the bigger cities and resorts. Helpful websites include www.gayscape.com, www.gaypedia.com and www.iglta.org (International Gay and Lesbian Travel Association).

Health

See your GP or travel clinic at least 6 weeks before departure for general advice on travel risks and vaccinations. Try a specialist travel clinic if your own GP is unfamiliar with health conditions in Costa Rica. Make sure you have sufficient medical travel insurance, get a dental check, know your own blood group and if you suffer a long-term condition such as diabetes or epilepsy, obtain a Medic Alert bracelet/ necklace (www.medicalert.co.uk). If you wear glasses, take a copy of your prescription.

Drinking water is safe in all major towns; elsewhere it should be boiled. Bottled water is widely available.

Intestinal disorders are prevalent in the lowlands. Malaria is on the increase: malaria prophylaxis is advised for visitors to the lowlands, especially near the Nicaragua and Panama border. Dengue fever has been recorded throughout the country, mostly in coastal cities. Having said all that, the standards of health and hygiene are among the best in Latin America.

Useful websites
www.btha.org British Travel Health Association.
www.cdc.gov US government site that gives excellent advice on travel health and details of disease outbreaks.
www.fco.gov.uk British Foreign and Commonwealth Office travel site has useful information on Costa Rica's people and climate and a list of UK embassies/consulates.
www.fitfortravel.scot.nhs.uk A-Z of vaccine/health advice.
www.numberonehealth.co.uk Travel screening services, vaccine and travel health advice, email/SMS text vaccine reminders and screens returned travellers for tropical diseases.

Insurance

Insurance is strongly recommended and policies are very reasonable. If you have financial restraints, the most important aspect of any insurance policy is medical care and repatriation. Ideally you want to make sure you are covered for personal items too. Read the small print before heading off so you are aware of what is covered and what is not, what is required to submit a claim and what to do in the event of an emergency.

Always buy insurance before setting out as your options will be more limited and generally quite costly once you've departed from your home country.

Internet

Internet cafés are popular and connections in the towns tend to be good. Prices vary but a rough guide is US$1-2 for 1 hr in the Central Valley; up to US$5 in beach towns and tourism areas. Rates are lower around colleges and universities.

Language

Spanish is the first language, but you will find someone who can speak some English in most places. In the Caribbean the Afro-Caribbean population speak a regional Creole dialect with elements of English.

While you will be able to get by without knowledge of Spanish in Costa Rica, you will probably become frustrated and feel helpless in many situations. A pocket dictionary and phrase book together with some initial study or a beginner's Spanish course before you leave are strongly recommended. If you have the time, book 1-2 weeks of classes at the beginning of your travels. The better-known language schools normally include a wide range of cultural activities and supporting options for homestays. A less well-known centre is likely to have fewer English speakers around. For details, see Language schools in the What to do sections of individual towns and cities.

Media

The best San José morning papers are *La Nación* (www.nacion.co.cr) and business-orientated *La República* (www.larepublica. net); there is also *Al Día*, *El Heraldo*, *Diario Extra* (the largest circulating daily) and *La Prensa Libre* (www.prensalibre. co.cr). *La Gaceta* is the official government daily paper. The *Tico Times*, www.ticotimes.net is no longer in print, but its website continues to publish news in English with classifieds.

There are 6 local TV stations, many MW/FM radio stations throughout the country. Local **Voz de América** (VOA) station. **Radio Dos** (95.5 FM) and **Rock Radio** (107.5 FM) have English-language DJs and music. Many hotels and private homes receive 1 of the 4 TV stations offering direct, live, 24-hr satellite TV from the USA. All US cable TV can be received in San José.

Money

£1=790 colones, €1=575 colones, US$1=526 colones (Dec 2015).

The unit is the **colón**, which in most years devalues slowly against the dollar. There are 5, 10, 25, 50, 100 and 500-colon coins. Notes in use are for 1000, 2000, 5000 and 10,000 colones. US dollars are widely accepted but don't depend on being able to use them.

ATMs and exchange

US dollars can be exchanged in most banks. Most tourist and 1st-class hotels will change dollars and traveller's cheques (TCs) for guests only; the same applies in restaurants and shops if you buy something. Hardly anyone will change damaged US dollar notes. All state-run banks and some private banks will change euro, but it is almost impossible to exchange any other major currency in Costa Rica. For bank drafts and transfers commission may be charged.

Banks are starting to stay open later and several open on Sat. Most banks will process cash advances on Visa/MasterCard. ATMs that accept international Visa and/or MasterCard are widely available at most banks, and in shopping malls and at San José airport. Credomatic handles all credit card billings; they will not accept a credit card charge that does not have the imprint of the borrower's card plus an original signature. This is the result of fraud, but it makes it difficult to book tours or accommodation over the phone.

If your card is lost or stolen, ring T0800-011-0184 (MasterCard/Visa) or T0800-012-3211 (AMEX).

Currency cards

If you don't want to carry lots of cash, pre-paid currency cards allow you to preload money from your bank account, fixed at the day's exchange rate. They look like a credit or debit card and are issued by specialist money changing companies, such as **Travelex** and **Caxton FX**. You can top up and check your balance by phone, online and sometimes by text.

Cost of living and travelling

Costa Rica is more expensive than countries to the north. While transport is reasonably cheap, you get less for your money in the hotels. If you are thrifty and stay in shared dorms, you may be able to survive on US$30-40 a day, but that does not allow for much in the way of travel or activities. A more comfortable and realistic budget is US$60-90.

Opening hours

Banks Mon-Fri 0900-1500.
Businesses Mon-Fri 0900-1200, 1400-1730 (1600 government offices), Sat 0800-1200.
Shops Mon-Sat 0800-1200, 1300-1800 (most stay open during lunch hour).

Post

Airmail letters to Europe cost 180 c, postcards 165 c; to North/South America, letters 155 c, 135 c for postcards; to Australia, Africa and Asia, letters 240 c, postcards 195 c. Expreso letters, 140 c extra, several days quicker to USA and North Europe. Registered mail, 400 c. Airmail takes 5 to 10 days. All parcels sent out of the country by foreigners must be taken open to the post office for clearance. **Lista de Correos**, charges 75 c per letter and will keep them for 4 weeks. For information call Correos de Costa Rica, T800-900-2000.

Safety

Generally speaking, Costa Rica is very safe but, as ever, there are some problem areas. Look after your belongings in hotels – use the safe. If hiring a car do not leave valuables in the vehicle and leave nothing unattended on beaches or buses. Theft (pickpocketing, grab-and-run thieves and mugging) is on the increase in San José, especially in the centre, in the market, at the Coca Cola bus station, in the barrios of Cuba, Cristo Rey, México, 15 de Setiembre and León XIII. Keep away from these areas at night and on Sun, when few people are around, as we have received reports of violent robberies. Street gangs, known as *chapulines*, are mostly kids. The police do seem to be trying to tackle the problem but help yourself by avoiding potentially dangerous situations.

You are advised to carry your passport (or a photocopy) with you at all times.

Tax

Departure tax US$29 per person. **Road tax** US$10, when entering Costa Rica by car or motorcycle. **Sales tax** 13%. The sales tax plus 3.39% tourism tax is added to hotel room prices.

Telephone

Country code T+506.
There are no area codes in Costa Rica, the **international direct dialling** code (to call out of Costa Rica) is T00. Dial T116 for the operator. In Mar 2008, Costa Rica changed telephone numbers from 7 to 8 digits. All landlines now have a 2 in front of the old 7-digit number and all mobile phones now have an 8 in front of the old 8-digit number. Nationwide phone changes are taken up by organizations and people at different rates. A few websites are still quoting the old 7-digit numbers. Be prepared when using phones and taking down numbers.

Using a mobile in Costa Rica can be very expensive. In addition to the hassle of having to charge your phone, research whether it is worth your while. Mobile phone calls will be cheaper if you buy a SIM card for the local network; in-country calls are likely to be considerably cheaper than using your home-based account. The initial cost of the SIM is getting more affordable, but check the cost of calls. Also bear in mind that the number you use at home will not work. Some networks, eg O2, provide an app so you can use the time on your contract if you access the app via Wi-Fi. Alternatively, you can keep in touch via services such as **Skype**, **Viber**, **Facebook Messenger** and **Whatsapp** if you have access to Wi-Fi.

Long-distance telephone services are handled by the state-run **Instituto Costarricense de Electricidad** (**ICE**) and its subsidiary **Radiográfica Costarricense SA** (**RACSA**), Telecommunications Centre, A 5, Calle 1, San José, Mon-Fri 0800-1900, Sat 0800-1200, closed Sun.

Public phones are maddening to use, various kinds are available: some use 10 and 20 colón silver coins, others use 50 colón gold coins, and still others employ at least 2 types of calling cards, but not interchangeably. The 199 cards are recommended, but it's often easiest to call collect inside (T110) and outside (T116) the country. Assistance for hearing impaired (Spanish only) is T137.

Phone cards with 'Personal Identification Numbers' are available for between US$0.80 and US$10. These can be used for national and international direct dialling from a private phone. Calls abroad can be made from phone booths; collect calls abroad may be made from special booths in the RACSA office, or from any booth nationwide if you dial T116 for connection with the international operator (T175 for collect calls to the USA). Phone cards can be used. Dial T124 for international information. Country Direct Dialling Codes to the USA are: **MCI/ World Phone** 0800-012-2222, **AT&T** 0800-0114-114, **Sprint/GlobalOne** 0800-013-0123, **Worldcom** 0800-014-4444.

Time

-6 hrs GMT.

Tipping

A 10% service charge is automatically added to restaurant and hotel bills, as well as the 13% sales tax.

Tourist information

Instituto Costarricense de Turismo (**ICT**), underneath the Plaza de la Cultura, Calle 5, A Central-2, T2223-1733, www. visitcostarica.com. Daily 0900-1700. All tourist information is given here along with a good free map of San José and the country. See page 37 for more details. Student cards give reductions in most museums.

Useful websites

www.centralamerica.com Costa Rica's Travelnet, contains general information on tourist-related subjects.
www.infocostarica.com A Yahoo-style search engine with information, links and maps for all things Costa Rican.

Tour operators

In the UK

Condor Journeys and Adventures, T01700-841 318, www.condorjourneys-adventures.com. Also has offices in France.
Costa Rica Revealed, T01932-424252, www.costaricarevealed.co.uk. Tailor-made holidays and honeymoons plus escorted small-group tours to Costa Rica and Central America by **Mercator Travel**.
Dragoman, T01728-861 133, www.dragoman.co.uk.
Exodus Travels, T020-8675 5550, www.exodus.co.uk.
Explore Worldwide, T0870-333 4001, www.explore.co.uk.

Rainbow Tours, T020-7666 1260, www.rainbowtours.co.uk/latinamerica. Tailor-made travel throughout Latin America.
Reef & Rainforest Tours, T01803-866 965, www.reefandrainforest.co.uk. Specialists in tailor-made and group wildlife tours.
Select Latin America, T020-7407 1478, www.selectlatinamerica.co.uk. Tailor-made holidays and small group tours.
South American Experience, T0845-277 3366, www.southamericanexperience.co.uk.
Steppes Travel, T01285-885 333, www.steppestravel.co.uk. Tailor-made and group itineraries throughout Costa Rica and the rest of Latin America.
Trips Worldwide, T0117-311 4404, www.tripsworldwide.co.uk.
Tucan Travel, T020-8896 1600, www.tucantravel.com.
Veloso Tours, T020-8762 0616, www.veloso.com.

In North America
Exito Travel, T970-482 3019, www.exito-travel.com.
GAP Adventures, T1-800-708 7761, www.gapadventures.com.
LADATCO tours, T1-800-327 6162, www.ladatco.com.
Mila Tours, T1-800-367 7378, www.milatours.com.
S and S Tours, T800-499 5685, www.ss-tours.com.

Visas and immigration

Nationals of most EU nations, the US, Canada, Israel and Japan do not need visas for visits of up to 90 days. Nationals of the Republic of Ireland, Australia and New Zealand do not need a visa, but visits are limited to 30 days. For more information, check www.migracion.go.cr.

If you overstay the 30- or 90-day permitted period, you must report to immigration before leaving the country. For longer stays ask for a *Prórroga de Turismo* at Migración (Immigration) in San José. For this you need 4 passport photos, an airline or bus ticket out of the country and proof of funds (for example TCs); you can apply for an extension of 1 or 2 months, at 300 colones per month. The paperwork takes 3 days. If you leave the country, you must wait 72 hrs before returning, but it may be cheaper and easier to do this to get a new 30-day entry. Travel agents can arrange all extension and exit formalities for a small fee.

Monetary fines for overstaying your visa or entry permit have been eliminated; if you plan to stay longer, be aware that immigration officials have said that tourists who overstay their welcome more than once will be denied entry into the country on subsequent occasions – part of government efforts to crack down on 'perpetual tourists'.

An onward ticket (a bus ticket, which can be bought at the border immigration office or sometimes from the driver on Tica international buses, or a transatlantic ticket)

is asked for, but can be refunded in San José with a loss of about US$3 on a US$20 ticket. Cashing in an air ticket is difficult because you may be asked to produce another ticket out of the country. Also, tourists may have to show at least US$300 in cash or TCs before being granted entry (especially if you have no onward ticket).

Volunteering

2 main areas provide opportunities for unskilled volunteers: childcare – often at orphanages or schools – and nature projects. Be warned, spontaneous volunteering is becoming more difficult. Organizations that use volunteers have progressed and plan their personnel needs so you may be required to make contact before you visit. Many organizations now charge volunteers for board and lodging and projects are often for a minimum of 4 weeks.

Variations on the volunteering programme are to enrol on increasingly popular gap-year programmes. These normally incorporate a period of volunteer work with a few months of free time at the end of the programme for travel.

Volunteering to help with environmental and conservation work is very popular, well developed and organized. Normally you have to pay for food and sometimes lodgings. (Charges usually vary from US$75-150 a week.) The workload and type varies enormously. Most volunteers organize a placement before arriving. Once working you will normally work a shift pattern with 2- to 4-day breaks for travel.

Volunteering at national parks can be organized through **ASVO**, www.asvocr.org. You can also contact organizations direct:

Hacienda Barú near Dominical (see page 120); **Caño Palma Biological Station** in Parque Nacional Tortuguero (see page 147); **Los Aviarios del Caribe**, south from Puerto Limón (see page 153); **ANAI** (see page 153) and the **Talamanca Dolphin Foundation** on the south Caribbean coast close to Puerto Viejo de Talamanca; the **Children's Eternal Rainforest** in Monteverde (see page 78) and **Campanario Biological Reserve** in Bahía Drake; and **Rara Avis** near Puerto Viejo de Sarapiquí (see page 141).

Weights and measures

Metric.

Women travellers

Some women experience problems, whether accompanied or not; others encounter no difficulties at all. Unaccompanied Western women will at times be subject to close scrutiny and exceptional curiosity. Don't be unduly scared. Simply be prepared and try not to overreact. When you set out, err on the side of caution until your instincts have adjusted to the new culture. Women travelling alone could consider taking a wedding ring to prevent being hassled. To help minimize unwanted attention, consider your clothing choices. Do not feel bad about showing offence. When accepting an invitation, make sure that someone else knows the address you are going to and the time you left. Ask if you can bring a friend (even if you do not intend to do so). A good rule is always to act with confidence, as though you know where you are going, even if you do not. Someone who looks lost is more likely to attract unwanted attention. Do not disclose to strangers where you are staying.

Index → *Entries in bold refer to maps*

Advertisers' index

Credits

Footprint credits
Editor: Jo Williams
Production and layout: Emma Bryers
Maps: Kevin Feeney
Colour section: Angus Dawson

Publisher: Patrick Dawson
Managing Editor: Felicity Laughton
Administration: Elizabeth Taylor
Advertising sales and marketing:
John Sadler, Kirsty Holmes, Debbie Wylde

Photography credits
Front cover: Anna Omelchenko/
Shutterstock.com
Back cover Bottom: Rosapompelmo/
Shutterstock.com

Colour section
Inside front cover: Richard Cummins/
Richard Cummins, ACME Imagery/ACME
Imagery, Mint Images/Mint Images,
Richard Cummins/Richard Cummins.
Page 1: robertharding/robertharding.
Page 2: Minden Pictures/Minden Pictures.
Page 4: Westend61/Westend61.
Page 5: Minden Pictures/Minden Pictures,
Hemis.fr/Hemis.fr, Christian Kober/
robertharding.
Page 6: Alvaro Leiva/age fotostock.
Page 7: Martin van Lokven/NiS/
Minden Pictures.
Page 8: LMspencer/Shutterstock.com.

Duotone
Page 28: Mark Bridger/Shutterstock.com.

Printed in Spain by GraphyCems

Publishing information
Footprint Costa Rica
3rd edition
© Footprint Handbooks Ltd
February 2016

ISBN: 978 1 910120 70 5
CIP DATA: A catalogue record for this book
is available from the British Library

® Footprint Handbooks and the
Footprint mark are a registered
trademark of Footprint Handbooks Ltd

Published by Footprint
6 Riverside Court
Lower Bristol Road
Bath BA2 3DZ, UK
T +44 (0)1225 469141
F +44 (0)1225 469461
footprinttravelguides.com

Distributed in the USA by
National Book Network, Inc.

Every effort has been made to ensure that
the facts in this guidebook are accurate.
However, travellers should still obtain advice
from consulates, airlines, etc about travel
and visa requirements before travelling.
The authors and publishers cannot
accept responsibility for any loss, injury
or inconvenience however caused.

Footprint story

It was 1921

Ireland had just been partitioned, the British miners were striking for more pay, and the Federation of British Industry had an idea. Exports were booming in South America – how about a handbook for businessmen trading in that far-away continent? The Anglo-South American Handbook was born that year, written by W Koebel, the most prolific writer on Latin America of his day.

1924

Two editions later, the book was 'privatized', and in 1924, in the hands of Royal Mail, the steamship company for South America, it became The South American Handbook, subtitled 'South America in a nutshell'. This annual publication became the 'bible' for generations of travellers to South America and remains so to this day. In the early days travel was by sea and the Handbook gave all the details needed for the long voyage from Europe. What to wear for dinner; how to arrange a cricket match with the Cable & Wireless staff on the Cape Verde Islands, and a full account of the journey from Liverpool up the Amazon to Manaus: 5898 miles without changing cabin!

1939

As the continent opened up, the South American Handbook reported the new Pan Am flying boat services and the fortnightly airship service from Rio to Europe on the Graf Zeppelin. For reasons still unclear but with extraordinary determination, the annual editions continued throughout the Second World War.

1970s

Many more people discovered South America and the backpacking trail started to develop. All the while the Handbook was gathering fans, including literary vagabonds such as Paul Theroux and Graham Greene (who once sent some updates addressed to "The publishers of the best travel guide in the world, Bath, England").

1990s

During the 1990s the company set about developing a new travel guide series using this legendary title as the flagship. By 1997 there were over a dozen guides in the series and the Footprint imprint was launched.

2000s

The series grew quickly and there were soon Footprint travel guides covering more than 100 countries. In 2004, Footprint launched its first thematic guide: *Surfing Europe*, packed with colour photographs, maps and charts. This was followed by further thematic guides such as *Diving the World*, *Snowboarding the World*, *Body and Soul Escapes*, *Travel with Kids* and *European City Breaks*.

2016

Today we continue the traditions of the last 93 years that have served legions of travellers so well. We believe that these help to make Footprint guides different. Our policy is to use authors who are genuine experts and who write for independent travellers; people possessing a spirit of adventure, looking to get off the beaten track.

footprinttravelguides.com

Richard Arghiris

Richard Arghiris is a freelance writer, journalist, blogger and long-term traveller. He has been wandering the highways and unpaved back roads of Central America since 2003, contributing to magazines, newspapers, blogs, websites, documentaries and Footprint guidebooks. The region's diversity of remote landscapes, its vivid tropical ecology, and its patchwork of indigenous, Latin and African-descendant cultures – not to mention its swashbuckling sense of drama – are an ongoing creative inspiration for Richard. His blog, Unseen Americas, www.unseenamericas.com, features news reports, narrative journalism, and street photography from the sketchy US-Mexico border to the teeming rainforests of Panama.

Price codes

Where to stay

$$$$ over US$150

$$$ US$66-150

$$ US$30-65

$ under US$30

Price of a double room in high season, including taxes.

Restaurants

$$$ over US$12

$$ US$7-12

$ US$6 and under

Price for a two-course meal for one person, excluding drinks or service charge.